WILLIAM LANGEWIESCHE

# *Aloft*

William Langewiesche is the author of seven previous books: *Cutting for Sign*, *Sahara Unveiled*, *Inside the Sky*, *American Ground*, *The Outlaw Sea*, *The Atomic Bazaar*, and, most recently, *Fly by Wire*. He is the international editor for *Vanity Fair*.

ALSO BY WILLIAM LANGEWIESCHE

*Cutting for Sign*
*Sahara Unveiled*
*Inside the Sky*
*American Ground*
*The Outlaw Sea*
*The Atomic Bazaar*
*Fly by Wire*

# Aloft

*Thoughts on the Experience of Flight*

WILLIAM LANGEWIESCHE

*With an Introduction by John Banville*

VINTAGE DEPARTURES
*Vintage Books*
*A Division of Random House, Inc.*
*New York*

FIRST VINTAGE DEPARTURES EDITION, OCTOBER 2010

Library of Congress Cataloging-in-Publication Data
Langewiesche, William.
Aloft : thoughts on the experience of flight / by William Langewiesche.—
1st Vintage Departures ed.
p. cm.
Rev. ed. of Inside the sky.
ISBN 978-0-307-74148-6
1. Langewiesche, William—Anecdotes. 2. Air pilots—United States—Anecdotes.
3. Air travel—Anecdotes. 4. Flight—Anecdotes. 5. Aeronautics—Anecdotes.
I. Langewiesche, William. Inside the sky. II. Title.
TL540.L272A3 2010
629.13092—dc22
[B] 2010027345

www.vintagebooks.com

*In memory of Che Barnes, who disappeared over the Pacific, October 29, 2009*

# Contents

## Author's Note

With the exception of the 'The View From Above', the articles collected here were written for the *Atlantic Monthly* during its golden era from about 1995 to 2005, and more recently for *Vanity Fair*, which exists today as one of the few mainstream publications in the English language that allows for long-form narrative reporting. A few editors stand in the background – most notably the brilliant Cullen Murphy, a writer himself, who for thirty years has been expanding other writers' ambitions to match his own. I myself never intended to write about aviation, having left professional flying behind for life as an international correspondent. Indeed the aviation writing collected here constitutes only a fraction of the work I have done on a variety of topics largely related to conflict and change, from parts of the world both far away and near. Gangs in Brazil, wars in the Balkans, Iraq, and Afghanistan, Islamist radicalism in North Africa and London, ship-breaking in India, an environmentalist missionary in Patagonia – these are the sorts of subjects that have occupied my time. It is almost to my surprise therefore to find at this mid-point in my career that I have written enough on aviation, already, to make a book and call it *Aloft*.

The essays appear roughly in the order they were published. The first that I wrote, however, appears as the sixth in the collection: 'Valujet 592.' It is about the 1996 crash in the Florida Everglades of an airliner that burned in flight, and more fundamentally about the inherent inability of governments or the airlines themselves to keep such accidents from happening. Murphy and *Atlantic* editor-in-chief William Whitworth sent me to the crash site for the first week after the accident, and then encouraged me to wait a full year before returning to the story. That sort of approach has been typical for me. The Valujet piece was noticed in safety engineering circles. After its publication I was asked once a year for several years to address system specialists at Los Alamos, the US weapons laboratory where the atomic bomb was born. For the safety of the world, each year I politely declined.

I am not a reporter in the traditional sense, because I do not report the news. While others slave against the clock to meet daily or weekly deadlines, what motivates me is the prospect of having to complete a project at some distant date on the calendar. The only truly journalistic piece here is the one on air traffic control – called 'Slam and Jam' – where one of the points is that safety does not hang in the balance, and controllers do not have especially stressful jobs. It so happened that another writer did a piece on air traffic control for the *New York Times Magazine* at the same time, and drew the opposite picture. His work was picked up by Hollywood, and made into a bad movie called *Pushing Tin*. My piece elicited only a prank phone call from a British friend, who pretended to be a controller and threatened to burn down my house. Obviously there was something wrong with my take. No article of mine has ever been made into a movie.

I never wanted to write about flight. It is a genre too easily confused with false heroics, or, worse, with tedious transportation history of the British plane-spotter kind. So each time I had to be pushed. The pusher has always been Cullen Murphy, a man with no inherent interest in aviation, but with an insatiable curiosity about the world, and also, simply, with a love for non-fiction writing. The episode that stands out in my memory occurred on a wintry day in Boston, at the *Atlantic*'s venerable offices, in the years before the magazine moved to Washington. Murphy was dressed as usual in a jacket with elbow patches and a bowtie. I was slumped as usual in a chair. Murphy said he wanted me to consider writing another aviation piece, if any came to mind. I said, no, hell no, I was done with writing about airplanes because I had more important things to say – maybe something about the role of romanticism in fomenting war, or the history of the world since Jesus Christ, or, my favorite, the five primary fallacies of our time. Murphy is an imperturbable man. He quietly asked me to reconsider, and said he would publish anything on flight that I might choose to write. Anything? I proposed the most esoteric topic I could imagine – an article about turning an airplane – which surely he would reject. To my surprise he answered yes. The result was 'The Turn'. To my further surprise he published it, and somehow it was a success, however small.

Cullen Murphy, William Whitworth, Mike Kelly, and Graydon Carter. There have been others in the book world as well – in New York, London, Paris, São Paulo, and Milan. These editors represent publishing as a brave and decent trade. But of course there are frustrations, too. For years after I went to work for the *Atlantic*, I had a little side business of occasionally taking pilots – a few at a time – into the worst weather we could survive in small and intentionally-vulnerable airplanes. This was more technical and less adventurous than it might seem: it was training for the mind, a practical school in self-discipline and escape-route planning. Again, Murphy asked me to write about it. I wrote the piece called 'Inside An Angry Sky', and Whitworth decided to publish it. The manuscript found its way, however, into the New York offices of the real estate tycoon who owned the *Atlantic* at the time, and his lieutenant, an amateur pilot, happed upon it. Then the unthinkable occurred: the lieutenant violated the firewalls around editorial content, and raised a fuss about the article, which he believed exhibited reckless and dangerous behavior. Technically he was wrong, but such were the other pressures on Whitworth that he acquiesced and spiked the piece. Murphy was upset, and Whitworth may have been, too. I thought the episode was funny. Did this man in New York believe that our readers would go out and start flying storms? Furthermore, what constitutes dangerous behavior? I had just returned from an extended stay in Sudan, on an assignment for the *Atlantic* during which I had dodged Revolutionary Guards and been arrested three times. There was no complaint about that.

I could go on at length about the back stories here, but will not. Suffice it to say that 'The Crash of EgyptAir 990' was the *Atlantic*'s response to 9/11 – a parable about war; '*Columbia*'s Last Flight,' was written largely in Baghdad; 'The Devil At 37,000 Feet' required such hard driving in the Amazon that it largely destroyed a truck; and finally, 'The View From Above' in my own mind has always been a tribute to my father, a man who believed in the importance of simply looking around. Beyond that I will not burden these pages. The pieces can be read in any order. They do not require technical knowledge. They avoid jargon, over-simplification, or mis-statement of fact. Most of them are stories about matters somewhat larger than themselves. There are suffused with the wonder I still feel that as a species we now find ourselves in the sky

.

William Langewiesche
New York
November 2009

# Introduction

## The Lonely Impulse

That sky, that band of air between the earth's skin and the edge of space, is for most of us an alien environment, where clouds boil and roil, where headwinds howl, and where the outside temperature, as our pilot jauntily informs us, is low enough to freeze the blood in our veins. William Langewiesche is the opposite of an aerophobe, but even he acknowledges the uncanniness of that turbulent azure above our heads: 'We find reflections of ourselves there, but of all inhabited places the sky remains the strangest.'

The number of writers who have tackled the subject of flight is very small, and of that number Langewiesche is the least fanciful, the most vigorous – the most, we might say, down-to-earth. His writing is tough and tangy, and as bracing as the breeze that, in the days before air bridges, used to hit you when you stepped out on to the apron to walk to your waiting plane. He is a true heir of the Wright brothers, those quintessentially American gadgeteers, and while he is happy to grant the rest of the world a licence to fly he is in no doubt as to who really owns the skies; as he warns us, 'I am an American pilot with an American taste for waste, a nervous hunger for speed and power only half justified by the size of the continent.'

Note that his first claim is that he is a pilot. He recognizes clearly in himself the way in which the flying informs the writing, and the reciprocal nature of the two disciplines that together make up his livelihood and his obsession. This is what gives his work its authoritative note; this man knows what he is talking about. 'The airplane's forward motion imposes a crude immediacy on our thoughts, so that even when we do not understand the weather, we may pretend that we do. Flying as much as writing teaches the need for such fictions, for discerning the patterns in a disorderly world.'

Here again he shows himself a member of that American fraternity that includes Huck Finn, Hawkeye Natty Bumppo, even Jay Gatsby – though Langewiesche's green light is not at the end of a dock but on the tip of a wing – all of them seekers after 'the patterns in a disorderly world'. He is truly a native son, and for him the sky is one more frontier, reachable enough to be still a human zone, just about – space is another element, with no weather and nothing in it except stars and a few drifting bits of manmade hardware. His voice is inflected with that particular American tone which is a blend of fortitude, individualism and unassuageable loneliness. He is surely a student of Emerson, the Emerson who writes: 'Life only avails, not the having lived. Power ceases in the instant of repose; it resides in the moment of transition from a past to a new state, in the shooting of the gulf, in the darting to an aim.' Of which Langewiesche's version might be this:

The aerial view is something entirely new . . . It lets us see outselves in context, as creatures struggling through life on the face of a planet, not separate from nature, but its most expressive agents. It lets us see that our struggles form patterns on the land, that these patterns repeat to an extent which before we had not known, and that there is sense to them.

Here we are back again to the solitary man in the lonely sky, fastened into 'the cockpit as a monastic cell', discerning the patterns in a disorderly world.

Langewiesche has known his moments of dread, too, the dread that comes of the sudden realization of being aloft at 'an unbridgeable distance from the world'. It would be hard to think of a writer more dissimilar from him than Antoine de Saint-Exupéry – 'I rejected his work as inauthentic,' Langewiesche writes, 'disdaining its sense of the common good, its maudlin emotionalism, and its overwrought musings on the glories of the mission' – yet in a telling passage the American pragmatist confesses to a moment of fellow-feeling with the 'notoriously dreamy' Frenchman.

It was his first winter of cargo flying, 'dangerous, low-paid work', and he was not happy, lifting off in nights of black rain 'into the storms and the inner landscapes of the mind'. On one of those nights, crossing a clearing in the clouds, he glimpsed far below the lights of a single ranch house and remembered a passage in Saint-Exupéry's *Night Flight* in which the Frenchman spotted a similar farmhouse 'that seemed to be sailing backwards from him in a great prairie sea, with its freight of human lives'. Suddenly, his nerve began to fail, as he contemplated something that 'previously I had believed no real pilot would take the time to do', namely, the possibility that this time he might not return from the night sky. Return he did, of course, but the sense of doom remained with him, until another night when, flying through the last storm of a bleak winter, the 'sheer force of that storm forced me at last to look up from the instruments again – and when I did I discovered a place fantastic even to me, far away in the wild winds, where rain fell upward and blizzards blew among cloud mountains and the walls of great caverns erupted in light'. It was a cathartic vision, and, for all its savagery, a saving one:

After returning I stood in the wind-driven rain and watched the workers back their vans up to the airplane to unload its cargo. I did not tell them where I had been. How could they have understood? Even to me it was a wonder that this little metal machine, so battered and unloved, had carried me there. It was late at night, and I should have driven home and slept, but I was not tired. I felt renewed not because I had survived but because I had the means and the inclination to fly again into that angry sky. No pilot could ever be at home there, but I for one had stopped yearning for the ground.

These are wonderful essays, at once thrilling and informative, awe-inspiring and exact, in places frightening, in others reassuring, and always elegant. Langewiesche is a born flyer – his father was a famous pilot who wrote a classic text on flight navigation – and an inspired writer, one whom, like Yeats's airman,

> *A lonely impulse of delight*
> *Drove to this tumult in the clouds*

John Banville, 2010

I

## The View from Above

After a century of flying, we still live at a moment of emergence like that experienced by creatures first escaping from the sea. For us the emergence has been given meaning because we can think about it, and can perhaps understand the nature of our liberation. Mechanical wings allow us to fly, but it is with our minds that we make the sky ours. The old measures of distance no longer apply, in part because we hop across the globe in single sittings, but also because in doing so we visit a place which even just above our homes is as exotic and revealing as the most foreign destination. This book contains observations of that place, and it takes the form of a spiral climb, occasionally returning overhead of the point where now it begins, with the idea that flight's gift is to let us look around.

At first I mean a simple form of looking around, and one that requires little instruction – just gazing down at the ordinary scenery sliding by below. The best views are views of familiar things, like cities and farms and bottlenecked freeways. So set aside the beauty of sunsets, the majesty of mountains, the imprint of winds on golden prairies. The world beneath our wings has become a human artifact, our most spontaneous and complex creation. Tourists may not like to contemplate the evidence, with its hints of greed and self-destruction, but the fact remains that the old sterilized landscapes – like designated outlooks and pretty parks and sculpted gardens – have become obsolete, and that it is largely the airplane that has made them so. The aerial view is something entirely new. We need to admit that it flattens the world and mutes it in a rush of air and engines, and that it suppresses beauty. But it also strips the façades from our constructions, and by raising us above the constraints of the treeline and the highway it imposes a brutal honesty on our perceptions. It lets us see ourselves in context, as creatures struggling through life on the face of a planet, not separate from nature, but its most expressive agents. It lets us see that our struggles form patterns on the land, that these patterns repeat to an extent which before we had not known, and that there is a sense to them.

Discovering that sense requires not only that we look outside while flying but that we get over the illusion of smallness, the 'Everything looks like a toy!' that blinds us at first to what we see. I write 'us' but frankly mean 'them' or 'you.' The truth is I can only imagine learning to see from the air, because my father was a pilot with pilot friends, and I grew up inside their airplanes, gazing at the world below. Day after day through the seasons and years we wandered the sky, and I sat looking outside. To pass the time I picked points on the airplane – a strut, a rivet, a place on the leading edge of a wing – and used those points as sighting devices against the ground to measure the airplane's speed and to define flight's independent paths across the landscape: for a while along a country lane, but then straight across a field and through someone's swimming pool, over a factory, into a city and out again. It was quite early in my childhood, as these random paths began to fit together, that I developed a pilot's integrated sense of the earth's geometry.

This was in the 1960s, the merest moment after the Wright brothers. When I first flew alone, in a sailplane at the age of fourteen, the experience seemed so normal to me that I have practically no memory of it now. It wasn't until college, when I took an air-taxi job and began carrying passengers for hire, people unaccustomed to flight, that I realized there was anything unusual about the view. Of course, some passengers did not want to look outside. But others were curious. For me it was like witnessing Stone Age people seeing photographs for the first time, getting used to the scale, then turning with growing excitement from the magic to the content of the picture.

These passengers had ridden on the airlines but had been herded into their cabin seats, distracted by magazines, and given shoulder-height triple-pane windows at right angles to the direction of flight. They had been encouraged not to look outside but rather the opposite – to draw the shades for the movie and pretend not to fly at all. And now suddenly they found themselves in a cockpit wrapped in glass, awash in brilliant light, in a small airplane lingering near the ground.

Some passengers simply could not understand the view. I remember a pristine young woman who, ten miles off the San Francisco coast, looked down from our airplane at a ship plowing through the Pacific swells, then looked up at me and smiled prettily.

I was charmed. I said, 'What do you think?'

She said, 'Is this the Napa Valley?'

The airplane was noisy. I said, 'The what?'

She repeated it, less certainly. 'The Napa Valley?'

I may have laughed. She looked concerned. Only later did I understand. First flights can confuse the senses and cause normal people to stop thinking.

On another occasion I had a passenger who during a smooth flight at 15,000 feet over Baltimore suspected that perhaps he had died and gone not to heaven but to a suspended place in time. He meant this quite literally. His face turned chalky, as if he were about to faint. I asked him what was wrong.

He stammered his strange uncertainty: Had we by chance been in a mid-air collision back there over Wilmington when the controller warned us about that oncoming airplane which we never spotted? The question put me in the unusual position of having to assure someone that both he and I were indeed still alive.

He was a German art dealer from Berlin and New York, and he did not know Baltimore. The softness of flight had combined with the visible abandonment of the streets below to give him the feeling of death. I explained that it was Super Bowl Sunday and that all Baltimore was watching the game on television. He had been long enough in the United States to understand. The color returned slowly to his skin. I think then that he became interested in the view, which was indeed the view of a sort of afterlife – or of a city in decline.

The German would have felt better over Berlin or New York not because they are healthier cities but because reading the ground from an airplane is easier if you understand some of the local customs. Residents of Baltimore would see their city from the air more clearly than any transient foreigner, and would find the landscape not dormant or deadly, but compelling. Rather than simply knowing about the Super Bowl, they might share with the city below a genuine interest in the game's outcome – and as result they might not even see a Baltimore in decline. Who could say then whose view was deeper, theirs or mine? But I do know that they would not choose that moment in flight to prefer watching television, because television is dull compared to the view of home from overhead.

I have imagined teaching the aerial view. The best approach would be to apprentice young children as I was apprenticed, to teach them without elaboration simply by flying them to different places, encouraging them to navigate, and to make the translations between maps and the world. Effortlessly they would develop the habit of seeing the world from above, and the more subtle trick while on the ground of understanding the scale and orientation of their surroundings. Flying at its best is a way of thinking. Because of that, once having left the earth's surface, people never again quite return to it. But also because of that, adults often find it hard to make the leap. They simply have spent too many years on the ground. To teach them the aerial view you would have to overcome that landlubbing prejudice which equates driving on a country road, or sleeping in a hotel and visiting the restaurant part of town, with having 'been' somewhere, to the exclusion of other possibilities.

I have a friend, a historian at Princeton University, who upon my return from a low-altitude flight up the Eastern seaboard of the United States denied that I had actually visited the places I had overflown – the farmed and citied coastal plain from Georgia to New Jersey and in between. I did not invite my friend's judgment, but he offered it anyway, argumentatively, because he could not shake a certain cramped sense of possession that he had acquired while driving the same route the summer before. He was a jealous sort of traveler, like those who return from tours convinced that theirs is the only authentic experience among the natives of some faraway land. Pilots are generally less-educated types, but they are more charitable about geography. In all my time among them, the endless hours sitting in cockpits and waiting around airports, I have never heard one speak possessively of a landscape. Maybe because the aerial view is unrestrained, it can also be generous.

I offered to introduce my friend to it, not by following his road trip from above but by taking him on a shorter flight over Princeton, his hometown, where his sense of possession was justified. He accepted my offer, and on a crisp and sunlit morning was surprised by the density of the university campus, by the alignment of the streets, by the nearness of the New York skyline, by the extent of the new suburban forest. He was interested in the generational growth of office parks, the division of the farms, and the inflated architecture of new houses on small lots like the coming of California to the East. I thought, specialists may measure the increments of change on the ground and may disdain the 'naïveté' of the untutored aerial view, but with just one short flight almost anyone can read the outline of the story from up here – in this case, the conclusion of New Jersey's farming life. The aerial view is a democratic view. My friend was interested also in local details like the capricious turns of a certain Hopewell Valley road, and the full extent of a new golf course, and the pattern of old overgrown cow paths converging on a converted barn, and a hidden patch of wilderness by a brook, and the torn shingled roof of another professor's house. Each earned a comment. But he asked me to circle only when we came to his own house, built among others near an expensive day school. He was absorbed, as all people are, by the unexpected proportions and angles and by the strange lay of a familiar neighborhood.

'It's like seeing your face in the mirror for the first time,' I suggested.

My friend did not answer. From riding the airlines, he insisted still on the airplane as just a better sort of train, and he was secretly proud of his impatience with the tedium of flight – such impatience being the mark of the modern traveler. In life he had crossed those thresholds of success and self-confidence beyond which he could not easily learn or change his mind. After we landed, he said he remained unconvinced. Of course. And he will not read these essays, which are meant as a guide to a still unsettled place in the human experience.

But during the flight he did not once turn away from the view of the old settled place, and that was a start.

The best aerial views are low views, but only down to a certain altitude, because there is also such a thing as flying too low to see. This happens at that height above the ground where, depending on the airplane's speed, the scenery rushes by too quickly. From the cockpit of a jet flown at treetop level at, say, 500 miles an hour, the rushing-by is sometimes described in schoolchild terms as a blur. In fact, to the accustomed eye the land remains visually distinct – a complex mix of definable points, of trees and houses and mountaintops. The points slide by in a spectrum of softening speed, from brutally fast directly below, to merely brisk one mile ahead, to not quite stationary up on the distant horizon. There is no blurring to it. You register the points coming in time, and can slow things down by looking a bit farther away.

But if not a blurring, there is indeed a visual frustration to such high-speed treetop flight, and it is a structural one. The details which pass by slowly enough to make sense of are precisely those details which lie too far away to see clearly. For example, you know it's a house that just went by, but for lack of time or clarity you cannot consider its design and setting, or the litter in its back yard – the house as an expression of its inhabitants. The airplane jars through upwelling surface winds. Its speed dominates your thoughts like an obsession. No matter how you twist and turn, you cannot get beyond it.

Even at a relatively slow 200 miles an hour, speed may rob the low view of its content. The obvious solution is to throttle back and fly still more slowly – and that indeed you can do, though not economically in a jet. I will ignore the levitational magic of helicopters, which can hover in any direction, closely matching the contours of the land, but which are inefficient, disruptive, and nearly as expensive as a jet to operate. For about the cost of driving a car you can fly an old two-seat, propeller-driven airplane and float low across the countryside at road speeds – slow enough to see the hats on the farmers and to judge the quality of their work.

And even that now seems too fast. Let children dream of their supersonic futures. For today's practitioner, the advance is rather at the other end of the scale, with a foot-launched aircraft in which the pilot hangs on shrouds from a wing made of loose fabric like a sail. How appropriate that the French, who are good sailors, have championed this form of aircraft. Calling it the paraglider, they developed it in the 1980s as an alternative to standard delta-wing hang gliders, which are exhilarating to fly, and reasonably safe, but which suffer from the weight and bulk of their tubular frames even when disassembled. The paraglider by contrast has no frame, weighs about the same as a family's picnic lunch, and can be stuffed into a rucksack and carried easily up a mountain. In essence, it is a rectangular high-performance parachute, a close relative to the tethered 'parasails' pulled by powerboats at beach resorts, with the important difference that it has no connection to the ground and flies independently, under the pilot's control.

High on some mountain, you invert the fabric on the ground behind you, strap yourself into a seat-harness, and with a tug on the shrouds allow the wind to send the wing aloft directly overhead, where it assumes a cambered form and floats at the ready. With a short run downhill you give it flying speed. It answers by lifting you off your feet, and beginning to coast downhill toward the valley below. Once it gains speed it flattens its glide angle, and takes you out across the trees, the ravines, and the valley itself. The experience is primordial, a feeling of lift and wind like a throwback to the earliest elemental era of flight before the Wright brothers, when pioneers like the great Berliner Otto Lilienthal floated downhill on homemade wings.

Lilienthal was a mechanical engineer, the manager of a factory that manufactured small steam engines. He crashed and died in 1898, at age forty-eight, after having made 2,000 hang gliding flights, the longest of which lasted fifteen seconds. It seems quaint now that he flew only on weekends and that he fell to his death at walking speed from only fifty feet up – but he was doing serious work, and he knew it. The epitaph on his tombstone records his famous words, *Opfer müssen gebracht werden*, or 'Sacrifices must be made.' If that now seems like the wrong way to approach the weekend, it was the right way in the 1890s, because at any cost the time had come for human flight.

The difference for us today is not that the designs have improved, though they have, but that as a species we have now had a century of experience inside the sky. The modern paraglider does not advance history but offers the human animal a bit of stitched fabric, some lines, and a harness – a cheap personal portable wing. The flying of such aircraft has become an indulgence and does not call for heroics. In turn, this means that our flying is safer.

There is risk to any flight, of course, and pilots do die in paragliders. They die not because paragliding is unregulated – though in the United States it remains delightfully so – but because of the physics of flight. The slowest and simplest flying machines are particularly vulnerable to the winds and dependent upon the pilot's athletic reactions. Those reactions take a while to develop. Wilbur and Orville Wright, who started as bicycle builders in Dayton, Ohio, set about designing, building, and flying the world's first practical airplanes after reading Lilienthal's obituary in the local newspaper. Their most important insight was that lift alone was not enough – that once in flight the pilot would have to be given absolute control of the wing. They were careful, cerebral men, but also supremely Midwestern and pragmatic. During their early experiments with gliding in 1901, Wilbur wrote, 'If you are looking for perfect safety you will do well to sit on a fence and watch the birds, but if you really wish to learn you must mount a machine and become acquainted with its tricks by actual trial.'

This remains almost as true today. Despite our accumulated knowledge of the air, the best way to go about paragliding is not to sign up for a class but simply to borrow a wing and run downhill with it. Borrow a helmet, too, and choose a calm day and a shallow slope – but indulge in the risk. In each hand you hold a handle connected by shrouds to the trailing edge of the wing. Those handles function as the glider's only controls. To turn, you pull one or the other, twisting the fabric of the wing to spoil the lift in the direction you want to go. Because the paraglider flies slowly, at bicycle speeds, it requires only a shallow bank to turn quickly. At the end of the flight, as you skim the ground, you pull both handles at once, causing the entire wing to rear up and to slow further until against a light wind you put your feet down and land with a few steps – or instead, as I have, you go about gently crashing.

The slowness of the paraglider is the feature that interests me here, not because it makes for soft landings but because it promises in theory to provide ordinary humans with the most detailed yet of the aerial views. Sometimes I think that people should, after all, take classes in paragliding, but that those classes should be taught at every public high school in the country and offered as alternatives not only to gym but to the tedious courses in 'civics' and geography. This is not a serious proposal, of course, because we have taught ourselves if anything to worship safety – to fasten our seatbelts, to act responsibly, and to follow the well trod paths through life. *Opfer müssen* nicht *gebracht werden.* Imagine the price to pay each time a student landed badly and was injured or killed. But imagine also the arrival of an entire generation in which people truly had learned to see their world from above.

Such dreaming aside, paragliders in recent years have encountered a practical problem masked as an advance. Through steady improvements in their design and construction, the gliding performance of these sky-sails keeps getting better, and is now nearly fifteen to one, which means they can fly fifteen feet forward for every foot they descend. This does not approach the sixty-to-one ratios of enclosed sailplanes, but it is about that of delta-wing hang gliders. Accompanying the flattened glide angle is a lessening of sink rates to about 200 feet per minute. The numbers are important because they are more than matched by the vertical fluctuations of ordinary winds. As a result, paraglider pilots can now soar, which means they can ride updrafts, gain altitude, stay aloft for hours, and even fly trips of a hundred miles and more. My own small regret is that these possibilities encourage a record-setting mentality in which flying becomes a 'sport' turned in on itself and pilots come to consider the landscape only for the chances it creates – the coastal ridge, the sun-heated parking lot, the swirl of dust that marks the start of rising air. To soar you have to stay high and exploit every opportunity. The ground becomes the enemy. You can't afford to see it in detail.

One answer is to abandon soaring and strap an engine to your back, and this indeed is now done. Again the French have led the way. They call the result the powered paraglider and have established enough of a following to support two stores in Paris alone. The wing is slightly shorter. The engine is mounted on a backframe and drives a four-bladed pusher-propeller in a wire cage – an arrangement, including fuel and a small battery for in-flight electrical starts, which weighs about thirty pounds, and which the pilot wears in addition to the standard wing harness. This time along with the control handles, you hold a throttle lever connected by cable to the engine. You take off downhill or on level ground after a short run into the wind with the engine roaring. For the outside observer it is a peculiar sight: this two-legged animal with a parachute overhead and noisy machinery strapped to his back, running awkwardly across a field, then retracting his legs and flying. It is peculiar for the pilot too, until your wings take hold and pull you into the sky. Then suddenly it feels quite natural. The powered paraglider may be the most primitive airplane that has ever existed, but it offers a genuine form of flight. You can climb in it one mile high and hover there for hours.

Better yet you can pack it into an airliner, then unpack it somewhere new and fly it low. I have a Parisian friend named François Lagarde, a pioneer of this technique, who has flown his powered paraglider across Tunisia, Niger, Cameroon, Martinique, and Thailand. Even the most timid traditionalists would have to admit that thereby he has 'visited' those places. Other than making occasional adjustments to the wing, he has little to do in flight but to look around. Lagarde flies low, sometimes below the treetops, following footprints and trails, chasing rabbits. He maneuvers among giraffes and elephants and smells the dry dung and wet earth, the grasses, trees, and flowers. He waves to villagers and alights like a bird in those villages where people wave back. He flies in the United States and France as well, and he talks of China next. All this may seem like another exercise in European adventurism, but Lagarde is not a faddist. There are good reasons for his obsession. He is extroverted and social and unafraid, and he wants to experience the world in its full vitality. He knows that the view from above is frank and unobstructed. And he has learned that the very low view, when it is also very slow, is often also intimate.

But he and I have different goals in flight. Although my writing now takes me to far-off places in the world, as a pilot I am still most interested in the view of the place I know best, which is this country here. And although I understand the interest of the slowest European flight and admire the education that sustains it, I am an American pilot with an American taste for waste, a nervous hunger for speed and power only half justified by the size of the continent. It is true that I would rather fly my own propeller airplane where I choose to go than fly someone else's jet much faster where others choose to send me. But I won't pretend that I always cherish the view.

I have even used speed maliciously to blind my passengers. For several years I worked as an air-taxi pilot along the Mexican border of west Texas. It was a wild part of the world, infested with smugglers of drugs and guns, and potentially dangerous for any public for-hire pilot. I knew it when I moved there, and I was determined to stay out of trouble. When one evening a rancher from the Rio Grande offered me six months' earnings to 'repossess' an airplane in Mexico and fly it low into the United States, I easily said no. The rancher was feeling me out; it was clear that the repossessed airplane would be loaded with dope. But I was hungry, and I did take some of the more ambiguous flights that an older pilot might have declined.

I flew small single-pilot airplanes. The danger for me, as for ordinary taxi drivers, was bad neighborhoods and aggressive passengers. The threat came not from the big drug cartels but from random freelance operators who could cross the Rio Grande from Mexico with a small load of cocaine and, once having arrived in the unpoliceable no-man's land along the U.S. side of the river, call for an air taxi to fly in and pick them up, then turn around and fly them north, far beyond the border defenses. We were a local flying service with frequent and legitimate flights to the Rio Grande, which made us the perfect target for such a scheme. As a pilot, it was of little help not to know the contents of the luggage. You could be convicted of smuggling nonetheless, and even without going to prison you could lose your right to fly, which for a pilot is nearly the same. Worse yet, a high-strung passenger could, upon arrival at a lonely landing strip, simply decide to silence you. It was a real possibility. The ghosts of murdered pilots haunt isolated runways all through the Southwest.

I thought I could control the danger by bringing along a strong friend – a 250-pound Chicano named Tweeter who worked as a mechanic at the airport and who played the copilot, glowering beside me in the cockpit with his drooping mustache and his wrapped sunglasses, armed with a fire extinguisher and a baseball bat, hoping for trouble. The worst flights announced themselves beforehand by phone: a harried stranger on the river, wanting immediate service for no clear reason, forgetting to question the cost. I want to think that we never carried narcotics, though in truth I do not know. I did fly through troubled currents, and because of Tweeter I flew through them without fear.

But once when he was not at the airport I got a suspicious call for a pickup at a remote runway on the border, and I had to decide whether to set off for the Rio Grande alone. The caller was a woman, a stranger who spoke with the flat nasal vowels of the Midwest. She said her husband was sick and needed to get to Odessa, an oil town 250 miles north on the interstate. I took a minute to scribble a few calculations of time and fuel. She understood my silence as reluctance.

'Just hold on,' she said, and she muffled the phone with her hand. Then she said, 'He says we pay cash – dollars.' Apparently she was used to following her husband's lead.

I gave her an estimate of the cost. I said, 'It's a standard rate, by the hour, the return trip too.'

'Who's the pilot? Are you the pilot?'

'Yes.'

'He says just get down here fast.'

If the man was that sick, why didn't he go to a doctor there? The call was all wrong. The woman's urgency worried me – it sounded like panic. But I started the airplane anyway and taxied and took off, because I needed the work.

It was a summer afternoon, with clouds building over the jagged west Texas peaks and a dust plume rising from a cattle truck moving down a dry dirt road. My destination was the runway outside of Presidio, the last town in the United States, and the hottest. The route led south across a grassland basin divided by barbed wire into vast pastures, some cropped close by cattle to the color of dirt, others more luxuriant and nonetheless brown. Isolated ranch houses huddled with sheds under cottonwood trees. I had once loved that landscape self-indulgently, for the purity and beauty of its wide open space, and for its comforting diminution of my own existence – the scale it gave to my worries and ambitions and the reminder it offered me that these concerns mattered less than I tended to believe. Such was the appeal of the wilderness to me – something I no longer feel, the appeal of a surrender. But I was learning a new way of seeing the landscape now, which was more acute in its acknowledgment of the human presence there and of my own involvement. Flight forced this on me. The enormity and emptiness of the place suggested no longer its virgin splendor but rather its human history – from the first tentative routes along the dry creeks, to the assertive overlay of the transcontinental railroad, to the birth and now death of the small towns.

Despite their beauty, the ranches were dying, too. Evidence lay not only in the decay of the old buildings, some recently abandoned, but also in the blossoming of flamboyant new estates. The estates were built by rich outsiders who made their money elsewhere and cared more about the esthetic of the land than about its productivity. I thought this was probably a good thing, since there was little risk of subdivision here, and land once wrested from the grasp of authentic ranching did seem to return to a deeper state of grace. Preservation, too, is part of the human landscape.

But it was the international boundary that occupied me today – a trace on a map, a dirty little river where two unequal neighbors met, an artificial and dangerous and unfair and necessary line. The river glinted at the bottom of a deep geological rift. I came at it from the side, crossing the rift's mountainous lip and descending steeply. The grassland soon succumbed to the desert, nature's equalizer, so that along the river, by narrow scenic standards, both sides of the border looked about the same.

The narrowness of the view is a problem particular to the ground. Few tourists ever went to Presidio, but those who did often got the impression that the border there hardly existed. Residents, too, because they freely forded the river, could share that illusion. But from the air the view always widens. Forget the revelations of a shared humanity that astronauts are told to talk about. Such revelations are pitched to placate the opponents of rocket ships and their budgets. The astronauts simply fly too high to see. What the ordinary aerial view shows is quite the opposite of a unified world. Beyond wind and water, it is human history that now sculpts the earth.

In flight you could never have mistaken the Rio Grande for just a river. With the exception of tiny Presidio and its satellite settlements, the U.S. side had been abandoned on private as well as public lands to the preservation of a new wilderness. Mexico by comparison made no excuses for its humanity. Big tough Ojinaga spread its dirty streets over the hills and extended a network of rutted roads to fifty miles of river villages – a band of hardscrabble civilization fastened tightly to the Texan underbelly. Somewhere below, a highway sign mentioned 500-year-old fields, but there was little real farming left. The border people got by as border people do, by smuggling. A few smugglers became rich and built big houses in fortified compounds, but most people merely survived. They let their churches and villages fall into ruin. And this, too, was obvious from the air.

The Presidio International Airport had a single sloping runway just off the highway. It was called 'international' because it also had an outside pay phone from which, if you flew in from Mexico, you could in principle call on Customs to come up from the river for the entry formalities. This happened maybe twice a year. Presidio was probably the quietest international airport in the United States.

Mine was the only airplane there that afternoon. I shut it down in the sun beside a wrecked trailer in which for a while a missionary pilot had lived while proselytizing the river people. He had told me he was a soldier in the army of the Lord. After only a half-year he had retreated, leaving the trailer with broken windows to collect the desert air.

The sun lay low. My passengers came from the trailer's shadow and hobbled toward the airplane holding each other and carrying a satchel. The woman was tall and bony and wore her jeans too tight; her husband was taller, and muscular, but walked hunched over, so that his hair fell forward in greasy strands across his face. His clothes were soiled with dirt. He stumbled, and the woman held him up. They pushed into the airplane without a word and sprawled onto the back seats.

I said, 'Wait a minute.'

The woman snapped, 'Just get us out of here!'

'I want to know what's the matter with him.'

'He got a bug in Mexico.'

But his face was bruised, and his eyes were strange, both furtive and aggressive. I figured that he had been beaten and that he was drugged, maybe against his will. He glared at me and mumbled something I could not make out. The woman draped her arm across his chest, pushing him gently against the seat. She touched her head to his and murmured soothingly into his ear. This seemed not to work.

'What's in the bag?' I asked.

'Sneakers and a T-shirt.'

'I'd like to see.'

She handed me the satchel grudgingly. 'There's a gun, too, but it's safe, so go ahead and check it.'

It was a 9mm pistol. I dropped the clip, checked the chamber, zipped the gun into the bag, and put the bag up front beside me.

The man said, 'He's a bitch.'

The woman didn't care. She wanted to get away from the border. She gentled the man back into his seat again.

An admonition in the language of a commandant is often posted at airports: 'Maintain thine airspeed, lest the earth rise up and smite thee.' In straight English, something similar should be said about landscapes as well. With these two frantic people the border – with all its lurking menace, its incipient violence – had reached for me and laid claim to my involvement. I had become a local character, and it did not occur to me to refuse the flight.

Nonetheless I was angry about it, worried not about contraband or a violent end at the airport in Odessa, but about the threatening attitude of the man in the back seat, and his apparent unpredictability. If from a distance now it seems obvious that the danger lay mostly in my mind, at the time the situation was less clear. Various possibilities arose – that the man could lose his temper and attack me in flight, that either he or she was a pilot and could take over, that partway to Odessa they might put a second gun to my head and force me to some remote runway where they could pull the trigger. I did not know who these people were or how their deal had gone bad, but I sensed they were dangerous to me, and without Tweeter there to protect me I instinctively took the offensive.

After lifting off from the runway at Presidio, I leveled the airplane at fencepost height, so low that we were flying down *inside* the scenery, where the slightest distraction would drive us into the ground. It was a rough ride. For 200 miles I kept us there, without explanation, a short throw from oblivion. It was an act of self-defense but also, I admit, of aggression. These people had menaced me, and here in the air I could reciprocate. The landscape was my ally because I often flew it low when I was alone and I knew every rocky point and power line along the way. Now I could wield it like a weapon and assault my passengers with the airplane's speed. I gambled that even if they were pilots they would not dare to grab the controls or try to resist me. And indeed they did not, but submitted to the landscape's punishment, clutched together on the back seats in a beleaguered embrace. They were strangers to the aerial view – I saw that, and did not relent. Who knows what confusion passed before their eyes. After we landed in Odessa they shoved cash into my hands and fled without waiting for change. I flew home low, too, for the simple thrill of my escape.

I still enjoy the escape of low and fast flight, and sometimes go out into the desert to chase at head height along dirt roads, banking vertically to make the turns, pulling up to keep the wingtips from dragging. But it is the richness of the genuine aerial view, something both higher and slower, that I keep returning to. I realize now that the aerial view has formed me, and that I have carried it with me from the cockpit to my more recent work of wandering and writing and reporting about the world. And it is odd how even on the ground, weeks from any airplane, the aerial view seems still to fit. It carries with it the possibility of genuinely free movement, and allows just the right amount of participation with the landscape – neither as distant as an old-fashioned vista nor as entrapping as a permanent involvement.

## 2

# *The Turn*

For most of human history evidence suggested that the sky constituted a forbidden realm and that if God had meant people to go
there He would, for instance, have made them lighter than air. As late
as 1670 – by which time it was known that air is a gas and has weight
– a Jesuit monk named Francesco Lana who came up with an idea for
a balloon had to abandon its development for just such philosophical
reasons. Soon afterward, during Europe's conversion to rational belief,
the strictest religious doubts faded, but questions of safety remained.
Over the centuries a number of determined travelers had equipped
themselves with birdlike wings, stiffened coats, and various air paddles,
and from high towers they had bravely jumped to their deaths. It was
observed that shipwrecked sailors can tread water in the ocean, cling
to flotsam, and swim to the shore – but that shipwrecked 'aeronauts'
must fall from the sky.

This became a practical concern after two French brothers named
Joseph and Etienne Montgolfier seized upon the uplifting effect of
hot air. They began launching experimental unmanned balloons near
Avignon in 1783. As usual in the flying business, they soon had competition. After hearing of their success, a physicist named Charles
accelerated his own experiments with lighter-than-air hydrogen, and
on August 27, 1783, amid much fanfare, he released an unmanned gas
balloon from the center of Paris. The balloon climbed into the clouds,
drifted fifteen miles downwind, and landed near the village of Gonesse
– where the terrified villagers bravely attacked and shredded the
monster with sickles and pitchforks.

The destruction of their competitor's balloon came as good news
to the Montgolfiers. Three weeks later, following a royal banquet at

Versailles, the Montgolfiers launched another hot-air balloon, again unmanned, to which however they had attached a cage carrying a rooster, a sheep, and a duck. Why these particular animals, no one knows, but the general idea was to check the effects of high altitude on living creatures. The Montgolfiers predicted that the balloon would climb to 12,000 feet and float there for twenty minutes – and that the animals would encounter there the same atmospheric conditions they would have found in the mountains at similar altitudes. In fact, the balloon reached only 1,700 feet and after a brief flight landed about a mile away. Still, the flight was thought to have been a success because all three animals had survived – though the sheep had kicked the rooster's wing. Maybe because he was more used to the aerial view, the duck had simply sat.

The Montgolfiers now set to work on a larger balloon for the first manned flight. Since they were engineers and theoreticians, and did not propose to make the flight themselves, they had to find a pilot. King Louis XVI offered to lend them a prisoner for the ride – a hapless volunteer who no doubt otherwise faced a more certain death at the king's hands. Had the Montgolfiers accepted, the first person to escape from the earth's surface would have been a convicted criminal.

No doubt aware of this, a forward-thinking young aristocrat named Pilâtre de Rozier, already well known in Parisian society for his scientific demonstrations, insisted on himself instead. On the initial tentative flights he rose just above the trees and rooftops, stoking a fire of straw and chopped wool in a hot-air balloon that, however, remained roped to the ground. Such tethered flights were, of course, too timid to justify much excitement. For the far more ambitious step of true free flight, de Rozier enlisted another young aristocrat to serve as ballast and companion and to help stoke the fire. He was a cavalry officer named the Marquis d'Arlandes, a friend of a friend of Marie Antoinette. These two – Pilâtre de Rozier and the Marquis d'Arlandes – became on November 21, 1783, the first of our species to break free of the ground. They took off before huge crowds in the Bois de Boulogne, drifted over Paris for twenty-five minutes, and after a trip of about five miles, having crossed the river Seine, landed near the present Place d'Italie.

Though the flight was a success, the big *Montgolfier* balloon suffered from a serious flaw: Its envelope was made of canvas and paper and had a dangerous tendency at its base to ignite in flight. The two airmen carried a bucket of water and extinguished the life-threatening flames with wet sponges. They did this casually by today's standards, and floated over the city as if in a dream. If the marquis' written account of the flight was admirable for its tone of Gallic nonchalance, it became heroic two years later when Pilâtre de Rozier was burned and killed in a balloon of his own design, becoming not only the first man to climb free of the earth but also the first man to die for it.

This was less important than it seemed at the time. By modern standards ballooning turned out to be a limited and impractical pursuit – not the sort of act that could take people where they wanted to go. As a result, though the first feeble moves away from the ground remain a curiosity, they lack the intellectual content that can sustain our interest now. Nonetheless, one unexpected and apparently simple observation of the human landscape still emerges from the marquis' account to lead us farther into our sky.

Naïvely, he wrote, 'I was surprised at the silence and the absence of movement which our departure caused among the spectators.'

What interests me here is the likelihood that the Marquis d'Arlandes was wrong. Parisian crowds are hard to impress and harder still to silence, as Louis XVI discovered a few years later. But solitary observers can be self-centered creatures, innocently assuming that others enjoy the satisfaction of their own full bellies. The marquis, it seems, had been disoriented by his sudden separation from the earth. I wonder: In his confusion did he attribute to the crowds what he himself felt – the sudden peace within the gondola, the eerie smoothness of balloon flight, its windlessness in the wind?

That sort of transposition remains today the most common illusion in the experience of flying. People on the ground know milder versions of similar reversals, observing, for example, that the sun moves toward the west, when of course it is the ground that moves toward the east. But above that, deep inside the sky, the confusion is heightened by flight's strange motions and by its utter detachment from the earth. The full extent of that detachment takes years to understand and accept. Until then balloonists continue to have the impression during takeoff not that they are climbing but that the ground crew, faces upturned, is sinking away. Airplane passengers have the impression that they are holding still, suspended in space as, far below, a miniature nation slides by. When they overtake a slower airplane they say it seems to come swimming by them backward. When another airplane passes head-on in the opposite direction they comment on its startling speed. When they fly through billowing clouds they speak of the inevitability of head winds. And when in order to turn they bank to one side, expecting to feel the tilt, they find instead that the world outside has toppled in the opposite direction.

I was reminded of this one day while riding in the back of a Boeing 737 departing from San Francisco on a short flight down the coast to Los Angeles. The morning was bright. We swept up the San Francisco Bay in a gently banked left turn along the city's waterfront, out toward the Pacific. Despite the airplane's bank, most passengers peered through the windows, cautiously admiring the view. But the pilots were too enthusiastic. Directly over the Golden Gate, they rolled suddenly into a steep turn, dropping the left wing so far below the horizon that it appeared to pivot around the bridge's nearest tower. I imagine they thought of the maneuver in technical terms: We were turning already, and for just a few seconds we would exceed the airline maximum of a thirty-degree bank. The maximum is aerodynamically unimportant at cruising speeds and is imposed only for peace of mind. Sightseeing seemed more important now. The pilots probably figured they had done us a favor.

But they had not. As the airplane pivoted, the startled passengers looked away from the windows and met the eyes of their unhappy neighbors. A collective gasp rippled through the cabin. The reaction did not surprise me. Over the years I have learned never to bank steeply with my own passengers without first preparing them for the maneuver, and have noticed that even then many of them become helpless and disoriented. I do not blame them, either. As an instructor of experienced pilots, I have heard gasps and worse from my students. Pilots are merely well-trained passengers. They have to be reminded not to flinch, whimper, or make audible appeals to the Savior. They have to be encouraged to ride the airplane willingly, from the inside, and to think as it thinks. And they have to be convinced of the strange logic of the turn. At its center lies the peculiar relationship between the bank and the resulting movement of the airplane and the fact that neither can be felt. Such nothingness is what the passengers sensed when the airplane tilted over the Golden Gate – like the Marquis d'Arlandes' windlessness in the wind, an eerie lack of feeling where feeling should be.

Indeed lack of feeling associated with the bank is so disorienting, so unlike experience on the ground, that many people refuse to accept it – even after they have had the turn carefully demonstrated to them. This is because they may feel the lurch as the airplane dips its wing, starting into a turn or starting out of it, and they allow this to fool them into believing that they can feel the bank itself. When the bank is visible, they ascribe their unease to fears that the airplane might slip to the side, or capsize, or somehow tumble. When the bank is not visible, during flight inside the clouds or on black nights, they no longer worry because, in their minds, that which cannot be felt does not exist.

Over history, pilots have made the same mistake. The airplane is such a simple device. Certainly the wing's profile is one of nature's purest forms. And our species was given its use before anyone knew even its most basic characteristics. Pilots as a result had to go about teaching themselves to fly. It took several generations. Eventually they had to admit that instinct abandoned them in the clouds and that they needed special instruments to tell of the bank. Without the instruments, they went into mysterious and uncontrollable turns and sometimes died. With the instruments, they maintained control and survived. Thus was born the most basic distinction in flying, between conditions in which the turn is visible and conditions in which it must be measured. And since the ability to fly through the weather has proved to be more important than speed in the conquest of distance, the mastery of the turn is the story of our sky.

The bank is a condition of tilted wings, and the turn is the change in the direction which results. The connection between the two is inexorable: The airplane must bank to turn, and when it is banked it must turn. The reason is simple. In wings-level flight, the lifting force of the wings is directed straight up, and the airplane does not turn; in a bank, the lifting force is tilted to the side, and the airplane therefore must *move* to that side. It cannot slide sideways through the air because it has a vertical fin on the tail, which forces the turn by keeping the tail in line behind the nose. The result is an elegantly curved flight path, created as the airplane lifts itself through the changes in direction.

The miraculous part of the maneuver is that the turn has an important balancing effect on the bank that causes it. The same effect, in cruder form, steadies cars on banked roadways, and bobsleds on the vertical walls of icy tracks. The difference in airplanes is that as the bank angle increases, the turn also quickens and by doing so automatically delivers a balance that is perfect. Bicycles react similarly: When they start to topple, they turn and thereby keep themselves up. Airplanes are even steadier. They operate in three-dimensional space and do not rely on tires to keep from sliding to the side. They will never capsize, no matter how steeply they are banked.

Consider for contrast the primitive banking or 'heeling' of a sailboat, which does not cause a turn and which amounts to a simple trick of balancing the forces of the sail against those of the boat's ballast – whether a heavy keel or some other form of counterweight. The magnificent sensation of speed it gives is all froth and spray. The truth is, heeling slows most boats. Racers accept it as an unfortunate byproduct of the conflicting forces that allow the boat to proceed upwind. Passengers do not enjoy it in boats any more than in airplanes, but they understand it better: Heeling a boat is a thrill seeker's gambit; if it goes too far, the boat will capsize and perhaps fill with water; if people don't brace themselves, they will slide across the deck and slip into the waves. It is ironic that the physics intend boats to move on level bottoms, but require of airplanes the banked turn.

It is true that as the bank steepens in flight, directing more of the wings' lifting force into the turn, the airplane has greater difficulty holding its altitude. Flown at bank angles approaching ninety degrees – in which the wings point straight up and down – no normal airplane can keep from descending. (Some fighters can, but only because at high speeds the fuselage itself creates lift and becomes a wing.) In such 'knife-edge' flight the wings exert all their lifting force in a direction parallel to the earth's surface, and gravity pulls the airplane down. But if the pilot controls the airplane carefully and allows it to keep turning, it will happily roll past the vertical, onto its back, and finally right side up again. During such a maneuver, San Francisco Bay momentarily appears *above* you, and the Golden Gate Bridge seems to hang from the water. This is fine, if you are prepared for it. Full rolls are the purest expression of flight. They are normally flown only in fighters and other acrobatic airplanes, but if you ignore convention you can safely fly them in any airplane, including a Boeing 737.

None of this would have comforted the man sitting next to me during that steep turn over the Golden Gate. He was large, sharp-eyed, and very alert. When the wing dropped, he said, 'Hey!' and grabbed the armrests. Now he rode 'above' me in the bank, leaning into the aisle as if he feared he might topple into my lap. He need not have worried. If he had dropped his pen, it would not have fallen 'down' in the conventional sense – toward me and the earth – but rather toward the tilted carpet at his feet. If he had dangled the pen from a string, it would have hung toward the floor.

A dangled pen is a primitive inclinometer, like a plumb bob or the heel-meter of a sailboat. On land or at sea, it hangs toward the center of the planet. But in flight, it hangs toward the floor, no matter how steeply the airplane is banked. A carpenter's level would be equally fooled. This peculiar phenomenon is another manifestation of the turn's inherent balance. The earth's gravity acts normally on an airplane, but so do the forces of inertia. Inertia is the desire of any mass to keep doing what it has been doing – in an airplane, to keep moving, and moving straight. During a turn, inertia pulls horizontally. In cars, it causes people to skid off roads. In airplanes, it combines with the downward force of gravity to create a new force that pulls constantly toward the floor. Actually, the force pulls toward points in space, but by banking, the airplane places its floor directly in the way – it has to, in order to turn. The neatness of this Newtonian package is beautiful to behold. Bob Hoover, a legendary stunt pilot, used to set an empty glass on his airplane's instrument panel and pour himself a drink while flying full rolls. Our 737 pilots seemed inclined to fly the same way. If they had, as we passed through the inverted position and saw the Golden Gate Bridge hanging from the water, my sharp-eyed neighbor could have watched his pen dangling toward the sky. The flight attendants could have walked upside down. And some passengers, too self-occupied to look outside, would not have even noticed.

The human body is just another inclinometer. Undisturbed by the view, it sits quietly in its seat, dangling its feet toward the tilted floor, churning out reports for the home office. This is difficult to accept about ourselves. The inner ear, and with it any useful sense of balance, is neutralized by the motion of flight. It is our greatest weakness as fliers that, having acquired wings, we still lack an instinctive sense of bank.

For passengers this actually offers certain immediate advantages. The man next to me, for instance, was not about to fall into my lap. He could have relaxed, lowered the tray in front of him, and called for a coffee. Unlike the table in a sailboat, an airplane tray requires no gimbals. Flight attendants brew coffee on fixed counters, deliver it without worrying about the airplane's bank angle, and fill cups to their brims. Full cups make people behave during turns: if they try to hold them level with the earth, the coffee pours out and scalds their thighs. If this seems unusual, imagine the alternative, an airplane in which 'down' was always toward the ground. Bedlam would break loose in the cabin during every turn. Unless people held their coffee just right, they would scald their neighbor's thighs.

Better to leave physics alone. As it is, as long as you contain your curiosity about what is happening outside, the inside of the cabin remains a steady and unsurprising little world. The turbulence which causes an airplane to shudder and buck is less important than people imagine. After hours on their feet, flight attendants do not develop sea legs. Passengers need no encouragement to stand and walk about. If he had stopped leaning, my neighbor could have stood up and danced the length of the tilted aisle.

The situation is not quite so carefree up front in the cockpit. In fact, the forces which tame the cabin during turns are the very same forces which over time have provided pilots with the most deadly problem of flight control. As long as its wings are level, the airplane is by nature a well-mannered animal, and slow to anger. If you pull its nose up, then release the controls, it puts its nose back down; if you push its nose down, it answers by rearing back up. Like horseback riding, flying consists mostly of leaving the beast alone, allowing it to do its own thinking. The problem is that this particular beast does not stay on the trail unguided. And once it strays, it develops a strong impulse to self-destruct.

Unguided, any airplane will eventually begin to bank. That in itself is fine if you don't mind the resulting turn, meaning the change in direction. But as the bank tilts the lift force of the wings, reducing their vertical effectiveness, it erodes the equilibrium that previously countered the pull of the earth. The airplane responds to the loss by lowering its nose and accelerating. Sitting in the cockpit with folded arms and watching it proceed is like sitting on a temperamental horse and letting it gallop down a steepening slope: It requires a morbid curiosity and steady nerves. In flight, the slope steepens because the acceleration tightens the airplane's turn, which increases its bank angle, which causes further acceleration. A sort of aerodynamic lock-in occurs. The airplane banks to the vertical or beyond and points its nose straight down.

That is the spiral dive. In its most virulent form pilots sometimes call it the graveyard spiral. The airplane descends in ever steeper circles and either disintegrates in mid-air from the air pressures of excessive speed or shatters against the ground at the bottom of a screaming descent. All flights would suffer this end if the pilot (or autopilot) did not intervene.

In good weather the intervention is easy. You hold the controls lightly, and when you see that the airplane has banked, you unbank it. During turns you hold the controls more firmly and keep the nose from dropping. The increased loading created by inertia during such a well-flown turn is felt within the airplane as a peculiar heaviness – a 'pull' not toward the ground, of course, but toward the cabin floor. Pilots measure it in 'Gs,' as a multiple of gravity's normal pull on the surface of the earth, or in steady wings-level flight. An airplane that banks to thirty degrees, the airline standard, creates a loading of 1.15 Gs: The airplane, and everything in it, temporarily weighs fifteen percent more than normal. Fifteen percent is just barely noticeable. But only a bit steeper, at a forty-five-degree bank, the load increases to 1.4 Gs: People feel pressed into their seats, and if they look outside they may notice that the wings have flexed upward. Technically, such loadings are not important. Airplanes are strong and flexible, and pilots shrug off 2 Gs and may feel comfortable at twice as much. But passengers are unaccustomed to the sensation. As we pivoted over the Golden Gate, the man in the seat beside me suddenly gained about eighty pounds. Had he dangled his pen toward the tilted floor, it would have pulled on the string with surprising force. This might not have reassured him. But the extra heaviness was a measure of the pilot's success in resisting the spiral dive. If we had felt 'normal' during the turn, it could only have meant that the nose was dropping fast toward the water.

No pilot would make such a mistake on a clear day. The view from the cockpit is dominated by the horizon, the constantly renewing division between the sky and the earth. It forms a line across the windshield and makes immediate sense of the airplane's movements. Birds, too, use the horizon. The sight of an angled and shifting world must act powerfully on them. They are subject to the same laws of physics as airplanes, but they fly with insouciance, neither worrying about their inability to feel the bank nor pondering the explosive nature of the spiral dive. They can get away with this not because they are better fliers than we – in truth, they are worse – but because they can wait out bad weather and usually do. People do not have that luxury. We fly on schedules, through clouds and storms and across the blackest nights. When no useful horizon is visible outside the cockpit we maintain control of the airplane by reference to an artificial horizon on the instrument panel. And so we outdo the birds.

But the use of that tool is not as obvious as it might at first seem. The artificial horizon is a gyroscopically steadied line which stays constantly level with the earth's surface. The airplane pitches and banks in relation to this steady line, which in spatial terms never moves. The problem is, in *airplane* terms it does move. And pilots are part of the airplane – they fly it from within, strapped to their seats, sensing like the Marquis d'Arlandes their own full bellies. In clear skies they would never misjudge a bank as the tilting of the earth, but with their view restricted to the abstractions of the instrument panel they sometimes do just that: They perceive the airplane's lateral motion as a movement on the face instrument of the artificial horizon line. This causes them to 'fly' the wrong thing – the moving horizon line, rather than the fixed symbolic airplane. For example, as turbulence banks the airplane to the left, the pilots, banking with it, notice the artificial horizon line dropping to the right. Reacting instinctively to the indication of motion, they try to raise the line as if it were a wing. The result of such a reversal is murderous. Pilots steer to the left just when they should steer to the right, and then in confusion they steer harder. While maneuvering calmly inside the clouds, I have flown with students who for this reason suddenly tried to flip my airplane upside down. They were rational people, confronted by the turn.

This has become a basic reality of our time. We are the energetic, self-centered, adaptable species, carving a landscape of motion through the sky. If we try to fly by instinct through the weather, even the best of us will roll into spiral dives. If we misread an artificial horizon, or follow one that has failed, we will take a shortcut to the same destination. The circumstance that causes the spiral is the very circumstance that prevents its solution. The bank itself cannot be felt. Pilots experience the fury of the dive and die in confusion. That is the inside history of human flight. The Montgolfier brothers gave us the balloon and introduced us to the peculiar egotism of flight. The Wright brothers gave us the wing and confronted us with the dilemma of the turn.

The Wrights flew straight and level at Kitty Hawk, North Carolina, on December 17, 1903, and a bewildered press paid little attention. The flight was the culmination of an almost incredible four-year story – two unassuming bicycle builders engaged in a process of problem solving so sure-footed that it left the world behind. The Wright brothers were simply smarter than their peers – much smarter. If their insight was to understand the importance of flight control, it was only with the mastery of the bank that they achieved their purpose. After their initial straight-ahead runs, they went home to Ohio, rented a cow pasture on the trolley line outside of Dayton, and spent the following year stretching their flights and learning to turn. At a time when higher authorities continued to proclaim that such acts were impossible, deep in the American countryside there were a few farmers who came quietly to know that the Wright brothers could fly.

The first detailed account of the Wrights' success appeared not in the *New York Times* or the *Scientific American*, but in *Gleanings in Bee Culture*, a little magazine for beekeepers published in Medina, Ohio. The editor and publisher was Amos Root, a typically moralistic Midwesterner with a taste for practical technology. In an aside intended as a parallel to the Wrights' experience, he admitted that as a young man he had imported the first modern bicycle to Ohio.

The whole town jeered at me, and the story of the 'fool and his money' was hurled in my teeth so many times I almost dread to hear it even yet. Men of good fair understanding pointed their fingers at me, and said that anybody of good common sense ought to know that *that* thing would not stand up with a man on it, for that would be an utter impossibility . . . Finally I rented the largest hall in the town, went in with one trusty boy who had faith, for a companion, and *locked the door*. After quite a little practice on the smooth floor of the hall I succeeded in riding from one end to the other; but I could not turn the corners. When, after still more practice, I did turn one corner without falling, how my spirits arose! A little later I went in a wabbly way clear around the room. Then my companion did the same thing, and, oh how we did rejoice and gather faith! A little later on, with a flushed but happy face, I went out into the street and rode around the public square.

Thirty years later now, Amos Root had a car, which he drove 350 miles round trip to visit the Wrights' cow pasture near Dayton. There on September 20, 1904, he happened to witness Wilbur fly the airplane's first full circle.

Bees, of course, are the great specialists of full-circle flying; they spend their days on round-trip missions and construct whole landscapes out of their ability to turn. Root must have been influenced by that knowledge. It is clear that he felt a general enthusiasm for circular movement, which meant that he of all people was predisposed to appreciate the significance of the flight that day. He labeled it 'the first successful trip of an airship, without balloon to sustain it, that the world has ever made, that is, to turn the corners and come back to the starting-point.' And he was right. It is the turn that makes the airplane practical.

The U.S. Army was slower to catch on. Five years later, after much convincing by the Wrights, it reluctantly took delivery of its first airplane. In 1909, horses still seemed more glorious. The war in Europe changed that. By its end in 1918, the cavalry had been slaughtered, and flying was all that remained of chivalry and adventure. Unsullied by the carnage in the trenches, pilots chased across the sky, turning hard on each other's tails. The war taught them to fly with confidence and encouraged among them the myth of inborn ability. They called it flying by the seat of the pants.

As in all wars since, more pilots died by error than by enemy action. Those who died in spiral dives left no records. Those who survived made the dangerous discovery that people can feel at home in the sky. They learned to accept the strangeness of a steep bank – the G-load and the sight of a tilted horizon – and the magic of a full roll. Nonetheless, they still believed in balance. When they ducked through small clouds and emerged with their wings slightly tilted, they did not suspect the importance of the unfelt bank. Luckily for them, when the weather was bad, or on black nights, they waited on the ground. German pilots called good conditions 'flight weather,' because they could fly, and bad conditions 'flier's weather,' because they could stay in bed. By happy coincidence, pilots had no reason to fly when they had nothing to see.

After the war, regular airmail service started in Europe and the United States. It made airplanes useful to the public for the first time, gave birth to the airlines, and placed pressure on the pilots to operate on schedules. They followed rivers and railroads in open cockpit biplanes with no gyroscopic instruments and flew under the weather, sometimes at extremely low altitude, dodging steeples and oil derricks.

One of those early airmail pilots, Dean Smith, wrote about getting his first route briefing for a bad weather run, west across the Allegheny Mountains to Cleveland:

From the field here at Bellefonte you head west through the gap in the ridge. Climb as you veer a bit north, passing over the center of this railroad switchback up the side of Rattlesnake Mountain, then due west again to clear the top of the ridge at, say, 2,200 feet. After about ten miles you hit the railroad again at Snow Shoe – look sharp, it's only four or five houses – then follow the railroad on down to the other side of the Rattlesnake to the valley where you pick up the West Branch of the Susquehanna River, winding along to the town of Clearfield, which you will know by three round water reservoirs just south of town. Next, you have to get over about thirty miles of plateau to Du Bois. This is pretty high, about 2,200 feet, but it is fairly smooth on top and there is a white gravel road cut through the trees straight to Du Bois. As you come into town you will see the railroad to your right, and just south of the railroad a piece of flat pasture you can land on in a pinch. Then the highway leads you for fifty miles through Brookville to Clarion. Each of these towns has a half-mile race track. The one at Clarion is half full of trees, but the one at Brookville is clean and hard, and it's the best emergency field from here to Cleveland: as soon as you land you will be met by a girl named Alice Henderson, driving a big Cadillac, who will be pleased to look after you. After Clarion, the country gradually gets lower until you cross the Allegheny at Greenville, which you can identify by a big S bend in the river. From then on it's clear sailing.

After such a flight, no one could accuse a pilot of not having 'been' to the mountains. Many were killed for the attempt; in fact, the early airmail flying was the most dangerous flying the world has ever known. But still the globe refused to shrink. Fog, night, and heavy weather continued to ground the airplanes. Some pilots did have a rough, though technically uninformed, respect for the disorientation lurking deep within the clouds, but most pilots simply stayed below the weather. In pride and ignorance they told themselves that this was because without radio navigation they needed to see landmarks to find their way. It was another happy coincidence.

In the winter of 1925, a young Army pilot named Carl Crane got caught in the clouds at 8,000 feet directly over Detroit while trying to fly a congressman's son to Washington, D.C., in a biplane. Crane later became a famous master of the turn. Speaking of the flight, he said,

In a short time, I was losing altitude, completely out of control. I could not fly the airplane at all – it had gotten into a spiral dive. Half way down I looked around at my boy in the back, and he was enjoying the flight no end. He was shaking his hands and grinning, and I was slowly dying because I knew we were going to crash.

The boy in the rear cockpit was just unaware. Crane had an altimeter and airspeed indicator. He thought he was dying 'slowly' only because of the way experience is compressed when an airplane goes wild. Pilots then tend not to think about God or their lives but about solutions. Once when flying a series of ill-considered acrobatic maneuvers, I stupidly lost control of an airplane and started into a flat spin – a dangerous condition from which there may be no recovery. On that particular flight a video camera had been mounted behind me in the cockpit, and as a result I later saw the whole thing on tape: the nose rising unexpectedly, the forested horizon swirling, and the uninformed attempt to find the answer – the systematic control stick motions, the experimental bursts of power, the reach for the canopy jettison knob, the inexplicable return to normal flight. The experience was frightening, even though I was wearing a parachute and flying in the clear. But what surprised me most about it later, when I saw it in on the tape, was the speed with which it was over.

Carl Crane's loss of control, which was both more dangerous and more prolonged, must have seemed at the time to stretch on for an eternity. Neither he nor his passenger was wearing a parachute. From his training he remembered only vague admonitions to stay out of the weather. But he was in the weather now and couldn't see a thing. He knew he was turning but could make no sense of the compass. It is a notorious problem: Because the earth's magnetic field does not lie parallel to the globe's surface but dips down toward the magnetic poles, the compass card responds to banks by spinning erratically, jamming, and sometimes showing turns in reverse. Crane did not know which wing was down, let alone by how much. If he tried to level the wings, he was just as likely to roll upside down as right side up. If he tried to raise the nose, the effect would be to quicken the turn and steepen the dive. Crane understood none of the details at the time, but he sensed that his situation was hopeless.

Dean Smith, the early airmail pilot, had gone through a similar experience. His memoir of a weather flight, written thirty years later, still rings with the authentic confusion of the time:

Now followed a long period of fighting to keep control of the plane while all the time my equilibrium became steadily more confused. I succeeded in climbing to 8,000 feet; then the plane began to get more and more out of control. It lost altitude until I was back down to 5,000 feet . . . At last I fell. The plane stalled and whipped off into a spin, although to my bewildered senses it did not seem to be spinning down, but impossibly up and to the side. I cut the throttle and held the plane in the spin for a few seconds to be certain I was in a known condition and to force my mind to reorient. When I broke the spin, I couldn't pull out level from the resulting dive. By the time I got the wires to stop screaming the plane promptly stalled again. The plane floundered through the dark muck in a series of stalls, spins, dives, and pull-outs. I struggled and fought with it all the way down, working with desperate concentration, but that little corner of my mind that detachedly views such things said, 'My friend, you are a dead duck.'

Dean Smith happened to survive, but others even today do not. The physics have not changed. In modern times, air traffic control recorded the radio transmissions of an unskilled pilot who, with family on board, tried to descend through an overcast. After he lost control, he began to sob into the microphone, begging the radar controllers to tell him which side was up. But radar shows air traffic as wingless blips on an electronic map, and is incapable of distinguishing banks. Controllers are in the business of keeping airplanes from colliding. Pilots are in the business of flight control. This one had instruments on board by which he could have kept his wings level, but in the milkiness of the clouds he became confused. The controllers listened helplessly to his panic and, in the background, to the screams of his children. The transmission ended when the airplane broke apart, somewhere far away inside the sky.

But Carl Crane's biplane – over Detroit in 1925 with the congressman's son – was stronger:

Finally it got down to under a thousand feet, and I said, 'Well here we go. I'm going to look at my boy once more.' And as I turned around to look at him, a sign went by my wing. It said 'Statler Hotel.' I had just missed the top of the Statler Hotel. In all the mist and rain, I could see the buildings and the streets. I flew down the street and got over the Detroit River, and flew down about ten feet high all the way to Toledo, shaking all the way.

Crane became obsessed. Shocked by the way intuition had abandoned him, he began to ask questions. For years he got no intelligent answers. He never met Dean Smith. Those veterans he did meet kept insisting they could fly by the seat of their pants, and they thought less of those who could not. Their self-deception now seems all the more profound because the solution – a gyroscope adapted to flying – was already widely available.

The gyroscope is a spinning wheel, like a child's top, mounted in gimbals that allow it freedom of movement. It has two important traits: Left alone, it maintains fixed orientation in space (in relation to the stars); and when tilted, it reacts in an odd but predictable way. Elmer Sperry, the great American inventor, started playing with these traits in the early 1900s. As a curiosity, he designed a gyro-stabilized 'trained wheelbarrow,' and he tried, without success, to interest a circus in it. Undiscouraged, Sperry turned to the U.S. Navy instead and interested it in gyro-compasses and ship stabilizers. Competitors in Europe developed similar devices and during the buildup to war interested their countries' navies, too.

Airplanes were an intriguing sideline. Sperry built a gyroscopic autopilot in 1910, not to enable blind flight but to stabilize the otherwise unruly early flying machines. In 1915 he began to ponder instrumentation and with prescient insight into the problems of flight was able after three years to produce the first gyroscopic turn indicator, an instrument still in use today. Its face consisted of a vertical pointer, which indicated turns to the left or right. (Necessarily, it also included a ball like a carpenter's level, an inclinometer that showed not bank but 'skid' or 'slip' – conditions of lateral imbalance.) Sperry called the instrument a 'crutch to the compass.' In his patent application he described its use as an instrument that would allow pilots to fly indefinitely through the clouds, implying that without it they could not.

It was hardly a secret. Already by the end of World War I, thinkers on both sides of the Atlantic had understood the difficulties of the banked turn, but the great majority of professional pilots continued to disdain the idea of any crutch. A group of Sperry's employees split off and, calling themselves the Pioneer Instrument Company, went into production with the device. They found the market difficult. For the next twenty years customers kept complaining to them about a mysterious problem: The instruments worked just fine in clear air, but as soon as they were taken into clouds they began to indicate turns.

Not all pilots were that stupid. One of the first cloud flights with this new device, the turn indicator, was made in 1918 by William Ocker, an Army captain and an experienced aviator. Though Ocker, too, lost control and spiraled out of the overcast, he assumed that the error was his, and he set off on an eleven-year quest for good answers.

During the 1920s a few of the more progressive airmail pilots, operating under deadly pressure to push the weather, began to admit the need to control their bank angles by reference to the instruments. Charles Lindbergh was one of those converts. When he crossed the Atlantic in 1927, he used a turn indicator with which he had first experimented only months before, and he readily admitted afterward that it had kept him from spiraling into the sea. His description of that historic piece of instrument flying holds true today:

What lies outside doesn't matter. My world and my life are compressed within these fabric walls. Flying blind is difficult enough in smooth air. In this swirling cloud, it calls for all the concentration I can muster. The turn and bank indicators, the air speed, the altimeter, and the compass, all those phosphorescent lines and dots in front of me, must be kept in proper place. When a single one strays off, the rest go chasing after it like so many sheep, and have to be caught quickly and carefully herded back into position again.

Two years later, in 1929, a young military pilot and engineer from MIT named James Doolittle made a 'blind' landing after flying a complete circuit around an airport in a special biplane modified with a domed cockpit from which he could not see outside. The landing itself was a technical dead end. Once Doolittle was over the field he reduced the power and waited until the biplane plunked onto the grass – an impractical technique for airlines then or now. More significant were the special devices that made the precisely flown circuit possible. The airplane was equipped with navigational radios, an airspeed indicator, an improved altimeter, a turn indicator, and two new gyroscopic instruments which Sperry's son, also named Elmer, had developed with Doolittle's guidance – a gyroscopic compass and an artificial horizon. This combination was so effective that it still forms the core of instrument panels today. Doolittle reported that using the artificial horizon was 'like cutting a porthole through the fog to look at the real horizon.' But that was the easy part. There remained the more stubborn problem of belief.

Marked for life by his near collision with the Statler Hotel, Carl Crane read the descriptions of Doolittle's 1929 flight with fascination. He was now an Army instructor at a training base near San Antonio, Texas. Though his superior officers disapproved of instrument flying, Crane was convinced of the need for gyroscopes. He finally got permission to cover over a cockpit and turn one of the biplanes into an instrument trainer. While he was at work on this, William Ocker wandered into the hangar.

Ocker was the man who had lost control of his airplane while flying with one of Sperry's first turn indicators back in 1918 – and he had been worrying about it ever since. He didn't look like much of a pilot, with his bifocals and his mournful puritan's face, but he had a powerful mind and all the conviction of a missionary. The truth about instrument flying had come to him in 1926, during a standard medical examination at Crissy Field in San Francisco. Part of the routine was a crude test of balance involving the use of a Barany chair, a rotating seat on which the pilot spun with closed eyes. Ocker easily passed the required test, but afterward the examining doctor, who was an old friend, told him that he would now demonstrate to him that his senses could indeed be fooled. This time Ocker felt the chair begin to turn, and he guessed the direction correctly – but when the chair slowed, he felt that it had stopped, and when it stopped, he felt that it had started to turn in the opposite direction.

For the doctor the demonstration was a parlor game, a gentle amusement with the inner ear. For William Ocker, however, it amounted to a stunning revelation: The sense of accelerating into a turn is the same as that of decelerating from the opposite turn. Here at last was the explanation for the persistence of so much confusion and death. The chair had induced the same false sensation that eight years before had caused him to lose control while flying with the turn indicator and that still today was leading even those few pilots who accepted their inability to feel the bank to distrust their instruments and roll for no apparent reason into dangerous spiral dives.

It was a moment to equal the Wright brothers' first full circle. The story goes that Ocker said nothing but left the doctor's office, went immediately to his airplane, and retrieved his personal portable air-driven turn indicator, which he proceeded to rig up inside a shoe box. He cut a viewing hole into one end of the box, attached a penlight and a black fabric hood to it, and returned that afternoon to the office, where he challenged his friend the doctor to trick him again – with the difference that this time he would look into the shoe box. Again Ocker experienced the false sensations, but because he refused to believe them and relied exclusively on the turn indicator, he could not be fooled. The doctor could hardly have grasped the significance of what he was seeing, but there on his simple spinning chair the bespectacled pilot William Ocker was giving birth to modern instrument flying. He had discovered the most disturbing limitation of human flight – that instinct is *worse* than useless in the clouds, that it can induce deadly spirals, and that as a result having gyroscopes is not enough, that pilots must learn against all contradictory sensations the difficult discipline of an absolute belief in their instruments. Perhaps equally as important, he had invented a way to prove it.

Ocker became so obsessed with the spinning chair that the Army hospitalized him twice for sanity tests, then banished him to Texas. Still he refused to quit. When Ocker met Crane in the hangar in Texas, he invited him for a spin in a revolving chair, and then and there Crane became Ocker's disciple. The two men began a joint exploration of all known aspects of flight inside the clouds. In 1932 they published *Blind Flight in Theory and Practice*, the first systematic analysis of instrument flying. It was dedicated, no doubt with some bitterness, 'To those courageous airmen who have risked criticism and loss of professional prestige by precisely relating their own difficult experiences during bad weather flight.'

The book had an enormous influence, though more at first with the Russians than with the U.S. Army Air Corps, which adopted it as a training text only at the outbreak of World War II. Never mind. The authors effectively laid to rest the old faith in flying by instinct. They described the physics of the turn and the confusion experienced by the inner ear, but their most dramatic argument grew out of an experiment with pigeons. From everything humans had learned after three decades of winged flight, it now seemed likely that birds, too, must be unable to fly without a visible horizon. Ocker and Crane decided to find out. They acquired a few pigeons, blindfolded them, took them up in biplanes, and threw them out. Sure enough the birds dropped into fluttering emergency descents – they panicked and went down like feathered parachutes. It is possible, of course, that they did not like the blindfolds, which were made of Bull Durham tobacco pouches. But anyway, the experiment was the kind pilots could understand. If God had meant birds to fly in the clouds, He would have given them gyroscopes.

Birds cannot fly through heavy rain. They get sucked up by thunderstorms, frozen by altitude, and burned by lightning. They lose control and crash, fly into obstacles, wander offshore, drift off course, get hopelessly lost, run out of fuel, and die by the millions. They would rather not migrate in bad weather, and they usually don't. Nonetheless, it appears that Ocker and Crane may have been wrong. There is evidence now that perhaps some birds do occasionally fly inside the clouds.

This is big news, though as time has shown it is not news of the sort that people seek out. Word of it first appeared back in 1972, in the proceedings of a NASA symposium on animal navigation. Hidden among reports like 'When the Beachhopper Looks at the Moon' and 'Anemomenotactic Orientation in Beetles and Scorpions' (When a Bug Feels the Wind) was a paper entitled 'Nocturnal Bird Migration in Opaque Clouds.' It was written by Donald Griffin, a Harvard zoologist who earlier had discovered the use of sonar by bats. Griffin reported that he had borrowed a military radar and on overcast nights in New York had tracked birds that seemed to be flying *inside* the clouds. There were only a few such birds, and Griffin was able to track them only for a couple of miles, but they appeared to be proceeding under control.

Griffin's biggest problem was uncertainty over the precise flight conditions at the birds' altitude. Was the weather really as thick as it looked from below? Were the birds really flying blind? Griffin had good reasons to believe so, but as a scientist he had to be cautious. His final report, in 1973, reinforced the earlier findings but was more carefully entitled 'Oriented Bird Migration in or between Opaque Cloud Layers.'

To ornithologists interested in bird navigation, the difference between 'in' and 'between' seems to be an unimportant detail – their concentration being instead on the observation that Griffin's birds could apparently find their way without reference to the stars or the ground. But to the birds, whose first job – like that of pilots – must be to control their bank angles, the distinction might be crucial. The ornithologists seem not to know that they should care, as if for all their curiosity about the birds' earthly habitats, the issue of the spiral dive has never even entered their minds. Griffin, a former pilot, understands the issue's importance. I once sought him out and expressed my frustration that so many ornithologists seem to be stuck on the ground. He laughed. 'I keep telling them, "Gee, birds fly!"'

Assuming they fly in the clouds, the question is, How? Ornithologists have no answer, and they shy away from speculation. It is known that birds navigate by watching the ground and the positions of the sun, the moon, and the stars – none of which would help them maintain control in the clouds. But they may also use a host of nonvisual clues and may use mental 'maps' based on sound, smell, air currents, variations in gravitational pull, and other factors. Experiments have shown that some species are extremely sensitive to magnetic forces. The heads of these species contain magnetite crystals surrounded by nerves, which may give them an intuitive knowledge of their direction (and possibly location) in the earth's magnetic field. A highly refined and error-free sense of direction, or of *change* in direction, could in theory amount to a non-gyroscopic turn indicator – a biological crutch for winged flight in the clouds.

The other possibility is that some birds actually do have gyroscopes of a primitive sort. This is less far-fetched than it seems. The rhythmic flapping of wings could have the effect of Foucault's pendulum, allowing a bird to sense turns without any external cue. A pendulum is more than a hanging weight; it is a hanging weight that has been pushed and is swinging freely. Swinging gives the pendulum its special ability to maintain spatial orientation. Léon Foucault was the French physicist who first used one, in 1851, to demonstrate the rotation of the earth: Though the pendulum appeared to change its direction as it swung, in fact the plane of its motion remained constant, and the apparent change was caused by the turning of the earth underneath it. Foucault knew that a spinning wheel would possess the same properties of spatial orientation, and though he never perfected such a device (largely because he could not figure out how to drive it), he coined the term 'gyroscope' for it – from the Greek *gyros*, for 'rotation,' and *skopeein*, for 'viewing.'

If birds do rely on the pendulum effect in some sense to 'see' through the clouds, they are not alone. Flies and mosquitoes (among more than 85,000 other species of Diptera) use specially adapted vibrating rods to maintain spatial orientation in flight. Not only can they turn sharply, roll inverted, and land on the underside of leaves, but they can do it in a fog.

Pilots, too, have relied on pendulums. It is said that an airliner inbound to New York in the 1950s lost all its gyroscopes in heavy weather over Block Island. The captain was a wise old man who had risen with the airlines from the earliest airmail days and was now approaching retirement. A lesser pilot might have fallen for the trap of intuition. But the captain simply took out his pocket watch, dangled it from its chain, and began to swing it toward the instrument panel. Flying by the pendulum and the compass, he proceeded the length of Long Island in the clouds. After breaking into the clear near the airport, he landed and wished his passengers a good day.

The story is not impossible. It came to mind one night when I flew out over the Pacific Ocean, off the coast of Oregon, alone at the controls of a borrowed single-engine airplane. High clouds darkened the sky. The light of a lonely fishing boat drifted by below. Flying a mile above the water, I headed beyond the boat and into the complete blackness of approaching weather. It was an experience of solitude: in dark clouds over a wild ocean, an absolute night, the cockpit a world of its own, the instrument panel a landscape within it. The instruments glowed in a warm light, abstracting the strange story of flight's pure motion.

The gyroscopes functioned perfectly. The radios were blissfully silent. I hooked a metal pen to a fishing line and dangled it from a knob on the ceiling. Flying by the artificial horizon, I made a steep turn and watched the pen dangle toward the titled floor. Then I straightened out, pushed the pen toward the instrument panel, and released it. It swung for almost thirty seconds before requiring another push. The problem, of course, was that each renewal would erase the pendulum's spatial memory. Nonetheless, I thought the device might work. After turning north, the direction in which the compass is most confused by the bank, I covered the gyroscopes with slips of paper.

The night air was smooth. The pen swung rhythmically toward the panel and back. Eventually it redirected itself to the left. This could only have meant that the airplane had banked and turned to the right. I rolled to the left gingerly, hoping to raise the right wing just enough to return to straight flight. The pen seemed to stabilize in its new direction. I renewed the swing, shoving the pen again directly toward the panel. It soon confirmed that the airplane had indeed leveled its wings and stopped turning. The compass settled, showing that earlier I had strayed twenty degrees to the right. Lowering the left wing cautiously, watching the pen swing to the right, I crept back to the original heading. Later, when I tried to make a large turn, I lost control and spiraled and had to peek at the gyroscopes. But with the wings level again, I flew on for miles, learning to work with the swinging pen. Trust comes slowly in the indication of turns. It is a small faith that allows us to fly so deeply into the sky.

# 3

## *On a Bombay Night (The Turn continued)*

This is a story about that faith. On another black night, at the end of the first day of 1978, a Boeing 747 with 213 people aboard taxied for takeoff at the airport in Bombay, the great port city on India's western coast. The airplane belonged to Air India and was operating as Flight 855 bound for Dubai, an oil-rich city of the United Arab Emirates, where many of the passengers worked. In its belly it carried a cargo of betel leaves, a mild stimulant chewed by Indian laborers and destined in this case for the homesick expatriates of the Arabian Peninsula.

The night sky over Bombay was clear, moonless, and hazy with smoke from the city. A balmy ocean breeze blew across the airport from the nearby Arabian Sea. The Boeing had arrived from New York the day before and had flown on a local training mission, during which it had struck a bird, damaging the right wing's leading edge. Twelve hours late now because of the subsequent repairs, it moved into position at the head of Bombay's main west-facing runway.

The man in command was Captain V. I. Kukar, at age fifty a senior pilot who had logged nearly 18,000 flight hours during twenty-two years with the airline. His copilot I. Virmari, age forty-three, was also highly experienced. Slightly behind them sat a man named Faria, age fifty-three, the flight engineer, whose job was to look after the 747's intertwined and redundant operating systems. Tonight all the systems looked good. The airplane was light and had ample margins of performance. Despite the size of the cabin that trailed behind it, the cockpit itself was a contained and intimate place, glowing in the warm lights of the instrument panels and not appreciably different from the cockpits of less imposing airplanes. The crew must have felt entirely at home there.

They expected to reach their initial cruising altitude of 31,000 feet by following a standard departure procedure known as the 'Seaweed One,' which called for them after crossing the coastline to make a gentle right turn and climb away from Bombay over the night ocean.

Cleared for takeoff just before 8:09 PM, the big, well-lit Boeing rumbled down the runway and lifted gracefully into the sky. Captain Kukar was at the controls. He held the airplane's nose a bit lower than usual, possibly for the pleasure of a good acceleration, and called in sequence for the landing gear and flap retractions. At 8:11 the Bombay departure controller spotted Flight 855 on radar and asked it to report passing through 8,000 feet.

Kukar answered, 'Happy New Year to you, sir. Will report leaving eight-zero, 855.' He was a mile offshore, climbing through 1,200 feet and rolling smoothly into the expected right turn, doing about 280 miles per hour. It was his last radio transmission. Twenty-two seconds later he and everyone else on board hit the water and died.

Air India 855 dove steeply and at high speed into the Arabian Sea. A great number of Bombay citizens were outdoors enjoying the evening air and mingling along the shore, and many of them saw the airplane fall. We can understand why their impressions were confused. If it is hard to believe that something as massive as a 747 can lift into the sky, it is harder still to accept, once it is engaged in forward flight, that something so stately and certain might come plunging back down. Many years later and on the other side of the world, this is what bewildered the observers of TWA's catastrophic 747 fuel tank explosion off New York. The fireball in the sky seemed to have been caused by a missile fired from the surface, not only because the flaming fuselage soared momentarily upward, but also because the mind required some such immediate explanation for what could only have been the unthinkable reality of a great airplane going down.

Air India went down much closer to the shore – so close that people clearly heard the boom of the impact. At least one witness believed that a meteor had fallen. Others saw the airplane explode in flight, or plunge in a streak of fire, or explode on impact, or slip fully intact beneath the waves. It was all over so very quickly. Afterward the sea lay as black and untroubled as it had lain before. The wonder is that a few witnesses actually did understand what had happened, as the subsequent investigation verified, and that they were able to describe with some precision the external appearance of the accident: the proud flight passing overhead and climbing offshore, the beginnings of the shallow right turn, then the strange reversal – the sharp roll to the left, and the dive at impossibly steep bank angles into the ocean.

The newspapers naturally speculated on the possibility of sabotage and political terrorism. An anonymous letter described a conspiracy involving counterfeit dollars and a bomb in the betel leaves. But as the Indian Navy began to salvage pieces of the airplane, the investigators found no signs of fire, heat, or inflight breakup. The airplane's crash-proof 'black boxes,' the flight-data and cockpit-voice recorders whose purpose is to provide a history of the details leading to an accident, were recovered intact. They indicated that the airplane's engines and controls had functioned normally, but that – on the basis of the recorded conversations and control wheel positions – something in the cockpit had gone terribly wrong. The fault appeared to be Kukar's. On a quiet night in Bombay after twenty-two years of steady service he had flown a perfectly good airplane into the water.

Kukar was flying by the big artificial horizon in front of him, the so-called attitude director indicator, or ADI. The copilot, whose tasks included monitoring the captain's flying, had his own independent artificial horizon. At the center of the instrument panel, easily visible to both pilots, was a smaller standby horizon, which also was independent. In addition, each pilot had a gyroscopic compass and turn indicator, along with the standard clusters of nongyroscopic instruments – airspeed, altimeter, and vertical speed, among others. Over history these instruments have been steadily consolidated in an effort to reduce the difficulty of the pilot's visual scan – the ghostly 'herding' that kept Lindbergh busy during his flight across the Atlantic. Nonetheless, even in the most recent 'glass' cockpits with their crisp and minimalistic displays, the instruments have changed surprisingly little since those first developed by Sperry and Doolittle in the open-cockpit biplanes of the 1920s. For all its apparent complexity, Kukar's 747 panel was largely just an answer to every biplane's needs.

What *has* changed is the way the instruments are used. Flight in the early years was an immediate and tactile experience, a short step away from the ground, and it required instrumentation only during passage through the clouds. Flight in a jet is a more distant experience and a condition more completely of the sky. Isolated not only by the quiet of the cockpit but by climb performance and high cruising altitudes, pilots are taught to 'fly the numbers' and to rely on their instruments for all stages of flight. The amateurish distinction between visual and instrument conditions, like the antique one between 'flight weather' and 'flier's weather,' seems hardly to matter anymore. Airplanes shrug off most weather. And we have come to a time when the least curious (and usually least competent) pilots hardly bother to look outside at all except during takeoff and landing. Even so, the physics of flights have not changed. The bank still cannot be felt. When it also cannot be seen outside the airplane, even peripherally, it must still be treated with great care – measured and controlled on the inside with gyroscopes. Ocker and Crane are long forgotten. Working pilots now accept their teachings as their own. But when it comes to a showdown, some still fall apart.

Kukar's trouble started when he began the right turn, at about the same time he wished the departure controller a happy New Year. The airplane was still heading west, into the blackout conditions of the night sky. A moment later, according to the flight-data recorder, Kukar made an unnecessary and unusually large control wheel movement to the left. The airplane answered appropriately by rolling out of the right bank, passing through wings-level flight, and dipping into a left turn. Kukar must have thought he was still turning to the right, because he now steered the control wheel even farther to the left. The airplane's left bank angle passed through thirty degrees, and the nose began to drop, flattening the climb. All this happened in three seconds.

Kukar knew something was wrong. The cockpit-voice recorder picked up the surprise in his voice. He swore, '*Arey Yar!*' and said, 'My instrument!'

His 'instrument' was of course Sperry's device, the all-important artificial horizon.

Kukar brought the control wheel back to neutral – a position to which the airplane would have responded, if only temporarily, by holding a steady bank angle. But Kukar was confused. Again he steered hard to the left.

The copilot looked down at his own artificial horizon, and saw the indication of a steep and unexpected left bank. He said, 'My . . . Mine's . . .'

Kukar said, 'Mine's just . . .'

The copilot said, 'Mine's is also toppled!'

Kukar said, 'Check your instrument!'

This conversation took four seconds, during which Kukar continued to swing the control erratically to the left. Though he did not know it, the airplane was banking past seventy degrees and accelerating through 300 miles per hour, and the nose was dropping swiftly below the unseeable horizon. It was the moment of maximum altitude, 1,462 feet, twelve seconds past 'Happy New Year.'

It is possible that Kukar remembered the bird strike of the day before, and he may have wondered if his controls had quit working. He kicked the rudder pedals once, hard, as if to check the response, although in an airplane the rudder is not normally used to get into a turn and cannot be used to get out of one. Kukar was flailing. Evidently he thought the airplane was still banked to the right, because he continued to steer and roll hard to the left.

If people on the shore noticed a falling comet, the passengers aboard the airplane probably noticed nothing at all. They sat easily in their seats and felt none of the heaviness of a well-flown turn as the Boeing, dropping its nose in perfect 1.0 G synchronization, rolled past knife-edge flight, and began to turn upside down. If the passengers had looked outside and behind, they would have seen a lit-up Bombay turning silently on its side and then floating above them like some strange city in the sky. They might have noticed the lack of feeling where feeling should be. Just then they could have poured themselves drinks without spilling a drop. For all the good it did them to remain seated, they could have stood up and danced the length of the inverted aisles.

That lack of feeling was of course precisely the problem for Kukar and his crew. The airplane was expressing a perfect spiral dive. Simulator studies at Boeing later showed that this moment, when it first rolled inverted to the left, was the pilots' last chance for recovery. If they had rolled fast to the right to level the wings and had aggressively raised the nose, subjecting the airplane to 2.5 Gs, they could have pulled out of the dive about 100 feet over the ocean. But that would have required them to know which way to turn.

In his blindness, Kukar did swing the control wheel hard to the right, and the airplane wobbled back to a ninety-degree bank.

The copilot repeated, 'Mine has also toppled!'

The flight engineer may have leaned forward to point at the third, standby horizon. He said, 'No, but go by this, Captain!'

But Kukar was still confused. He swung the control wheel back to the left, and again the airplane rolled inverted. Seventeen seconds into the upset, the nose had dropped twenty-two degrees below the horizon. Though the airplane was still 1,100 feet above the water, its descent rate was shooting past 10,000 feet per minute, and before the end would reach three times that.

Only four seconds remained. Kukar said, 'Just check the instrument! *Yar!*'

The copilot asked desperately, 'Check what –' and was answered by the impact.

In the course of its spiral dive, Air India's Flight 855 had turned from west to south. It hit the water doing 380 miles per hour, with its nose pitched thirty-five degrees down and its wings banked inverted, eighteen degrees past the vertical. Kukar remained confused to the end and died steering left.

The Indian government convened a court of inquiry to establish an official cause for the accident. The hearings lasted several months. They took place in the heart of Bombay, in a sweltering courtroom whose latticework walls let in the dust and noise of the street outside. Pedestrians peered in through the openings. The inquiry was presided over by Justice M. N. Chandurkar, of Bombay's High Court, who had no previous experience in this area. A clerk recorded the testimony by pounding on an antique manual typewriter loaded with carbons. Flight 855's instruments had been shattered and dispersed by the impact, so the case was complicated by a lack of good physical evidence. Chandurkar, however, turned out to be an effective and intelligent questioner, unintimidated by the technical complexities of the case and unwilling to brook the double-talk of the interested parties – Air India, the pilots' union, Boeing, and their various expert witnesses, along with a slew of American attorneys who had converged anxiously on Bombay to monitor the proceedings. Chandurkar sorted through the conflicting testimonies with a fairness and certainty that ultimately won over all but the most partisan of the observers. The final report, written by Chandurkar himself, still stands as a quiet and credible piece of work, the expression of an almost naïve belief in the possibility of truth – this in contrast to the cynical rewriting of the story that took place later.

Chandurkar's first conclusion was simply that Kukar's artificial horizon had failed. During the hearing, expert witnesses had advanced three theories about such a failure. The first was that the instrument had frozen during the gentle right bank and had never moved again. The second was that the failure was 'ratcheted,' meaning that the instrument had responded normally to right rolls but had jammed whenever the airplane had rolled to the left. The third and most likely was that the instrument had not stuck at all but had failed by showing a steady and fictitious roll to the right, to which Kukar had slavishly responded by rolling to the left. Chandurkar did not try to decide among the three but reduced them to the essential: Kukar had rolled left and had died while trying to fly an indication that had gone bad.

Which raised the question of the warnings. The best artificial horizons, such as those on the 747, constantly test themselves; and when they detect a problem they drop a red warning 'flag' across the face of the display. If such a flag had dropped, Kukar would certainly have seen it, and would have known to switch his focus immediately to the small standby horizon, or to hand over control of the airplane to the copilot. The airplane would hardly have wobbled. But as all pilots know, the flags themselves fail, and such failures, of safety systems generally, are especially dangerous because of the trust invested in them.

It was never Chandurkar's intention to absolve Kukar, and in the end he did not. At the same time, however, maybe because of his lack of previous involvement with the flying business, he was determined to describe the crisis in the cockpit not as others insisted it should have been but as he himself believed it was. After uncovering cases of flag failures in other 747s, he concluded that Kukar's instrument had deceived him twice over.

Chandurkar then went farther. The Air India cockpit was equipped with another safety device called a 'comparator,' which continuously compared the flight attitudes shown on the pilot and copilot artificial horizons and in the case of a disagreement between the two flashed a light on the master warning panel. Chandurkar agreed with the manufacturers that the comparator must have functioned correctly and that in the dimness of the cockpit the warning light must have been visible. But he pointed out that the warning had obviously been of no use to the pilots anyway, and he questioned the value of such a device in this particular case, when survival depended on the immediate interpretation of the panel's main instruments.

Chandurkar had glimpsed an especially modern aspect of human flight, and something that crews themselves need clearly to understand – that the cockpit's automated warnings, horns, and flashing lights provide largely just the appearance of safety and that for a variety of practical reasons no amount of automation can yet relieve pilots of the old-fashioned need to concentrate and think clearly in times of trouble.

Having examined the failures of the instruments, Chandurkar turned his attention to those of Kukar, who may once have been a good pilot but who at the time of the accident clearly was not.

'*Arey Yar!* My instrument!'

There it was on tape. Kukar had suspected a failure of his artificial horizon in plenty of time to keep the airplane under control if only he had been able to convince himself of it. If this lack of conviction seems hard to understand, remember that in the complete blackness of that night, a toppling artificial horizon line would have looked level to Kukar as he, in equal reaction, toppled the airplane to follow it. As an experienced airman, he seems to have noticed a bewildering discrepancy between his hard left steering and the lack of normal response on the face of his instrument. '*Arey Yar!*' Such a disconnection would have given him an intuitive perception of trouble, perhaps of control failure, and would explain his single exploratory kick of the rudder. A momentary confusion was inevitable. The sadness is that he sustained his confusion when directly in front of him a host of secondary instruments in a little stampeding herd clearly showed that the airplane was turning to the left, diving, and gaining speed. Kukar ignored them all. He had fixated on his artificial horizon, and in the urgency of the moment he could not summon the discipline to look away from it. His visual incapacitation is the most frustrating part of the story. He flew as if shackled to a single indication of the turn.

As the captain of the flight, Kukar was to blame for his copilot's errors as well. Pilots communicate with each other in unspoken ways, by the way they slouch in their seats, or throw the overhead switches, or handle the controls of the airplane in flight. The airlines fight back with standardized procedures and try to encourage enlightened regimes of teamwork and safe behavior. Nonetheless, the cockpit is like a club, and in the privacy of flight the sloppiness of a senior pilot will encourage the same attitude in his subordinates.

Kukar's copilot must have noticed what the airplane's 'black boxes' later indicated – that Kukar made sloppy and unnecessary control motions on the runway, that he lifted off the pavement late and fast, that he rushed the flap retractions, that he climbed at too flat an angle, and that he started the right turn 500 feet below the altitude called for by the departure procedure. Less experienced pilots would not have made such mistakes. Kukar had proved capable of greater precision during his periodic flight checks, and he would no doubt have disapproved of such flying among his juniors, but he may also have felt that his improvisations were the prerogatives of a high-time pilot. And in the immediate sense he was right, too: Nothing he did during that takeoff was unsafe. But on the basis of his subsequent performance, his looseness now seems to indicate that he had grown careless. And to make matters worse, his copilot clearly did not think less of him for it.

Relaxing in the right seat, the copilot did not even bother to monitor the flight. When he heard Kukar's 'My instrument!' he looked down at his own artificial horizon, expecting to see it showing the standard right turn, and was shocked to find it showing something quite the opposite – a nearly vertical bank to the left. Feeling nothing of that turn, checking none of the other instruments, he declared like some early airmail pilot that his indication was in error.

His stuttering 'My . . . Mine's . . . Mine's is also toppled!' was not what Kukar needed to hear, and it marked the actual point – no matter what the simulator later showed – from which no recovery was possible.

The confusion was now absolute. Kukar said, 'Check your instrument!' But against what? The circumstance that causes the spiral is the very circumstance that prevents its solution – in this case the collapse not just of one gyroscopic instrument but of the two pilots who refused to cross-check all the others.

From his position in the back of the cockpit, the flight engineer had the largest view of the instrument panel and therefore in this case the most accurate. The last seconds must have been frightening to him. The passengers and flight attendants knew nothing of the dive and had their lives extinguished so mercifully that they will in some sense forever be flying to Dubai. The pilots knew something, but not what, and they were fully occupied with their confusion. Only the flight engineer clearly saw the errors being made. It was not a nightmare, though that possibility must have crossed his mind. After so many years during which these things had happened only to others, he was the one now actually going down, out of control, crashing. There was no reason for this, and it didn't feel wild, but the instruments told an undeniable story. And yet he could do nothing but point.

'No, but go by this, Captain!'

Kukar did not even answer him. It is impossible to know what denials he was engaged in. Pilots train in simulators to handle all sorts of failures, sometimes heaped one on top of the other. But even the best of the simulators require a suspension of belief that never quite overcomes the understanding that they are pretend airplanes built for the purpose of experiencing failures and that no matter how poorly the pilots perform they will walk away unscathed. That, of course, is not true of failures inside the sky, where the first challenge is to suspend *disbelief* and where the urgency is real.

In any case the flight engineer's advice came too late. I refuse to turn away from the thought that the airplane's lights illuminated the ocean's surface at the last instant, that the surface appeared to surge at the airplane from somewhere above, and that the flight engineer flinched as the water exploded through the cockpit. It does not help to be polite about these details. The tangible consequence of any serious failure in flight can be just such an unstoppable insider's view.

Chandurkar was appropriately severe in his final judgment. He placed responsibility for the 213 deaths squarely upon Kukar and blamed the tragedy entirely on his inability, in a cockpit full of functioning instruments, to handle the failure of just one gyroscope. He wasted no emotion blaming the instrument itself, since it was obvious to him that even the best equipment can fail, which is one reason why pilots are needed. Instead, he recommended changes to Air India's recurrent training program and a renewed emphasis not only on the basics of instrument flying but also on the principles of communication within the cockpit. It all made perfect sense.

Nonetheless, Boeing was unhappy with Chandurkar's work – and for good reason. Armed with the official finding of an instrument failure, the families of the victims hired a New York law firm to bring suit in the United States against Boeing and the instrument manufacturers. The plaintiffs contended not only that the artificial horizon had caused the accident but that the comparator had failed as well, and furthermore that the designers of both devices had been negligent.

After years of maneuvering, the arguments were finally presented in a federal court in Seattle, at the heart of Boeing country. They were heard in 1985, in a proceeding without a jury, by a judge named Fitzgerald. The first problem for Boeing and its codefendants was to persuade him that the artificial horizon and comparator had been well designed. This was not difficult. For every criticism of the designs made by the plaintiffs, Boeing had a credible answer. It so happened that Fitzgerald had been a pilot, and he understood the compromises – lightness, reliability, size – necessary in the practical world of flight. He must also have understood, given Boeing's reputation, that this was simply the best technology that money could buy. When Boeing asked the plaintiffs' experts to describe better designs, they could not. Fitzgerald decided against all claims of negligence.

Boeing's attorneys had a more difficult problem in attempting to maintain that Chandurkar's findings were wrong – that Air India's artificial horizon had indeed never failed. A more likely explanation, they said, was that Kukar had succumbed to vertigo. This goes back to William Ocker's discovery on the spinning Barany chair – that the sense of balance is worse than neutral in flight. A half-century later, while flying an airplane that Ocker could not have imagined, Kukar was overcome by a false sense of turning right, and he rolled left in response to it. His 'My instrument!' was an expression of his primitive disbelief. His artificial horizon showed the same extreme left bank as the copilot's. The copilot's 'Mine's is also toppled!' was evidence that he had looked across the panel and had seen that the instruments agreed. The comparator had worked perfectly because it had never illuminated. The flight engineer's recommendation of the standby horizon, 'No, but go by this!' was meant as good advice on what to do when in doubt.

Chandurkar had heard these arguments in Bombay and had found them unconvincing, but Boeing's attorneys had now had years to refine them. To the question of how an experienced pilot could succumb to vertigo, they asked the equally difficult question of how such a pilot could succumb to a simple instrument failure.

Then they went after Kukar. He was an easy target – a heavy drinker and a diabetic who had temporarily lost his pilot's license for medical reasons three years before the accident. This too had been known to Chandurkar and dismissed as unimportant, but Boeing's attorneys had dug up additional dirt.

On New Year's Eve, the night before the accident, Kukar had gone out drinking with his family. Boeing found a retired filmmaker named Saran who lived in Kukar's Bombay apartment building and who while riding the elevator with him on New Year's morning had noticed that Kukar was in a particularly friendly mood, and that he smelled of alcohol.

Saran was a thin and ascetic man, a strict vegetarian, and for good reason something of an anti-American. It turned out that his son had been murdered while visiting Texas, and Saran held a grudge. He had no desire to help Boeing and the American insurance industry defend themselves against the families of the Indian dead. Nonetheless he was also a moralist, and because he did not approve of Kukar's intemperance, he allowed himself finally to be flown to Seattle for a deposition, which was recorded on video.

The camera focused tightly on Saran's face, creating the suspicion of a halo around his head. Saran told his story of smelling Kukar's breath.

Off camera, a voice asked aggressively, 'How can you be sure you weren't smelling shaving lotion?'

Another voice said sarcastically, 'Ah yes, the famous shaving lotion defense!'

In astonishment, Saran raised his hands to his mouth and said, 'Do you mean he drank shaving lotion?'

When Judge Fitzgerald saw the video during the hearings he smiled for the only time.

No one claimed that Kukar was drunk when he got to the airport. But Boeing discovered that he was fasting and taking an oral hypoglycemic in order to fool a glucose tolerance test that he was scheduled to take the following week. The combination of the drug, the fasting, and the drinking of the night before meant that when Kukar taxied out for takeoff he was suffering from low blood sugar – a dangerous condition for a diabetic, and potentially disturbing to the functioning of the inner ear.

That was Boeing's pitch. Kukar was an experienced pilot but also a diabetic with a dangerous sense of balance. The sloppiness of his takeoff and departure fit the profile of someone who already was suffering from vertigo and ignoring his instruments. After he crossed the shoreline and no longer had a visible horizon, he inevitably lost control. And his copilot was simply incompetent.

The same medical evidence could have been used to explain why, after the failure of his artificial horizon, Kukar was unable to cope. Even so, Fitzgerald accepted Boeing's scenario and declared in the end that no failure of the instrument had occurred. It is hard to know whether he really believed this or whether perhaps he was engaged instead in a deeper, airman's understanding of justice. When later I asked the plaintiffs' attorney about it, he called the decision terrible. On the narrow question of the instrument's failure, he was probably right. Boeing's attorney disagreed, and called the decision wise. And in a larger sense than he intended, he was right. The killing was all Kukar's fault anyway.

In the final analysis, the underlying cause seems oddly enough to have been the very extent of Kukar's flying experience. Although this is difficult for outsiders to comprehend, there comes a point in a pilot's life when the sky feels like home. In my case it came after 4,000 flight hours, during a certain takeoff on a bright winter morning in Lincoln, Nebraska, westbound to California. Once airborne I retracted the landing gear and rolled into an early left turn, and as I looked back at the leading edge of the wing slicing stiffly above the frozen prairie, I realized that no difference existed for me between the earth and sky; it was as if with these wings I could now walk in the air.

Kukar too must have known such a moment and may have fallen into the trap which in later years can lie beyond it – a frustration with the complexities of life on the ground, and a lack of control in personal affairs heightened by love affairs or drink or failing health, which defeats old pilots and leads them to the tragic conclusion that they have ever only been truly at home when seated in their obedient airplanes in the sky.

Yes, the sky at times can seem as familiar as a familiar landscape, but on dark nights and inside the clouds its alien nature reemerges. Again then it becomes a surreal and dangerous place across which we humans may move, but only with care and wonder. The cockpit at such times is like a capsule hurtling through some distant reach of space. And yet that reach of space may lie just overhead, and may be entered only seconds after an airplane lifts off the runway. Pilots going out into those conditions need to hesitate before they power up for their takeoffs. They need that moment to run through the first critical moves of the flight, to shift their thoughts away from the ground, and to summon the concentration necessary to navigate the strange sky ahead. Kukar did none of that. He flew badly and crashed because he leaped too willingly into what even for him remained the unknown.

# 4

## *Inside an Angry Sky*

The first winter of my cargo flying was the worst because my days spent writing seemed increasingly wasteful, and I had yet to understand my nights. As others sat down to their warm dinners, I headed out alone and in darkness from the San Francisco airport, on routes across all the mountainous West, through a steady succession of weather fronts and violent low-pressure systems spinning in from the North Pacific. It was dangerous, low-paid work, in battered old airplanes that were poorly maintained by mechanics who joked about 'pencil whipping' the equipment into the air. It taught me hard lessons about in-flight failures – of engines, electrical systems, and instruments. More important, it taught me about the cockpit as a monastic cell – to hold myself in it at the head of rain-soaked runways under heavy clouds, and to reduce the instrument panel to its barest indications, and only then to push the throttles forward and allow the wings to lift me into the storms and the inner landscapes of the mind.

It was during that difficult winter that I reread *Night Flight*, Antoine de Saint-Exupéry's classic romanticization of self-sacrifice among the pioneering French airmail pilots in South America. Although Saint-Exupéry was one of those early pilots, he was a notoriously dreamy one; and it was as a working pilot myself now that I rejected his work as inauthentic, disdaining its sense of the common good, its maudlin emotionalism, and its overwrought musings on the glories of the mission. Closer to my own emotions then was another old novel, *The Death Ship*, written by the German anarchist B. Traven, which I stumbled across in paperback at the airport newsstand in El Paso among the usual cowboy stories and religious tracts. Presented as a sea adventure 'by the author of *The Treasure of Sierra Madre!*' with a cover drawing of men swimming away from a sinking ship, it was in fact a bitter political manifesto written in a false proletarian voice, the story of a doomed and nationless stoker who cursed the society that excluded him and the commerce that sent him to sea. I myself had nothing to be bitter about – I had chosen this path – but I was cold and tired and underpaid, and I could not help resenting my cargos of last-minute gifts and unimportant documents, the casual spinoffs of smarter or more certain lives than mine. That winter threatened never to end.

And then one dark night, while strapped into a cockpit spitting snow, I crossed a cloud crevasse and glimpsed the lights of a single ranch house far below. Despite my earlier disdain, a scene from Saint-Exupéry came to mind. I have read the words again since.

*Sometimes, after a hundred miles of steppes as desolate as the sea, he encountered a lonely farmhouse that seemed to be sailing backwards from him in a great prairie sea, with its freight of human lives.*

My airplane was running poorly, and shuddering at times as though it might shake itself apart, and staggering under a load of ice that had accumulated along its leading edges because its deicing system had once again failed, but it was the view of those lights that unnerved me.

*Gathered round their lamp-lit table, those peasants do not guess that their desire carries so far, out into the vastness of the night that hems them in.*

The depth of the clouds, fleetingly apparent through the crevasse, forced on me the realization of an unbridgeable distance from the world. Saint-Exupéry had after all known something about this night sky. Like one of his imagined characters, I began actively to contemplate the possibility that I would never return from it – something that previously I had believed no real pilot would take the time to do.

I told myself that I was just discouraged. But for weeks afterward I could not shake the sense of doom. The weather did not relent. Every evening I drove in isolation to the airport, away from the satisfied city crowds, away from friendships and the beauty of women, to endure the delays for takeoff under black rain, when sometimes a terrible sleepiness would overcome me. Saint-Exupéry knew that sleepiness, too; he called it an inertia which paralyzes men who face the unknown. To me it felt like complete physical relaxation, anticipation, the slowest form of fear. A more active fear took its place after takeoff, causing me to fly slavishly, without raising my eyes from the instruments. It was dangerous because I kept yearning for the ground.

The winter closed with a violent storm that flooded the rivers and blew down power lines and trees. The sheer force of that storm forced me at last to look up from the instruments again – and when I did I discovered a place fantastic even to me, far away in the wild winds, where rain fell upward and blizzards blew among cloud mountains and the walls of great caverns erupted in light. The passage of my flight through that weather attracted an electrical charge from the clouds, a flash and bang that burned a hole in the right engine nacelle and mushroomed the top of the tail – and the airplane just shrugged it off. After returning I stood in the wind-driven rain and watched the workers back their vans up to the airplane to unload its cargo. I did not tell them where I had been. How could they have understood? Even to me it was a wonder that this little metal machine, so battered and unloved, had carried me there. It was late at night, and I should have driven home and slept, but I was not tired. I felt renewed not because I had survived but because I had the means and the inclination to fly again into that angry sky. No pilot could ever be at home there, but I for one had stopped yearning for the ground.

That little piece of history may explain why, years later, I sometimes still go out hunting for bad weather, flying low in simple airplanes to explore the inner reaches of the clouds. Less experienced pilots occasionally join me, not to learn formal lessons about weather flying but with a more advanced purpose in mind – to accompany me in the slow accumulation of experience through circumstances that never repeat in a place that defies mastery. Our destinations lie in the turbulent eddies of the lower atmosphere, places called 'cyclones' or 'lows' on the weather maps, but also known simply as 'storms,' a word which better reflects their effect on the sky.

It is obvious that flying intentionally into such places, and lingering there, is the kind of behavior easily disapproved of. We have critics for whom the intentional pursuit of severe weather amounts to heresy; they grow angry about the risks we take, and about our apparent lack of judgement. I have always understood their concern. But the pursuit of such weather is an internal act, not a public one, and it is neither as reckless nor as arbitrary as at first it may seem. It involves dangers, of course, but to a degree unimaginable to the critics, those dangers are controllable. Because of the mental concentration required by such flying, there is never the slightest question of survival – in fact, it is such discipline that gives the exercise its content.

The secret of good storm flying is to stay low, in slow and vulnerable airplanes, and to resist the pursuit of performance. By the standards of practical transportation, therefore, it is an artificial problem. Most weather lies within the first 20,000 feet off the ground, where gravity compresses the atmospheric mass into a dense soup, and above which the airlines for economic reasons as well as safety and comfort must climb and cruise. Engineers have designed away the storms, leaving professional pilots to fret about the kind of unimportant turbulence that startles their most anxious passengers. It seems a pity. With a few simple equations, meteorologists can prove that the lower atmosphere, where the simple airplane must fly, remains rich with surprise.

That is the allure of storm flying. There is no graduation from the experience, only an end to each flight. The techniques we practice involve a certain calmness under pressure. More important, they involve ways of picturing the storms, of understanding the weather from the weather's inside. The airplane is merely our tool. We ride it aloft, descend in it to refuel or sleep, then ride it again, mixing nights into days, listening to the changing accents of air traffic control, exploring a continent that lies entirely within the sky. We fly the forecast, turn, and probe the forecast's flaws. But we are not theoreticians. The airplane's forward motion imposes a crude immediacy on our thoughts, so that even when we do not understand the weather, we may pretend that we do. Flying as much as writing teaches the need for such fictions, for discerning the patterns in a disorderly world.

On a recent Christmas, for instance, a storm was born above the Pacific in a place which for most of us can exist only in the imagination.

Picture an air-world of mountains and valleys through which strong eastward winds meander. The air is a gas, and like other gasses it is compressible, and has weight, and is subject to the simple physics of motion. The winds are air molecules driven by the sun's heat and steered on a global scale by the earth's rotation. The mountains and valleys through which they move are immense. They consist of semi-permanent 'highs' into which, strangely, the winds descend, and 'lows' into which the winds climb. The explanation for this apparently peculiar behavior lies entirely in the language: The terms 'high' and 'low' refer not to altitude but to pressure, variations caused by the sun's unequal heating of the earth's surface. When the molecules are cooled, they compress downward into a 'high,' and when they are warmed, they expand upward into a 'low.' These pressure variations constitute the sky's elemental topography.

Now imagine something equally elemental, an atmospheric war caused by the same solar inequality. Across the Pacific theater, past China and Siberia to Canada, lies a great front, an undulating zone of conflict between jealous masses of polar and tropical air. The front shifts with the seasons but endures year after year. It is accompanied by high-altitude winds that have been squeezed and accelerated into a jet stream flowing at speeds over 100 miles per hour. Swooping and swerving among the contours of the sky, the jet stream serves as a powerful catalyst. East of the Aleutians, it catches a high-altitude corner of the North Pacific's largest permanent low, in a part of the sky where already the atmosphere is unsettled. The immediate effect is a further drop in air pressure as molecules begin to scatter more quickly than they can be replaced. Such high-altitude scattering, known to meteorologists as 'horizontal divergence,' is the most important mechanism in the life of storms. It creates a form of hunger whereby a pocket of low-pressure air sucks at the denser air immediately below.

That is what happened that Christmas. The storm's birth was typically fast. Cooling as it rose, the Pacific air condensed into cloud and worked up an appetite of its own. The pressure continued to drop. The result was an odd sort of digging at the sky – the creation of an atmospheric hole through which the air surged upward, away from the earth. The hole steepened as it deepened, the upward surge intensified, and rain began to fall. Satellites photographed it on the second day. From across the horizons, low-altitude winds rushed forward, only to be deflected to the right by the globe's rotation. The deflected winds gave the storm its counterclockwise twirl and an indication of its power. Inexorably it drew the opposing air masses into direct conflict. Steered by steadier winds aloft, the storm drifted eastward toward the continent like an eddy spinning downstream. By the third day it appeared on the map as a massive winter storm, centered 500 miles west of the Alaskan panhandle, sending the long arm of a cold front toward the California coast, where I waited with two other pilots.

Our airplane was a single-engine Bonanza, a weather-scarred veteran that we had used before. The plan was for the two less-experienced pilots to swap legs – for each to fly in turn as the other observed from the back seat – and for me to remain up front throughout. We gave ourselves a week. On the eve of the departure, we discussed where to meet the storm. It was due to hit the West Coast by morning, bringing low cloud, rain, and snow from Vancouver to San Francisco.

We considered flying north to Seattle, toward the storm's center, where even after its passage the weather might linger. Seattle is famously good for cloud. It also offers the upslope of the Cascade Mountains, where we were likely now to be blocked by heavy icing – a deadly condition into which our airplane was not equipped to fly. The challenge for us would to find a way *around* such conditions, rather than through them. Moreover, the same Cascade upslope threatened to wring the wetness from the storm, leaving it to cross the western deserts in a dry and weakened form. The deserts are deserts for a reason. By flying to Seattle we might put ourselves into a corner of the continent, and after a day finish with no weather at all. The forecasts seemed uncertain. So we decided to leave the storm temporarily behind and spend the first day jumping east to Kansas City, where a smaller disturbance had stirred the clouds. There, we would reassess the map. The forecasts seemed contradictory and uncertain. We had to trust that the storm would survive its mountain crossings, reassemble, and catch up with us in a more difficult form.

At 200 miles per hour, the flight from San Francisco to Kansas City took all day. We climbed out of northern California through the storm's bands of rain and cloud and, in search of tail winds, headed into the warm and clear skies of the Southwest. We refueled in Winslow, Arizona. Toward evening, as we crossed the Rockies, we checked by radio and found that Kansas City was reporting lowering clouds and snow, an unexpected downturn to threaten our arrival. It seemed possible now that the weather would continue to worsen and, because of ice and low ceilings, block the flight during its final stage, when our choices would be limited by lack of fuel.

We kept going but discussed an escape plan that would allow us to retreat even from retreat. Such planning is a large part of storm flying. Airplanes give pilots plenty of time to consider possible trouble, but when the trouble hits, it hits fast. Retreat then means climbing, descending, turning, or slowing to save fuel. Preparing those moves in advance – and preparing for their failure – involves a layered logic that is not difficult to understand, but it also requires that pilots confront their worst fears. Unfocused anxiety is the emotion people must avoid. Circumstances in the atmosphere combine to kill the wishful or the distracted.

After dark at 11,000 feet over Kansas we hit the weather, which opened like jaws above and below, then closed firmly around us. The clouds on the inside were pitch black. The engine sounded rough only to the imagination. The instruments glowed reassuringly in soft yellow light. The outside observer would have noticed little action: three ordinary Americans dressed in ordinary clothes, watching nearly motionless dials, talking in half-sentences about the flight, talking about politics, occasionally transmitting to air traffic control. We flew on into the night, took a frosting during the descent, broke free of the clouds about a mile from the runway on final approach, and landed with plenty of fuel in the tanks. In downtown Kansas City, where we slept, steam rose from the manhole covers. The streets looked abandoned to an Arctic winter.

Spring blew in overnight. Already by breakfast, under leaden clouds, the temperature had climbed to forty degrees, and Missourians were talking about mud. The tone was apocalyptic, as it often is when people wake up to the weather. A bookish waiter at the hotel blamed global warming. Out at the airport, the Christian pumping fuel mentioned trouble in the Middle East.

Our own interests were more immediate. Shepherded by upper winds, the Pacific storm had barely endured the climb across the mountains and had emerged onto the Wyoming plains in a mechanically weakened condition. Once there, however, it reformed and gathered strength on the southern flank of a great dome of cold Canadian air that was spanning the continent. Spinning purposefully again, the storm attached itself to that boundary – the line where the cold air met the warmer air to its south – and drifted eastward, chewing deeply into its air-mass hosts. On the scale of a continent, the map was clear. The air-mass boundary formed a single deeply curving front that extended for nearly 2,000 miles across the American heartland, from Wyoming to upstate New York. The storm swirled like a cataclysmic whirlpool along that line. To the west of its center, the counterclockwise circulation had swept the Canadian air mass far to the south, bringing cold temperatures to Salt Lake City and Las Vegas. Here in Kansas City, to the east of the center, the same whirlpool circulation had generated a powerful southerly flow, forcing the winter temporarily from the streets. In other words, our gamble had paid off. The unusually warm weather in Missouri meant that a big disruption was under way.

The official weather briefing sounded shrill. The storm center was moving fast and was expected to cross the Mississippi by afternoon. Already the worst weather lay to the northeast, where the warm air aloft was overriding cold air close to the ground. We heard reports of moderate and severe turbulence, ice, and snow falling hard across the Great Lakes. The shadow of Lake Michigan promised near-blizzard conditions. Huddled over our maps, we prepared to fly into it with a 500-mile run to South Bend, Indiana. The ground rules were clear: Safety would lie in the ready retreat, but success would depend on our determination and mental flexibility. Storm flying in such an airplane is more a negotiation than a brawl. You slip through a few miles at a time, judging and probing the clouds, moving higher or lower, turning, detouring, rarely surrendering. That was all we could be sure of in advance. On the intimate scale of an airplane, the weather promises eternal complexity.

We took off over the downtown and climbed into warm gray clouds. Moisture rolled up the windshield and became a tapping rain. The weather held clouds within the clouds, with textures and discernible edges. We rode the storm easily at first. At 9,000 feet, where we leveled, the temperature held a few degrees above freezing. Occasionally we emerged into cloud chambers with floors and ceilings joined by misty columns. They must have been beautiful. Maybe they were even interesting. But an airplane does not allow for an uninvolved appreciation of the weather. For the moment we had two specific concerns – the possibility of dangerous icing at our altitude ahead, and the certainty of it already directly below. Shuddering through light turbulence, shoved by the winds, we approached the Mississippi and asked for updates on the winter now enduring beneath us. Moline, Illinois, reported low clouds, snow, and a surface temperature of only thirteen degrees. In the worst case now, retreat might require a slow run against head winds all the way back to Kansas City. The forecast called for freezing temperatures to return there by afternoon. If they returned sooner, even that retreat could be cut off.

Pilots are forever being pestered with platitudes, including that which advises them to know their limitations in order to stop short of them. But there is no reason to enter into storm flying only to give ground. And there is also such a thing as being too careful. If you give in to your fears, if you don't push gently against them, you will turn around too soon. And the next time you fly, you will turn around sooner. Eventually you will turn around before takeoff, which is the unhappy fate of some pilots: to choose finally never to fly again.

So past the Mississippi, when we ran out of warm air, we accepted the risk and kept going. The air temperature dropped through freezing, and our wings began to ice over dangerously. Hoping only for a temporary reprieve – an increase of merely two degrees would have melted the ice – we descended to 7,000 feet and found clear air between cloud layers. Without the clouds' sustaining moisture, the wing ice slowly evaporated. Once again, an outside observer would have noticed little. We watched the instruments. We made a mental concession to the weather and stopped anticipating our arrival in South Bend. It was too far ahead to matter. Deep inside the storm, we worked mile by mile.

The temperatures aloft continued to fall, just as the barometric pressure rose. A meteorologist would say we had passed north of the volatile air-mass boundary, into a dome of Arctic air. But seen from within, there wasn't much change; the weather remained thick with cloud. Icing occasionally, maneuvering to stay between the layers, climbing once to 13,000 feet, we continued for another hour. Snow blew in through the ventilators. Somewhere over central Illinois the clouds opened for a few miles and we glimpsed a frozen strip mine, a high school, and fields colored the same whitish gray as the sky.

Chicago passed in the chattering of air traffic control. By the time the cloud layers merged, the temperature had dropped to minus five degrees, and the clouds consisted of frozen crystals that bounced harmlessly off the wings. We had won a temporary victory over the ice and could plan again for South Bend. The airport there was equipped with a standard instrument approach, a radio beam we could follow to a point 200 feet above the ground and a half-mile short of the runway. From there, we would have to see the runway to land. On the basis of the reported weather, we expected to. The South Bend approach controller greeted us as we drew near and he watched us on radar as we flew a fast descent and shot the approach. We landed in falling and blowing snow. We intended to refuel, talk through the flight, and set out again in the afternoon. The temperature registered ten degrees as we taxied slowly in. No one emerged from the hangars. We found the ground crew inside watching football. They looked up at us blankly, as if they could not imagine where we had come from. Had they asked, we would have answered, Kansas City.

Months later, armed with old weather maps from our flight, I drove to the National Weather Service's Operations Center, in suburban Camp Springs, Maryland. The Operations Center is the collection point for weather observations nationwide. A staff meteorologist there, Paul Kocin, had agreed to go over the record of the flight with me and to make sense of my memories.

Kocin turned out to be an affable New Yorker in his thirties, neatly dressed in jeans and a checked shirt. He led me through humming rooms where banks of electronics monitored the mass of incoming observations and meteorologists worked in teams to meet the schedule of summaries, weather maps, and national-scale forecasts necessary for the regional offices. Giant TV screens flashed satellite sequences of a growing Gulf Coast storm, adding urgency to the day. At a special briefing, the sector chiefs reported in expressing concern about the storm's overnight movements. Despite the placidity of their expressions – they yawned and slouched and doodled – it was clear to me that the meteorologists there felt a certain thrill at working on the front edge of time.

Kocin's duties included supervising the three-hour surface analysis chart, the basic weather map from which most of the nation's forecasts are derived. He led me to a large horizontal screen on which an electronic outline of the United States was filled with symbols representing the latest weather observations.

Rhetorically Kocin asked, 'What's going on here?'

He answered himself, 'I have no idea.'

Nonetheless, after peering at the electronic chart for a few minutes, he used a pointing device to take the indication of a cold front from Arkansas and casually stretch it eastward. He said, 'I don't even really know what I'm looking for. I hope it'll become obvious.'

He said that experience still plays an important role in weather work, and to show me what he meant, he pivoted to look at the satellite and radar displays. 'Is there a squall line there? Yeah, sure is. A good one.'

As a result, he rearranged the map again, hooked the front through Nashville, and zoomed in on Ohio to study wind and pressure changes there. This sort of redefinition of the weather lasted an hour. I sat on a high upholstered stool and watched – my government in action, producing an orderly and convincing view of the sky. I sipped coffee. The operations room felt as comfortable and secure as a command bunker. It amused me to give no thought to the pilots out there in the confusion of the real world.

The next day, over a sandwich in the lunchroom, Kocin confided,

'People around here know this about me. I try to keep it from my outside friends. It's not so bad anymore, but I used to be a real weather-weenie.'

Politely, I acted surprised. 'What do you mean?'

'You know, in high school I started keeping temperature and pressure logs.'

I nodded sympathetically, because in recent years I myself had taken to reading *Weatherwise*, a magazine that promotes just such behavior.

*Weatherwise* is published in Washington, D.C., by a nonprofit foundation that rescues worthy periodicals. Its circulation has recently doubled to 13,000, largely due to the efforts of its young editors, the sort of fresh college graduates who take the job on a whim and discover only afterward their own fascination for the subject. They know how to satisfy their readers, offering up the earnestly informative essays the readers expect – on blocking highs, jet streams, and Doppler radars – but also digressing into the sort of surprising subjects that keep the magazine fresh. In a recent issue, for instance, they ran a cover story on the importance of 'weather spying' in nineteenth-century Central Asia, along with another piece on exciting careers in forensic meteorology – the plaintiff says she slipped, but was the driveway icy?

*Weatherwise* gets read cover to cover, then passed around. The letters to the editor are passionate. And the ads – for home weather stations, computer services, forecasting contests, conventions, and videos – are almost as interesting. 'Watch *Camille* in action!' The ads hint at a large and closeted population of weather watchers.

*Weatherwise* writes up the action heroes. There are, for instance, the diehards who drive against the fleeing traffic, flash press credentials at the police, and head into the center of tropical hurricanes.

The electrical explosions across the city grew more intense, yet the fury of the wind swallowed up all the sound save the car alarms whining inside the garage. Eventually even the alarms were overwhelmed by the whistling wind. Around 4 AM all hell broke loose. I have experienced severe storms with winds in excess of 75 mph, but these gusts were blowing at well over 140 mph

. . . By now only an occasional thud – some building collapsing or losing a roof – would punctuate the noise. Windows from the surrounding buildings imploded, scattering glass everywhere. I looked down at my arm and saw blood, not knowing when I'd been cut. Putting on my reading glasses to protect my eyes, I made a mental note: next time, bring goggles.

And there is Professor T. T. Fujita, the hands-on 'Mr Tornado,' who has devised a tornado scale based on destruction, from the mild F-0, which knocks over chimneys and billboards, to the full-blown F-5, which is the kind of twister that surprised Dorothy in *The Wizard of Oz:* 'Winds greater than 261 mph. Incredible damage. Lifts strong frame houses off foundations, sweeps them away, and dashes them to pieces; debarks trees; badly damages steel-reinforced concrete structures.'

Among hard-core weather watchers, tornadoes are known affectionately as 'beasts' and are considered to have one clear advantage over hurricanes: Because they are localized, only hundreds of yards across, you can drive right up to them safely. During the spring spawning season, hundreds of hunters chase around the Great Plains, trying to capture one on videotape from up close. There are risks, of course. The F-4 will make projectiles, for instance, of full-sized rental cars. Nonetheless, the hunt has become so popular that at least one bad movie has been made about it, and a man in Norman, Oklahoma, calling himself Whirlwind Tours, has begun to offer two-week tornado safaris. His game hunters come from around the world.

Most weather watchers are less adventurous. They set their computers to quick-start onto the best new radar maps, and they monitor the Weather Channel with its excited sky-is-falling banter and its occasional live reports of genuine meteorological disaster. But they seem perfectly happy to stay home and measure the weather, second-guess the official forecasts, compare notes, and quarrel over weather records.

One of the *Weatherwise* editors, a young man who also had a passion for baseball statistics, put it this way to me: 'Look, the weather is important. There is a strong feeling out there that you can't just let it pass by.'

But 'passing by' is precisely what the weather does.

This frustration is apparently what motivated the greatest living weather watcher, the weather historian David Ludlum, who in 1948 founded *Weatherwise*. Ludlum, who had earned a Princeton doctorate in conventional history, became an Army Air Corps meteorologist during World War II. For three weeks he delayed the crucial invasion of Cassino, Italy, until he could predict that the weather, would be favorable. In thanks, the Army named the invasion 'Operation Ludlum.' And you can still see Ludlum playing himself in the 1953 Paramount production *From Cassino to Korea*.

No wonder he returned from the war convinced that weather could not be ignored in the writing of history. We know about the wind's defeat of the Spanish Armada and about Napoleon's difficulties with the climate in Russia, but just how hot and humid were the American colonies on July 4, 1776? And what did Lincoln *really* feel at Gettysburg? More generally, what about New England weather during the last decade of the last century? This was the sort of question that came to obsess Ludlum. He wrote books full of answers.

As a reader of his magazine, I came to the conclusion that an interest in disembodied weather history – in weather history for its own sake – is the surest sign of the genuine weather-weenie. Paul Kocin did not need to admit his past to me. I had already seen his book, *Snowstorms along the Northeastern Coast of the United States: 1955 to 1985*, and I understood his predicament: We live in a society that does not reward these efforts. Try discussing forgotten weather with strangers and watch their reactions. Pilots, too, will grow impatient. They navigate through history without the education to make sense of it. That is why I felt lucky to find Kocin: He was just the man to rescue my storm from its passing.

We spread the relevant weather maps on a conference table. Kocin started with a regret that my students and I had missed the more interesting conditions. It so happened that the day before our departure from San Francisco, a tightly wound low had left the Canadian plains and sailed fast to Alabama. Kocin called it an 'Alberta Clipper' and said he remembered this particular one for its turbulent wake.

And that was nothing compared to events of the following morning when, as we lifted off from the West Coast, a complex system of twin storms and connecting fronts formed on the other side of the nation. Research meteorologists are still sifting the data to explain what happened next.

That gray winter morning Kocin had just assumed his duties in the operations room when he noticed that the atmospheric pressure at a weather station in Georgia had dived sharply and climbed again. Kocin watched with growing excitement as the next station to the north reported the same phenomenon. The pressure drop was as catastrophic as a crash, and it seemed to be moving quickly up the Eastern seaboard.

Kocin faxed the first hastily scribbled alert to the regional forecasting centers: 'Possible gravity wave!'

He got the warning out just in time. The wave sped into Pennsylvania and New England like the impulse of a whip. Cities reported incredible snowfall rates of up to six inches an hour. Weather enthusiasts rushed to their stations. Citizens were amazed to see lightning and to hear the snow thunder. Traffic snarled. Across the Northeast a million little invasions were delayed.

Our Pacific storm lacked that punch. Kocin worked diligently to help me understand its birth, but his attention kept drifting back to the pressure drop in the East. He truly regretted that we had missed it.

I did not have to remind Kocin that on that first day New England remained out of reach of our slow airplane. I wanted to keep the conversation focused on our storm, now in the Midwest. Kocin said he understood, but a little gulf had opened between us: Weather watchers are drawn to history's most violent weather, but pilots are drawn to the weather they have flown.

I tried to describe the conditions we had encountered on the flight from Kansas City to South Bend. Kocin listened politely but remained unimpressed. He had the advantage of trusting the weather map. This was hardly surprising. Theoreticians and practitioners will often disagree. And ordinary history usually looks more orderly from a distance than from up close. Kocin doubted, for instance, that we had found much bad weather in South Bend. He mentioned perhaps some trivial lake effect.

But the weather in South Bend seemed plenty bad to me. The storm was advancing fast and was now expected to slip eastward along the air-mass boundary and into Massachusetts by the next morning. We decided to cross the notorious Alleghenies and spend the night in Harrisburg, Pennsylvania. It would be a hard-fought flight most of the way there, but for the next day it would gain us maneuvering room over the coastal plain, with its low cruising altitudes and its frequent well-equipped airports. If everything went according to plan, the storm's center would pass over us while we slept. In the morning we would head for Boston and hit the weather again from the south.

In the meantime, the weather conditions had worsened in South Bend. Bundled against the cold winds sweeping the airport, we fueled and checked the airplane. By the time we taxied out, in late afternoon, the visibility had dropped to a third of a mile in heavy snow. In principle such visibility was less than we would need to see the runway at the end of an instrument approach should we encounter a problem after takeoff and need to return, though in a true emergency we felt we could in practice make it to the runway. Conditions ahead for 200 miles looked almost as low. The tops were expected to be at 22,000 feet, about our capabilities. The airlines were reporting moderate turbulence. The only good news was that the temperatures remained too cold, probably, for icing to threaten us.

We took off and were swallowed by cloud. The effect was immediate and dramatic – the ground vanished so quickly that it might never have existed. Indiana became an abstraction, South Bend an uncertain memory. The clouds were rough, but it was the psychological severity of this transition from the ground to the weather that made the airplane difficult to control. I asked the pilot beside me at the controls to stop throwing switches, to stop writing down frequencies and fuel settings, to stop listening to the Morse identifiers of the navigational stations, and please simply to concentrate on flying. A good pilot is one who knows when *not* to follow procedures.

The thin voice of air traffic control, with a woman's laughter in the background, offered a thread to the Midwest, but for us the world had been reduced again to the instrument panel. We were tired and did not talk. We were together, but also each of us was alone. The flight passed not by the minute or hour but, as flight often does, in a suspended condition of time, an abstraction of speed disconnected from progress across the surface of the earth. Harrisburg existed merely as the anticipation of a faraway descent through the clouds. There was nothing to do about it yet. We flew on in a meditative mood. The airplane ran strongly. The landscape that surrounded us was one of our own making.

Night came at 9,000 feet in continuing cloud and snow. Our forward lights bored horizontal holes into the blackness through which snow-flakes rushed back at us in frenzied assaults. Out at the wing tips, the strobes caused the night to bloom. We did not exclaim over the beauty of this wilderness but recognized it as fully involved participants, judging our surroundings critically because the conditions remained rough and hostile.

Over eastern Ohio we broke suddenly into the clear air of an Arctic night. The lights of Cleveland lit the northern horizon. The air-mass boundary lay just to our south, in the black wall of cloud from which we had emerged. Paul Kocin would have been delighted with the view: The weather lay exactly where the map said it should. We sailed over Pittsburgh, which was still digging out from Kocin's gravity wave, and we hit the clouds again for the brief crossing of the Alleghenies and the high-speed descent into Harrisburg, where we landed on an icy runway. We were content then to let the storm center pass overhead.

In the morning we woke to a heavy snowfall outside the hotel windows and realized immediately that the weather had gone wrong. Rather than tracking as forecasted to New England, the storm had slowed over the Mississippi and had assumed a classic stance, extending a cold front southwest across Oklahoma and a stationary front east-ward across the Virginias to the Chesapeake. Along the stationary front now, warm sluggish southern air was trying to climb the dense Arctic air that had parked at low altitude over the Northeast. Harrisburg lay in the thick of the resulting disturbance. The woman on the Weather Channel sounded tense and excited.

We got a ride to the airport and telephoned for a formal weather briefing. The ceiling and visibility were close to the minimum requirements of the instrument approach. And the temperature gradient looked ominous: On the ground it registered a normal twenty-one degrees, but rather than cooling further with altitude, it stayed about the same, just below freezing, to a point near the tops of the clouds. A DC-9 climbing out of Harrisburg reported heavy icing from the surface all the way to 16,000 feet – conditions too deep and dangerous for our unprotected wings. There would be no escape after a takeoff. The storm had grounded us. We settled by the hangar telephone and waited for a break.

Ice on any airplane is scary stuff. Allowed to accumulate, it disturbs the lifting air flow across the wings and tail and causes them finally to stop flying. When the wings stop flying, the airplane does one of two things: It descends into a flat, mushing, semi-controllable impact with the ground; or it shudders, drops its nose, maybe rolls, and hits the ground much harder. When the tail stops flying, the effect is even more dramatic: The airplane dives violently, irreversibly, and may gain so much speed that it breaks apart even before it hits the ground.

Other complications are possible. The American Eagle ATR turbo-prop that crashed at Roselawn, Indiana, in October 1994, was a new design with an unexpected vulnerability to ice, which under narrow circumstances caused the airplane to roll out of control. Immediately after the accident, pilots at the airline's Chicago base balked at continuing to fly that type of airplane into winter weather. The company answered with apparent concern, suggesting that the pilots seek psychological counseling. Pilots everywhere smiled bitterly. The fear of ice is a healthy and rational emotion.

Still, ice can become an obsession. Once you start looking for it you see it all around. Watch an airplane standing on the ground in sleet or freezing rain. Ice accumulates in glistening sheets across its top surfaces. Airport crews spray it off with an alcohol mixture before the airplane taxis. If there is a delay before takeoff and the ice comes back, the crews have to spray it off again. Some airliners have crashed because of the inconvenience of that second deicing, which may require a return to the ramp. The resulting delays are measured by the hour. In response, a few airports have installed taxi-through spray racks near the runways. Pilots need no counseling to use them.

Once an airplane takes off, the obsession changes. Now you see ice growing forward from the sharp leading edges – on the wings, tail, and engine nacelles. If the airplane is propeller-driven, you imagine it on the spinning blades, where it grows even faster. In-flight icing may come from sleet or freezing rain, but more commonly it comes from the super-cooled water particles that make up the clouds at temperatures between thirty-two and about fifteen degrees Fahrenheit. Super-cooled water particles are droplets floating in such perfect equilibrium that they maintain a liquid form in below-freezing air. Then along comes the below-freezing airplane. The disturbed droplets turn instantly to ice and stick to its leading edges. The effect is that of a telephone pole in an 'ice fog.' Only here the wind is blowing several hundred miles an hour. Because of the airplane's speed, the growth can be explosive and can lead to loss of control within just a few minutes. The critical load varies, but beyond perhaps three inches of ice, flight becomes a gamble. Airliners are protected by heated leading edges, or by rubber boots which inflate to knock off the load once it accumulates. Our airplane had no such devices. So we waited in Harrisburg.

By noon we had ruled out New England, where the conditions had started to duplicate our own, but the weather to our south was opening. Cloud bases at 2,500 feet were reported over Wilmington and Washington, D.C., and the surface temperature at Norfolk was an ice-melting forty-five degrees. The cloud structure looked loose enough to allow us escape routes once we got up into it. Harrisburg was still clamped down, but we prepared the airplane for a fast getaway and a flight to Norfolk.

The break came in mid-afternoon with a slight raising of the ceiling. Having warned the air traffic controllers that we would need an immediate return to Harrisburg should we discover no way through the ice, we took off and climbed aggressively into the weather. And we found a way through. Slipping and twisting to stay clear of the heaviest clouds, we passed Philadelphia and Wilmington. Near Baltimore, we began to see a bit of the ground – glimpsed through holes in the clouds, a patch of brown farmland, a forest of leafless trees, a stretch of sad gray water and marshland. Fifty miles later, over the middle of Chesapeake Bay, we ran entirely out of weather and changed our destination to Richmond, where we landed, refueled, and rethought the storm.

We went back into it after dark on a round trip to Wilkes-Barre, Pennsylvania, where the weather looked worst. The flight was not dangerous, but it was rough and involved. Again, ice was the problem. The stationary front had turned warm and was moving up the Eastern seaboard. In the blackness of the clouds we took ice and shed it, and kept repeating the cycle. At Wilkes-Barre we flew the instrument approach through cloud and falling snow, saw the runway lights, and pulled up without landing in order to avoid delays on the ground. Deep in the weather, we turned south for Richmond.

It was late at night. The storm had developed with unexpected strength. We stayed low, fighting forty-mile-per-hour head winds at 3,000 feet. To the left, the only other pilots on the frequency, a Delta crew, got blown off the instrument approach into Allentown and had to circle back to try again. Despite the south winds, the air temperature at our altitude was a frigid fifteen degrees. The clouds were thick with moisture. Outside of Philadelphia, with a splatter that sounded like sleet, we began to ice heavily. I shined a light on the wing and saw the ice growing like a voracious parasite. It looked white and crusty on the leading edge and clear where it streamed back over the wing. Within a minute we had taken more than an inch – a rate of accumulation that required immediate action. We gambled on a quick climb to 7,000, where we found warm Georgian air that melted the ice and slid it in sheets from the wings.

Had the gamble of that climb not paid off, and fast, we would have fallen back on our second plan – a quick retreat downwind into the frigid air to the north and a high-speed approach to a long runway. The high speed would have been necessary because iced-over wings stall at above-normal speeds. It would have complicated the landing, but we knew the airplane and thought if we could make the pavement, we could come to a safe stop.

All that proved to be academic, however. Having found the layer of warm air, we crept comfortably through the clouds to Richmond, welcoming the moisture rolling up our windshield, listening to the first reports of freezing rain on the surface in New Jersey. In the morning we saw the headlines about an unexpected ice storm in New York. People as usual were blaming forecasters for the mess.

Pity the forecasters. Of all the sciences, theirs is the most public. Here is a short version of its evolution. Emergence from the sea came first, followed by speech, followed by talk about the weather. Then came sacrificial rites, followed by the idea that peasants might pay a tithe to priests to keep the sky in order. Aristotle had the brains to separate the atmosphere from the heavens. He wrote *Meteorologica*, the first unified weather theory, around 340 BC. Two thousand years later, René Descartes doubted his methods and applied new rigor to the ignoring of God. In 1637, as an appendix to *Discours de la méthode*, he published 'Les Météores,' an explanation of the weather. Modern meterology is essentially his child. Descartes suffered from a lack of weather data, since in the seventeenth century the basic instruments for measuring the air were still being invented. Credit Galileo with the thermometer, his student Torricelli with the barometer, and French intellectuals in general with the discovery that atmospheric pressure rises and falls with weather and altitude. Acknowledge various Europeans for their wind and humidity instruments, for their discoveries in physics, then jump to the mid-1800s, to places like Ohio, where the telegraph suddenly allowed news about the weather to travel faster than the weather itself.

National governments now set up weather services to collect observations and issue forecasts. At last a modern relationship could develop between the weather wizards and the public they served. It was a terrible shock. In England, the esteemed meteorologist and admiral Robert Fitzroy, who had captained Darwin's *Beagle* on the famous voyage of scientific discovery, was in 1855 named director of the first British weather office. Fitzroy was a good man, but like other nineteenth-century meteorologists he suffered from some misleading ideas about the nature of storm systems. Over the next ten years, he issued a series of dramatically bad forecasts. When the public finally noticed, a popular new sport was born. Fitzroy's last forecast was apparently the worst. Ridiculed by loftier scientists, attacked in the press, he did the right thing and shot himself. Maybe his old friend Darwin could have explained why forecasters today seem less sensitive.

Some seem almost belligerent. At the Camp Springs Operations Center, I asked the forecaster in the office next to Paul Kocin's about the kind of forecasts that gave him satisfaction. He fixed me with a hostile stare.

Satisfaction?

In the winter, he wanted to know about his damned drive home from the office. In the summer, he wanted to know about his damned backyard barbecue. That was enough for him. He did not expect the National Weather Service to organize his life for him. In the days leading up to his daughter's outdoor wedding the weather was unsettled, and so rather than complaining about the forecast he put up a damned tent.

He was a wounded man. As I left he said, 'If people would just verify *all* our forecasts, all the times we call for *no* rain and get it right, they'd find our accuracy skills somewhere above 90 percent.'

Naturally. Most weather is good, most of the time. This means that most forecasting is inherently easy. For instance, I predict that Las Vegas will be hot and sunny on July 4, 2026. And at small risk, I can go farther. My forecast for Nashville on the same day is: partly sunny, high near ninety-two degrees, chance of afternoon thundershowers. Also, I think I'll issue a flood watch.

I mentioned my confidence to Keith Seitter, the assistant director of the venerable American Meteorological Society, based in Boston. His attitude was more philosophical than that of the angry forecaster in Camp Springs. He said, 'Sure, but we know those aren't the calls that buy us dinner. We get paid for the good storms, the ones where we say, "Okay, the time has come to batten down the hatches."'

Poor Fitzroy. He stumbled away from dinner in 1861, about fifty years early. At the start of the twentieth century a Norwegian mathematician named Vilhelm Bjerknes made an assertion that only then became obvious: The future form of the weather is determined entirely by its original form, acted on by the known mechanical and thermal laws of physics. This meant that numerical weather prediction was theoretically possible – you could start with a numerical map of a storm, and then apply a few equations.

Vilhelm Bjerknes and his son Jacob began working through the initial problems of quantification. They came to the conclusion – and forced the meteorological establishment to come to it as well – that the existing models were completely unable to explain the observable life cycle of storms. In the 1920s they shook the establishment again by proving the importance of air-mass boundaries, which they called fronts, and by providing a conclusive mechanical explanation of the weather's behavior which recognized storms as atmospheric waves.

Simple but functional numerical models might now be built, but a practical problem remained in a world before computers. The volume of calculations was so large that the process of forecasting was slower than the weather itself. To predict even the simplest storm only a single day ahead could take months of calculations. One British theoretician imagined a 'weather factory' in which 64,000 math workers, directed by the meteorological equivalent of a symphonic conductor, could barely keep up with the weather. And he vastly underestimated the problem. No wonder John von Neuman turned, in 1947, to weather forecasting as the perfect application for his new electronic computer. In April 1950, in Aberdeen, Maryland, under the guidance of von Neuman and meteorologist Jule Charney, the first successful numerical weather forecast was produced by a computer. Within a few years the computer results looked better than those of human forecasters.

That wasn't saying much. Theoretical understanding of the weather had advanced in recent decades, but under the pressure of a daily schedule, the forecasters still had to rely on gut feeling – the old-fashioned experience of having seen some weather pattern before. They called it the 'analog approach' but might more honestly have called it educated guesswork. The results were poor for the obvious reason that no two storms are ever the same. A weather pattern today that looks like one last year will become something quite different by tomorrow.

Computers promised to solve those problems by bypassing the

external features and working with the elemental equations of the weather process. The models were like electronic atmospheres within which mathematical storms could blossom. Meteorology suddenly knew no limits. With refinement of the models and closer weather observation, forecasters would be able to look a week, a month – why not an entire year into the future? The public would adore them. Until recently, faith in these principles was so great that you could almost overlook a persistent problem with the product: In practice, the computer forecasts still had to be judged and touched up with the old and unreliable methods. The models kept getting better, providing measurable improvements in the accuracy of short-range forecasts. But beyond one or two days, major inaccuracies crept in; and beyond five days, the forecasts proved nearly worthless. They still do.

The natural response was to blame the models or the sparseness of data. But already by the 1960s, an MIT meteorologist named Edward Lorenz had taken a different approach. He wondered whether the computers had so perfectly captured the functioning of the atmosphere that the forecasting errors were a manifestation of some unknown trait of the weather itself. Lorenz reduced a computer model to its essentials, then ran weather simulations from seemingly identical starting points. The results on the computer, as in the real weather, were wildly diverging patterns.

It was a fascinating observation. No wonder the new forecasts kept going wrong. Individuality appeared to be as fundamental to computer-generated storms as to those of the actual sky. Lorenz kept reducing the problem until he entered the realm of theoretical mathematics. There, he isolated the hidden and fundamental trait that he called chaos. You could say that pilots knew it all along: The weather is wide beyond the continents and wild beyond prediction. But Lorenz went farther than that. By separating chaos from its atmospheric effects, by giving it clear mathematical expression, he made one of the most important discoveries of our time.

And forecasters are bitter about it. The scientific recognition of chaos has only added to their personal gloom. Whatever hope they harbored of public adoration has now faded. They take it particularly badly that Lorenz was not awarded the Nobel Prize. Physicists and philosophers may glory in uncertainty, but meteorologists are scorned even in Scandinavia because by Monday they cannot be sure of Sunday's weather. Chaos could let them off the hook, if anyone cared to let that happen, but of course no one does. The Weather Service's recent lengthening of the forecast from five days to seven was the last cruel reflex of an old dream. The fact is that no improvement in the model and no amount of computer power can fix such a forecast.

So, quietly, there has been a shift. Gone is the talk of clairvoyance. The effort turns inward now to improved radars and automated observation posts designed not to extend the length of the forecast but to narrow its geographic scale. It may be possible, say the visionaries, to anticipate individual thunderstorms a few hours in advance. Chaos theory still permits that. The wild talk now imagines personal forecasts that will follow people across their daily navigational grids.

How tedious.

But rise above your disdain and remember Fitzroy. And pity the forecasters who are paid to predict the weekend's weather. Lorenz has explained why they will get it wrong.

Richmond in the morning was cloudy. The Weather Service had an office at the airport, and so we walked in to sample the informed opinion there. One of us made a joke about the unexpected freezing rain in New York. The forecasters acted offended and refused to talk. We looked at their maps. The storm center had floated east from the Mississippi River to the hills of West Virginia. The warm front of the night before had buckled and jammed against New England's stubborn winter. Just below it, the mid-Atlantic states remained locked in ice and would be for the rest of the day. However, a classic cold front now curved south from the storm center along the western slope of the Appalachians, out across Jackson, Mississippi, and into the Gulf of Mexico. The front was moving slowly and packing weather: Reported ceilings were low, and radar showed lines of building rainstorms that were especially active near Knoxville, Tennessee. We decided to try the storm at its roughest.

After climbing from Richmond through warm cloud layers, we flew past Raleigh to the point over coastal North Carolina where we could turn west and head directly for the front. The route from there would take us over the heights of the Smoky Mountains, past Asheville, North Carolina, and down into Knoxville, where within the hour the airport had reported a 500-foot overcast and 2 miles visibility in heavy rain.

Westbound through the cloud tops at 8,000 feet, we crawled toward the mountains against sixty-mile-per-hour head winds. A dark wall marked the front ahead. As we approached, we made out bulbous and hooked cloud shapes indicating power and turbulence. Onboard the airplane we had a device, known as a stormscope, that plots the direction and distance to lightning strikes. It showed the first ones now, ahead about fifty miles. Lightning means thunderstorms. We strapped down hard into our seats.

The pilot's claim to have known always about chaos is of course a sort of vernacular conceit. Edward Lorenz discovered and could describe a core element in the very functioning of history. Pilots discover the immediate sky and can describe only their current confusion. That may explain the sensitivity of the Richmond forecasters, who, working at an airport office, must have been tired of listening to pilots' ignorance and presumption.

For example, this Carolina front into which we now prepared to fly was for meteorologists on the ground nothing dramatic or difficult to understand. A wedge of cold dry air was driving under warm moist air and forcing it up to altitudes where it cooled and condensed into cloud droplets, which collected into rain. Within the clouds, the condensation released the moist air's store of latent heat in a molecular process opposite to that of evaporative cooling. The released heat caused the air to rise higher and condense faster, which in turn released more heat. Accelerated in places by uplift from the mountains, the chain reaction raged along the entire length of the front.

When later Paul Kocin studied my weather map, he said, 'Yup, a cold front.' He glanced at me with the disappointment I had come to expect. 'But you know, it really wasn't anything unusual.'

He was right. It was like flying into a slow, sustained explosion. The rain pounded at the windshield and tore paint from the wing's leading edges. Turbulence slammed the airplane from above and below, rocked it onto its side, stretched us against the seatbelts, and at times shook the instrument panel so violently that we had trouble focusing on the instruments. But that makes it sound worse than it was. You can fly an airplane like you ride a horse, refusing to be intimidated. It is one of the inside tricks of storm flying – based on the knowledge that airplanes are the most weather-worthy of vehicles, strong and capable beyond the imagination even of their pilots.

Passengers are not easily reassured because in the alien world of flight they lack a useful sense of scale. But here is some advice for nervous airline riders: The only reason to grip your seat is to keep the seatbelt from bruising your thighs. It may help in reverse to know that the trickiest turbulence is not rough at all but is the layered shift in the wind known by pilots as shear, which happens close to the ground and causes a notoriously seamless sink. There are solutions for that, too.

It was just as well that we had no passengers for Knoxville. Our ride kept getting rougher. The pilots with me were apparently unafraid. The man at the controls fist-fought the airplane with determination. I watched him carefully, alert for fatigue or any slackening of control. We measured the head winds in places now at eighty miles an hour. The clouds were swollen with rain and so dark that we switched on the cockpit lights. The weather at Asheville, one of our escapes if the weather became unflyable, had dropped nearly to the limits of the instrument approach.

We considered diverting while we still could but got a report that Knoxville, ahead, was holding steady. We continued westward. As we crossed the highest mountains, the stormscope showed lightning strikes off the right wing and ahead to the left. We heard the crackling on the radio. Lightning is an electrical reckoning. When it occurs between oppositely charged clouds, or between the clouds and the ground, airplanes will not get in the way. But airplanes do get hit by lightning – or a mild form of the same thing. As they fly through heavy rain or snow, they build up a static charge which normally bleeds off through metal wicks attached to the trailing edges. But if the wicks can't keep up, the charge builds until, with a flash and a bang, a stroke of lightning takes care of it. The stroke will usually not ignite the fuel, but it may damage a circuit or – as occurred to me during that first winter of my cargo flying – burn or blow small holes in the airplane. Airplane repairs are expensive. So we grew concerned when, with lightning around, the rain turned to sleet and our radios started hissing with static and began to fade. It was a sign that the wicks could no longer keep up.

The static charge grew so large that eventually it knocked out our ability to talk to air traffic control. This was less of a problem than it might seem, since there were no other airplanes out there and the controllers could see us on radar and knew our intentions. The static charge continued to build. We grew more concerned when next we lost the navigational radios as well, one by one, until for a while we banged through the crashing rain and sleet by compass and clock alone.

It would be ridiculous to say that we were not then afraid. The sky had gathered around us in a malicious display of its power. But the control of fear is a necessary part of the inner work of flight, and one of the reasons no doubt that each of us was there. We still had an escape route open to us – a 180-degree turn and a retreat downwind and down-weather, on compass alone if need be, into the warm coastal air of the Carolinas. We talked it over. We decided to keep going.

I tuned one radio to an inactive frequency and rhythmically keyed the transmitter, hoping to spark a discharge to help the static wicks dissipate the airplane's electrical shield. I don't know whether the trick worked, but we avoided any damaging strikes. Past the mountains the weather eased, the static wicks did their job, and the navigational radios sprang back crisply. Soon afterward we made contact with a Knoxville controller, who mentioned laconically that we seemed to have come through 'some pretty good cells.'

We had not seen the ground now for several hours. Angling for the approach into Knoxville, we descended rapidly through continuing rain and cloud. Ten miles north of the airport we hooked onto the instrument approach and began to ride its electronic beams like a downsloping rail to the runway. Five hundred feet off the ground, the clouds hinted at the green fields. Seconds later we caught the motion of trees sliding by below. The runway's pulsing approach lights materialized ahead, floating in the mist. We emerged from the clouds, crossed the runway threshold, and touched down on the glistening runway.

That afternoon we continued down the front in rain and ice, and spent the night in Montgomery, Alabama. By morning, the storm center had crossed Nantucket and was heading into the North Atlantic, where within a day, deprived of its sustaining temperature differences, it would quietly collapse into the Icelandic Low, the birth-place of European weather. The end of its weakened cold front curved through central Florida. We flew to Orlando and made an approach through gentle clouds that now seemed like old friends. Then we headed west and along the Gulf Coast finally flew into the clear skies behind the system. In mid-flight we radioed for a weather briefing. Already a powerful new system was bringing blizzards to the Great Lakes. The news encouraged us not to regret the old storm's passing. We turned north, in search again of our landscapes of solitude.

# 5

## *Slam and Jam*

At this point in our starting evolutionary development, hardly more than a century of human flight, the sky has become crowded with our egocentric species, each of us on self-important missions, and wanting to go first. Nowhere is this more true than in the New York area, where the runways of Newark's International Airport, for instance, now rank among the most heavily used in the world. Night after day, in good weather and in bad, the airplanes bear down on them. Their traffic is relentless. Drivers on the adjacent New Jersey Turnpike can count on the distraction: the procession of lights inbound to the runway, the graceful touchdowns, the taxiway parades, the miraculous, banked, nose-high departures. The equipment out there is complex, capable, even exotic, but it is the sheer quantity of it that commands our attention. The big orange radar that stands beside the turnpike can never stop turning.

The radar sweeps the sky beyond the eye, keeping watch on the intertwined arrivals and departures from New York's three major airports. LaGuardia and Kennedy each handle a third of a million flights annually, and Newark, which used to be called Sleepy Hollow and is still thought of as a lesser airport, is in reality even busier than the others, accounting for another half-million flights a year. Because jets fly fast and turn wide, these three airports, which once stood distinctly apart, now lie atop one another. Adding to the tangle, each of the smaller airports – White Plains, Teterboro, and Islip, to name just three – produces its own heavy flows of arrivals and departures. And just overhead pass the en route flights cruising to and from Boston, Philadelphia, and Washington, D.C. The result is the most congested air space in the world, a chunk of sky through which much of American air traffic daily flies, a special place where the usually reliable 'big sky' theory of collision avoidance simply does not apply.

It was because of the congestion that I chose Newark to flesh out my impression that, despite what the public has been led to believe, no immediate danger lurks within the system of air traffic control. This may come as a surprise. If there is one thing that nearly everyone can agree on, it is that air traffic control is critical to the safety of flight. Decades of moviemaking and superficial reporting have contributed to the idea that controllers 'guide' airplanes, that the task allows no room for error or inattention, that controllers must have superhuman reflexes and cool nerves, that only split-second timing and fast computers keep disaster at bay, that passengers' lives hang in the balance because of old and unreliable equipment – and that the work of air traffic controllers as a consequence is impossibly burdensome. These images jibe so neatly with people's sense of helplessness in flight that they have acquired the force of an accepted reality and have become the necessary starting point for any conversation about air traffic control.

But that reality is a myth. Controllers do not puncture it because it gives them leverage with the public and because they themselves have come to believe in it. To be sure, the potential for collisions exists, all the more so in the high-pressure environment of the big-city sky. Concern for safety is the bottom line of all aviation – in the control room as well as in the cockpit. But even in a place like New York, the controllers' real concern is with a set of work rules which operate narrowly atop the nearly absolute safety provided already by pilots and aircraft designers. Mistakes by controllers have led to accidents, but only as one link in a chain of failures. Air traffic control's main function is to provide for the efficient flow of traffic and to allow for the best possible use of limited runway space – in other words, not to keep people alive but to keep them moving.

Like jugglers, controllers are practiced at handling constellations of flying objects. There is an important difference, though. When jugglers get distracted, their constellations tumble to the ground, but when controllers make mistakes, or lose their radars or radios, their airplanes continue to fly. Even if these jugglers were to stop suddenly and walk away, the elements of their constellations would on their own eventually slow down, take in the situation more or less calmly, and by following a variety of well-accepted procedures discover places where they could land softly. Imagine juggling on a low-gravity planet using smart balls that knew how to navigate and to talk to one another and could find ways not to collide.

Of course, once the balls landed they would not rise again without the juggler. That, too, is the nature of air traffic control. Controllers have to work well and willingly in order to keep the air transportation system aloft. And only the most persistent glad-talker would deny that over the past decades controllers have had difficulty, for whatever reason, in living up to the demands placed upon them. But air traffic control's core problems are both less tangible and more difficult to resolve. Yes, the hardware can be modernized, and with sufficient political support new airports can be built, but air traffic control's greatest weakness is cultural and organizational and will not yield to the microchip and the dollar. This weakness lies deep inside the Federal Aviation Administration, a government agency now divided into two mutually antagonistic camps, management and the working controllers, each with its own traditions and memories.

The FAA has other problems as well. It has been accused of waste and stupidity and on a regular basis has been held responsible for airline crashes because of its role in certifying airline and airport operations. In response, it has promised to streamline itself and to pay closer attention to detail; Congress has occasionally decreed other changes. But such reforms, to the extent that they touch it at all, only brush the surface of air traffic control, an individualistic profession which relies on the willingness and creativity of each on-duty controller but within which old-fashioned class resentments and labor discontent now rise like specters from the past. A generation has passed since the great controller strike of 1981, when Ronald Reagan fired most of the work force, giving the FAA the opportunity for a fresh start. But there is a new union now, the National Air Traffic Controllers Association (NATCA), and it is growing as angry as the old one. Among the controllers a quiet and as yet unseen rebellion has broken out. The consequences are serious, if not for safety then for something more important still – the routine human flight that already, after only a century, we have come to believe is our right.

On a first visit to the cavernous radar room of New York Approach, the noise, commotion, and apparent chaos seem to validate the worst fears about air traffic control. Certainly air traffic control has become more dynamic than it was in days gone by – the days of men with crew cuts and white shirts holding binoculars and saying 'roger.' Controllers today wear T-shirts and jeans and have adopted the swagger of the street. Most do not work in towers. This place called New York Approach, which has responsibility for the low altitudes above the entire metropolitan area, is situated away from the airports, half an hour past Kennedy on Long Island. It is known throughout the world for the fury of its controllers, especially those assigned to the Newark sector, who work in a condition of permanent frenzy – shouting, complaining, joking, throwing plastic data strips the length of the consoles, staring at their screens with gum-chewing concentration, swearing at their supervisors, punching the keyboards, gesturing at the radio transmissions of the pilots who cannot match their pace.

This is the sort of intense activity cited in cases of 'burnout,' and it obscures the actual functioning of air traffic control. I spent days at the Newark sector, absorbing the technical details, and came away with the appreciation that the intensity was mostly self-induced and was actually what many of the controllers thrived on. The opportunity to indulge in it seemed, in fact, to be what had drawn them to the job.

The controllers did complain about the pressures, but largely because they would have been embarrassed not to. They complained also about the food in the cafeteria, the condition of the roads, and life on Long Island. One man finally admitted. 'How can you go home from this and be satisfied mowing the lawn?' It was practically a declaration of love. About the only time the controllers seemed genuinely upset was when they talked about their superiors in the FAA.

I don't mean to diminish the controllers or to belittle the experience and dedication they bring to the job. The sight of a radar scope swarming with little ovals, each representing a flight, is indeed daunting. But what does it mean that control rooms can sound like trading floors? Maybe only that air traffic control has become less regimented, more human, and more complex than originally anticipated. There is no doubt that air traffic control consists now of an accumulation of informal solutions pieced together at the last moment to cope with an overwhelming flow. In that sense it is a typically American institution – the problem coming first, the attempt to manage it coming afterward. And who knows, this may be for the best.

On a mechanical level, the most pressing issue that controllers face is a surge in air traffic without a commensurate expansion of runway availability. Since 1979, when President Jimmy Carter deregulated the airlines, unleashing competition among them, the number of scheduled flights in the United States has grown by nearly 70 percent. And the growth has been lopsided: Of the several thousand airplanes aloft during a typical daytime rush, most are headed for the same few cities. The busiest fifty airports, out of thousands of airports altogether, now account for more than 80 percent of the nation's traffic. The lopsidedness is in part a reflection of people's final destinations, but it also results from the airlines' competitive needs for efficient route structures centered on hubs – the now familiar passenger-and cargo-exchange airports that require flights to arrive and depart at about the same time, and that by their nature inflate the number of takeoffs and landings.

Newark, for instance, does double duty as a New York destination and as a Northeastern hub for Continental, United Parcel, and Federal Express. Faced with all the inbound airplanes, its controllers have no choice but to greet them. They grapple with the core problems of overcrowded air space – that flight is fast, fluid and determinedly forward-moving; that every airport, airplane, and pilot is different; that thunderstorms, fogs, winds, ice, snow, or merely low clouds can block a route or slow a runway; that even under a clear blue sky airline schedules push airports past their limits. The slightest bump then ripples backward, forcing the controllers to scramble. A flight may miss an early turnoff from a runway, or come in too fast or slow, or ignore a call on the radio, or jump out of line with an engine shut down. A new pilot may be unsure of the local procedures. An old pilot may get huffy and insist on having his way. These things happen constantly. The resulting complications are measured in wasted fuel, money, and time – but not in lives lost, or even in levels of danger.

Across the Newark controllers' radar screens I watched the targets move in short jumps, dragging identifying tags behind them: Lufthansa, United, Continental – dozens of airplanes at a time. By assigning headings and descent paths, the controllers angled the flights down from the mid-altitude collection points known as arrival gates, joined them up to the south, and swept them into an arc which took them north past the airport and skirted LaGuardia's air space before bending back around, straight in for the runways. The purpose of the arc was only secondarily to keep the airplanes apart. Its primary purpose was nearly the opposite: to give controllers the angular flexibility necessary to tighten the spacing and to exploit the occasional gaps by shooting airplanes in from the side, pushing them toward the airport ahead of sequence.

The most basic geometry of air traffic dictates that departing airplanes naturally fan out and so usually diverge, that cruising airplanes only sometimes cross, but that arriving airplanes must inevitably converge. Moreover, the inbound traffic compresses accordion-style as the airplanes slow toward their touchdown speeds. The compression does not mean that the airplanes are in danger of rear-ending each other; closing speeds are low between airplanes flying in the same direction. The formal separation requirements, which are measured in miles, are dictated ultimately by the civilian orthodoxy that requires one airplane to taxi clear of the runway before the following airplane lands. Military pilots routinely take off and land in formation, and safely. I don't mean that airline pilots should, too, but that the margins built into standard civilian procedures are large. That is why, between themselves, New York Approach controllers take their pride not in the collisions they avoid – an issue that almost never comes up in the manner the public imagines – but in the pressure they keep on the runways.

At the receiving end of that pressure stand the tower controllers at Newark International Airport. On the day I went to see them an overcast paved the sky. I wandered through the airport labyrinth to the service road that led between blast fences out across the vast concrete aprons toward the main runways. It was a bleak landscape, an industrial plain roamed by heavy machinery and scented by jet exhaust, a technical world that was practical and unadorned, a place to feel at home. At the end of the service road the control tower rose against oily winds.

The door at the base had a buzzer and was unattended. An elevator carried me up to the mid-level, where I met the tower's chief, an immaculate man who wore cuff links and a well-tailored suit in the typically dandified style of the FAA management. We sat in his government-issue office, with the clean desk and coffee table, the soft chairs, the FAA seal, the flag, the picture of the president. Drapes hid the view of the wasteland outside but could not exclude the roar of the jets, which regularly shook the walls. Airplanes were backed up fifteen-deep on the taxiways and for 200 miles out into the arrival flow. The chief volunteered that Newark had in recent times led the nation in delays, but he said the airport had improved its record for the current fiscal year. I asked him to be specific about the changes he had made. He admitted that the improvement was due mostly to an unusual stretch of good weather. I assured him that as a pilot I understood. I wanted him not to make the kind of excuses that would embarrass us both. You can do only so much with three cramped runways, and you can do less when the weather turns bad. Controllers do not fly airplanes. Controllers do not control the climate.

I rode the elevator higher and climbed the steel stairs into the tower's cab, the small glass-walled room where the work is done. The cab held a dozen controllers, ordinary-looking men in casual clothes, the sort of standard middle Americans bred by the outer city. In a shopping mall crowd you would never have picked them out. But if they were ordinary men, they were in this place, on the job, also impressively unsettled. Disdaining the swivel chairs, they worked on their feet, tethered by their headset cords, moving restlessly along the radio consoles, leaning toward the traffic outside, checking the radar scopes, issuing instructions, asking questions, barking into telephones, joking, swearing, shouting across the cab in a confusion of emotions difficult for any outsider to decipher.

At the center of the turmoil stood a slight young man with blond hair and birdlike reactions whom I will call Dobkin. He wore a light-weight headset and held a transmitter switch down low in his right hand. It was Dobkin's turn on the frequency known as 'local,' which gave him responsibility for the airport's two parallel runways, the narrowly spaced '22 Left' and '22 Right,' running southwest beside the turnpike. The third runway, a short east–west reliever called '29,' crossed the thresholds of the parallels and conflicted with their traffic. It was a cramped and awkward layout.

Dobkin said, 'We work with what we've got. The parallels were built way too close for simultaneous approaches. We use the outer runway for arrivals. We use the inner runway for departures. We try to run the props over there on 29, keep them out of the way of the jets, but we can't cross them into the main approach. When the wind's light we flip that runway back and forth, pump a load of departures to the west, then bring the inbounds around for landings to the east.'

The idea that such a controller is somehow in the business of 'talk-ing airplanes down' is the part of the myth fostered by the movies. Dobkin had ridden in cockpits a few times, but he knew little about the actual flying of airplanes. Between transmissions he told me how he had come to the job after a stint as a controller in the Navy. He had escaped home, had learned a skill, had grown tired of saluting, and had hired on with the FAA because the FAA was hiring. He had chosen a control tower over a radar room because he liked to look at airplanes. He had picked Newark for the money and action, and he sometimes now wished that he hadn't. He concluded his story with the false regret of a man proud of his skills: 'So here I am ten years later, just another keeper of the concrete.'

He had a high-strung personality, encouraged by the work. If the purpose of his game was simple – to squeeze the maximum possible use from these three runways – in execution it was fast-paced, complex, and competitive. He said, 'The hard part's not doing it, but doing it right. You've got to use every chance, every gap, to move the traffic. Slam and jam. The job keeps you on your toes.'

And safety? It intruded not as an active minute-by-minute concern but as a set of rules within which he had to perform, the most basic of which was the restriction against simultaneous operations on a single runway. Perspective is needed here. The deadliest airline accident in history was a runway accident that occurred in 1977, when two 747s collided on Tenerife (in a fog, one taking off, the other taxiing across); and other runway collisions have occurred. They have all, however, been freakish accidents resulting from multiple errors by both the controllers and the pilots. Except in the worst weather, or sometimes at night, pilots can easily see anyone lingering on the runway and on their own initiative can delay their takeoffs, or if they are landing can add power and climb safely away from the ground. It is primarily because such go-arounds waste valuable landing slots and further burden the final approach that controllers work to avoid them. In other words, Dobkin took the timing seriously, but as an efficient practitioner of traffic flow rather than out of a sense of averting disaster.

I had been told at the FAA headquarters in Washington that the capacity of Newark's runways was 180 operations an hour. When I mentioned this to Dobkin he said, 'Forget it. Not even if every airplane's a 737–400, and they're all flown the same.'

'Why the 400?'

'Land short, slow fast, hit the high-speed exit.'

He took a short break from the frequency and drank too much coffee. Washington's arrogance ate at him. He said, 'A hundred and eighty? With all three runways up and running, the most this airport can handle is 120 an hour. Weather slows us to 70. You tell me how headquarters is going to do better.'

I said, 'I think they've got ideas about personnel. They warned me about this place. They said the tower has been hijacked by union hotheads.'

Dobkin passed this news along to the others. The man working ground control asked about my sources at headquarters. Among others, I mentioned the FAA's administrator.

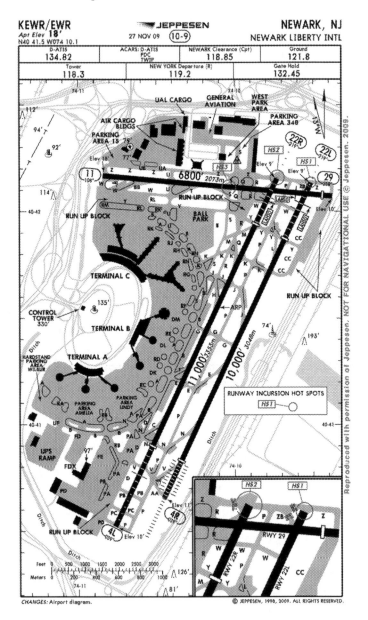

Ground said, 'Yeah? Who is he this week?'

The clearance man answered, 'He's the guy with the "courage" to kill "advanced automation." Didn't you hear?'

'How many billions did they burn on that one?'

Radar said, 'What a joke.'

Dobkin said, 'They should have asked you. You could have told them.'

The talk was constant, a condition of the job. On the frequency and off, it made no difference. The controllers shared with pilots an ease with the transmitter switch that allowed them to superimpose multiple conversations without mixing the lines. At the back of the tower cab, the shift supervisor listened quietly with the placidity of a commander who could no longer keep the pace. A trainee came around with a takeout menu from a cheap Chinese restaurant. Dobkin was cruel to him. In his presence he said, 'Here's a guy who just can't get the picture, but because this is the FAA he'll never wash out. It's a program they call "Train to Succeed."'

I did not mention what Dobkin seemed to have forgotten – that 'Train to Succeed' had been a union initiative.

The airport beyond the glass walls crawled with airplanes moving slowly toward the runways. Thousands of passengers sat like patient prisoners strapped into their seats, but Dobkin's attention went first to the traffic pouring down the final approach. He judged the inbound lights with a familiar mixture of confidence and concentration.

The inbounds tonight showed up first on the tower's radar screen, where we watched the work of an unseen Approach controller who was pushing the flights closer together than the runways would be able to handle for any length of time. Dobkin asked the pilots for speed reductions, which worked at first but soon echoed backward. The tower supervisor telephoned Approach for better service and was told irritably that Approach itself was being force-fed by the long-distance controllers over at New York Center, who in turn were squabbling with their counterparts in Cleveland. In the meantime, because of Teterboro and LaGuardia traffic, New York Approach could not swing the Newark inbounds any wider. Approach threatened to make space by freezing the 'commuter' turboprop departures off of Runway 29, a restriction which would have crowded the turbo-prop departures over to the parallels.

There simply was not enough space for all the airplanes, not in the air and not on the ground – at least not without delays. Dobkin cursed Approach nonetheless. He thought he was doing the controllers there a favor by cleaning up their mess on final. So far he had avoided any wasteful go-arounds, but the airplanes now were barely clearing the runway before the traffic behind flared down across the threshold. After a Delta flight checked in with a stately drawl, Dobkin knocked twenty knots off the Continental that followed. To me he said, 'You learn to read the signs.' Delta dawdled after landing. Off the radio Dobkin snapped, 'Come on dumb boy, clear the runway.' Delta did and Continental landed short, with company behind.

The unfortunate consequence of Dobkin's success was the speed with which it was filling up the airport. To make room for the new arrivals, ground control kept pushing loaded airplanes up the taxiways toward the departure runway, 22 Right. Dobkin cleared them for take-off as aggressively as spacing within the outbound corridor allowed. With relief provided by Runway 29, the tower had managed to avoid gridlock on the ground; nonetheless, the departure delays were stead-ily growing longer. The reason had to do with aircraft performance: While descent angles and final approach speeds can be matched for most inbound traffic, optimal climb rates and speeds vary widely between departing airplanes; moreover, because the heaviest airplanes generate dangerous wakes immediately after liftoff, additional spacing behind them is required.

For Dobkin the result was an inevitable irregularity in takeoff timing which translated into the inefficient use of 22 Right. Ground control worked to reduce the effect by bunching airplanes by type so that they could be launched in quick order. The success of this strat-egy then created another problem: Having landed on 22 Left and pulled onto the taxiways between the runways, the arrivals could not cross the departure runway to get to the terminals. They accumulated between the runways until, by threatening to block the runway exits for landing traffic, they forced Dobkin to hold the takeoffs. Dobkin tried hard to avoid such hangups by exploiting the natural gaps in the departure flow. He said, 'It's Traffic 101. You cross behind a heavy jet, a seven-two, a prop. You use every chance you've got. You don't forget any part of it. You *keep* this traffic moving.'

What he did *not* say was, 'You keep this traffic apart.'

Not that the lives-hanging-by-a-thread idea was entirely absent. I asked Dobkin about the toll on controllers in shattered health, divorce, and drink. 'Sure,' he said uncomfortably. 'It's hard sometimes – I've known guys who had to get out.'

Earlier a controller had said to me, 'Stressed out? If you're the type, sure. But then it's the freeway traffic when you're driving to work that will really do it to you.'

Pilots do not believe that air traffic control is in the business of keeping them alive, or that it should be. This is not a matter of principle or bravado but simple observation. The surrounding sky is so large that even when another airplane passes nearby it remains by comparison very small. Like other pilots who fly in crowded air space, I have had close calls with traffic. But 'close' can mean many things. Is it a crossing that surprises you, or one that requires an evasive maneuver, or one so tight and fast that no maneuver is possible? Or is it – most likely – merely the violation of an official standard that may to some extent be arbitrary? I talked to a controller involved in research with radar simulations, who said, 'You'd be amazed how hard it is to vector two airplanes into each other.' The sort of head-on encounter in which another airplane appears as a dot and within ten or twenty seconds fills your windshield is very rare. Neither pilots nor controllers need gunslinger reflexes. Airplanes sidle slowly toward each other. Can you wonder why a pilot would feel detached from the newspaper and television treatments of his experience? Airplanes will continue to collide, but the reporters who speak so urgently of confusion aloft, of all the accidents avoided by chance, seem to have discovered some separate sky.

Moment-by-moment air traffic control has less to do with the safe operation of the airplane than with the forward progress of flight. From tower control, to radar, to tower again, a procession of voices accompanies each airplane across the map. Their presence is humanized by accents, moods, and informalities and by a shared sense of accommodation and competence. Good controllers are neither automatons nor traffic cops. At the start of a trip they deliver a 'clearance,' assigning the pilots a computer-generated route to the destination. In an uncrowded sky such a clearance might stand alone as a guarantee of traffic-free flying, eliminating the need for controllers. In the actual sky, it serves instead as a plan in the event of radio failure and as an approximate prediction for the actual flight path.

The details fill in after takeoff. Controllers thread the departing airplanes through the first busy altitudes with headings and climb restrictions. Pilots are expected not to comply blindly but rather to judge and agree. They distinguish between the controllers' wrongs and rights. By visualizing the subtleties of a changing technical geography, they can even predict their instructions.

Eventually the pilots are turned loose to proceed high and fast on course, either along the airways that zigzag across the grid of navigational stations on the ground or, more commonly, in airplanes equipped with independent long-range navigational devices, directly toward the destination. Over the continental United States, the airplanes cruise under the surveillance of 'centers' – en route radar facilities whose role, despite the increase in traffic, remains less interventionist than passengers might imagine. Across a sky so deep and wide, 'control' consists mostly of monitoring flights as they proceed by routes and altitudes that have been approved by the computers but that remain essentially the pilot's or airline's choice. With controllers' routine approval, pilots cut corners, deviate around thunderstorms, ride good winds, slide above or below the reports of turbulence. Controllers intervene if they see a traffic conflict developing, or if other controllers elsewhere ask for delays or route changes. The respective roles are clearly defined: Controllers may separate airplanes, but pilots still navigate them.

Controllers do make errors, routinely. Pilots judge the errors, just as in turn the controllers judge theirs. For the participants it is hardly worth commenting on. Few of the errors are serious. The system works in any case only because of the unspoken compensation that goes on within it, the subjective reading of the traffic and the endless adjustments that define the art for everyone involved. You play with speed and descent rates, with bank angles and headings; you measure your transmissions and words; you anticipate the other pilots, their skills and their airplanes; you calibrate the controllers in their own calibrations of you. Busy air space functions on the inside like an ethereal community, a radio village rich with understandings. Machines move through it, but it is a community of the mind.

It is obvious that you cannot just elbow your way through bad weather and into crowded airports. Still, let us imagine a total collapse, one day, of the nation's entire air traffic control system. Even then, airplanes would not simply begin to blunder helplessly into each other. Transportation would of course grind to a halt and the nation would soon be paralyzed, but safety would probably not be affected. Pilots in flight would sit up and pay attention, but they would continue to fly and navigate normally. They would find frequencies on the maps, and talk to their airline dispatchers, and radio to each other as they do already at the many uncontrolled airports. If they were originally headed for hubs like Newark or O'Hare, they might turn and fly somewhere else. Some would have to revert to cumbersome arrival routes, and many would have to hold for a while. But few pilots would feel seriously threatened. This is all the more true in modern cockpits equipped with traffic displays. In the airplane I fly today, I often spot other airplanes electronically (not to mention by looking outside) before the controllers call them out to me.

Certainly the air traffic control system has become an ill-planned patchwork with geographic overlaps, conflicting procedures, and chance redundancies that exist as remnants of earlier times. Airplanes move from one little zone of control to the next, are spoken to across overloaded voice-radio frequencies, are handed off from one controller to another, and are given the sort of customized service that often preempts the needs of the larger traffic flow. Individual control facilities function as parallel fiefdoms, each with its own traditions, procedures, and compromises, each speaking directly to (and quarreling with) its neighbors, without passing through a central command. If you were to design a system from scratch, you would never design this. Nonetheless, one consequence of the system's haphazard structure, of its decentralization and its very inefficiency, is to scatter its many failures, and to provide pilots and controllers with a rich weave of choices when something goes wrong – a radio quits, a radar quits, a computer stops calculating. Perhaps partly as a result, no air traffic control equipment failure has ever yet caused an accident.

I do not mean that the hardware is good enough but that as an educated user I do not feel threatened by its imperfections. Within such a large and complex system, we can assume that the equipment will wear out or become obsolete and that the government will compound the problem by reacting incompetently. It is of course absurd that the FAA has not yet replaced all the old unreliable IBM computers that contain routing information for flights. And it is annoying that the addition of new power supplies in several centers caused outages that in turn led to major delays. And it is disgraceful that the FAA wasted hundreds of millions of dollars between an overambitious attempt to consolidate control rooms and a poorly managed, ill-conceived, and now abandoned 'advanced automation system' – an attempt to automate a wide range of internal air traffic control transactions. But on what basis, exactly, do people care that a controller's radar display does not contain the processing power of a personal computer? And why, precisely, do we worry that backup flight information is still written out on strips of paper? And what was the point, technically, when a secretary of transportation, who was an ex-mayor of Denver, held up an old vacuum tube for ridicule? The controllers, whose workplace he meant to improve, are said to have jeered at his theatrics. Even he must have known that vacuum tubes are not the problem.

The real problem lies not in hardware but in human relations. From its origins in the 1920s among the agencies responsible for the fresh and bewildering endeavor of human flight, the FAA developed an institutional personality, unrestrained by history or tradition, that was raw, arrogant, and domineering – an exuberant expression, some observers still believe, of the twentieth-century form of big government. For generations most controllers came from the military, bringing with them a hierarchical view of organization, which was further encouraged by the nature of the work. The managers were controllers who worked their way up through the ranks, taking pride in each small step, savoring the distinctions which marked their rise. Those distinctions may have been subtle at first, but they grew and strengthened and eventually came to define the management's style.

To explain the resulting tensions then and now, a controller in New York mimicked his bosses for me. He said, 'When I was a controller, I worked aircraft. It was easy. I told them what to do and they did it. Now that I'm management, I work controllers. Same deal. I tell *you* what to do and *you* do it.'

But by the 1970s, a younger generation of controllers was no longer willing to comply. Faced with a rebellious work force, the bewildered FAA management commissioned a psychiatrist, Robert Rose, then of Boston University, to conduct a study of controllers' mental health. The Rose report, published in 1978, confirmed the popular impression that controllers had stressful jobs (they suffered disproportionately from hypertension and certain psychological difficulties, including uncontrollable anger and anti-social behavior), but it concluded in typically stilted language that the causes had less to do with the pressures of traffic than with divisiveness within the FAA: 'This finding of "It's not so much what they are doing as the context in which they are doing it" holds definite implications for changes that might be considered in the work environment to reduce the risk for future morbidity.'

In short, the problem lay with the way the FAA was run. Then came deregulation and the steady growth of air traffic. At New York Approach, a controller with tattooed forearms and a ponytail told me his insider's history of the Newark sector. He meant it as the insider's history of all air traffic control. He said, 'For years you're sitting around Sleepy Hollow eating your brown bag lunches, then one day you look up and, Jesus, you've got a hundred airplanes inbound and every one of them is low on fuel.'

This happened with the deregulation of the airlines, when People Express, then Continental and others, rushed into the Newark void. The controller said, 'The managers and headquarters types, the paperpushers, they would have run away. The only reason the system survived was the skill of the guys working the mikes. They dropped their sandwiches. They threw away their manuals. They stood up to the traffic. They managed to patch things together.'

The real history is less tidy, because nationwide in 1981 most of those same valiant controllers went on strike and lost their jobs, and it was then the turn of the managers and headquarters types, emerging from the back offices and reviving old skills, to stand up to the traffic for the year that followed. The pressure was eased by a stopgap reservation system and an enforced reduction in flights. Nonetheless, to everyone's surprise, the managers actually did as good a job of controlling as had all those 'irreplaceable' union members. Working with small and enthusiastic teams, they handled nearly as many airplanes, safely, and demonstrated convincingly that parts of the old system had indeed been overstaffed. But to accomplish this they, too, had to 'throw away the manuals.' For several years after the strike very little of the normal paperwork got done.

It should have been a lesson but was not. The frustrating part of this story is that after the FAA hired and trained a new and smaller work force of 'permanent replacements,' the managers returned to their offices and again lost respect for the job.

The permanent replacements – strikebreakers by another name – were naturally compliant at first. They were blank slates, the sort of fresh young recruits harboring hopes for promotion who could have been made to share the perspectives of friendly, flexible, and competent management. They gave the FAA an opportunity that other troubled organizations can only dream of – to shed the burdens of the past and move beyond outdated concepts of hierarchy and conflict. But quickly then the recruits became working controllers and came face to face with the airline boom, the congestion around hub airports, the front-line problems of sequencing converging airplanes. To keep the traffic moving, they had to disregard a growing stream of impractical directives from the managers. There was no mystery to why the pre-strike pattern of distance, distrust, and hostility was reasserting itself (everyone involved knew the history), but it seemed all the worse for its institutional inevitability. At New York Approach, I met two brothers – one a manager, the other a controller – who had stopped speaking to each other because of it. In their anger and intractability I could see the emotionalism dividing all air traffic control.

The resentment today is so strong that for many controllers their hatred of the FAA has become a burden against which the original pleasures of the job – the 'slam and jam' and giving of good service – has to be weighed. A controller from California wrote this to me:

You seemed to be surprised that controllers now have a vested interest in the failure or embarrassment of the FAA. But 'they' have taken our profession and our air traffic control and completely screwed it up. 'They' have blown every opportunity to do what is right. 'They' have devoted their efforts to the goddess Bureaucracy. 'They' have relegated us to second class status. 'They' have completely forgotten why 'they' and 'we' are here.

Management, for its part, must cope with a profound political uncertainty. This is usually explained as a confusion between two missions – the need simultaneously to promote and to regulate civil aviation – and though Congress has eliminated the agency's formal responsibility for promotion, that confusion remains real. But the political uncertainty also stems in many cases from something even more difficult to legislate away: the managers' envy of their natural adversaries, the unfettered executives of the airline industry. Those executives are the same people who crowd airline passengers into hub airports and then denounce the FAA for the resulting delays. And the FAA does not really disagree.

The politics play like a cultural revolution in which disdain for government becomes an orthodoxy required of the government itself. This, too, we can now see in the still, fresh realm of the sky. Moreover, it is generally agreed that airline deregulation is an experiment that has worked and that the very growth of traffic is one proof of it. When forced, the FAA managers can still talk tough about maintaining standards, but they do not dare suggest that the market has created imbalances and that through re-regulation or more clever mechanisms the hubs may someday have to be abolished and the traffic dispersed. They cannot even state the obvious, that air traffic remains a classic example of the legitimate need for public control.

Self-disdain is of course not the FAA's official policy. The senior managers of air traffic control run 75 percent of the agency's $10 billion budget and direct a force of 20,000 employees. They are strong operators, intelligent, energetic, and decisive, but their work is also heavily saddled with bureaucratic procedure – the yearly uncertainty of congressional appropriations and the endless consultations which slow or kill their initiatives. But you need only to listen beyond their words to hear the themes of regret.

The ambivalence at headquarters only reinforces a sense among the controllers, incident by incident, that their managers do not stand up for them but instead, for example, side with the airlines in the persistent and irritating disputes over delays. These disputes have become systematic because to a degree unimagined even by active pilots the FAA has surrendered to free enterprise, allowing the airlines to penetrate every level of air traffic control. Beyond taking a hand in the planning and architecture of the system, the airlines now employ full-time representatives at all the major facilities to question the smallest operational details – a certain flight forced to hold, a certain runway selected because of weather, priority given to one airplane or denied another, a routing or even an altitude assigned. For the airlines big money is involved. But among the controllers the feeling of abandonment is so strong in certain radar rooms that some controllers would be willing to take the entire structure down. The managers know it and in turn feel betrayed by the controllers.

What makes this fight peculiar is the coding which allows it to be waged invisibly. Practically everything about air traffic control – whether it emanates from the controllers, their managers, or the airlines – now has a private as well as a public meaning. For instance, a proposed new arrangement called 'free flight' would give pilots more freedom to pick their own routes and more cockpit technology to do it safely, with less guidance from controllers. 'Free flight' may mean 'smart technology' and 'progressive thinking' to outsiders – and it probably *would* increase the capacity of the sky – but it means something quite different to hard-pressed controllers. To them, it is a policy so obviously irrelevant to the bottlenecks on final approach, which greater pilot freedom can only make harder to manage, that it must be interpreted as a coded taunt about the value of controllers and a mean-spirited (if empty) threat about their future. Even when new policies make sense – like the recent systemwide elimination of obsolete flight restrictions, or the reintroduction of inflight holding pools as a way of deriving maximum efficiency from the final approaches – they are interpreted as personal assaults on the working men and women. The controllers fight back through alarmist 'equipment failure' articles in the press and through careful cultivation of the safety myth – a tactic especially galling to the managers because of their own lack of credibility with reporters.

The managers like to reassure themselves that many controllers have not joined the union and that at certain Sunbelt facilities nonunion controllers still constitute more than half of the work force. But that hardly means that those controllers have taken their side. The angry Californian who wrote to me had feelings against the union nearly as strong as those against the FAA headquarters. As I sat beside him one evening at his radar screen, he said, 'We made a big mistake when we let in the AFL-CIO. Look at these guys around you, look at their attitude, look how they're dressed. Where's their professionalism? A "safety issue" for them is a tripping hazard on the stairs. The problem is, *labor* unions represent *laborers.*'

He glumly watched the airplanes moving across his screen. 'But you want to know the real problem? Go outside and look how empty the parking lot is after 5:00. Do you remember how full it was this afternoon? What were all those people *doing* today? They can prove in triplicate that the system works. So what? I've gotten so I'm just running out my time. Give me a year and I'll be retired in Florida. I never thought I'd say it, but I'll wish the union well.'

When I asked another nonunion controller, at the Fort Worth Center, about the low rate of union participation in Texas, he said, 'It's simple. We can afford to watch and wait. It's the big dog theory. Everybody knows it. How goes the Northeast, so goes the country.'

And how goes New York, so goes the Northeast.

Also hotly contested is the use of Flow Control, a command facility with formal responsibility for the hour-by-hour functioning of the national system and the power to intervene. Flow Control originally achieved prominence as a rational response to the 1981 strike, enabling a small team at the FAA headquarters, when necessary, to delay take-offs across the nation in order to keep the reduced staffs at the busiest destinations from being overwhelmed. It was meant to be a fraternal player, the controllers' friend and adviser. Since then, however, it has turned into something quite the opposite. Based in a futuristic radar room near Dulles Airport, it has become a master center with electronic vision that sees every airplane in the system and the authority to question and, in some circumstances, to countermand decisions made by individual controllers. Though it still initiates the departure holds which frustrate pilots and passengers, and though inevitably it miscalculates, causing needless delays, it now sees its mission largely in opposition to the individual control facilities – to keep as many airplanes in the air as possible and maintain pressure on the final approaches. The problem is not simply that controllers and Flow Control often now work at cross purposes; there is also the matter of symbolism. Flow Control has inserted teams into all the regional facilities – specialists who dress better than controllers and work under more relaxed conditions, sometimes from raised islands at the center of the control room floors. Those who say that Flow is just another bureaucratic empire have vastly underestimated it: Whatever its impact on air traffic, it is also Headquarters' greatest hope, free flight's natural companion, a Big Brother with the ability to identify recalcitrant controllers and the authority to intervene and fight back against them. The controllers' union would like nothing more than to break into Flow Control. So far it has been unable to. Now the angriest controllers accuse the union itself of selling out. It is a dangerous sentiment. A similar escalation preceded the ill-considered strike of 1981, but that experience is well remembered, and no one expects the controllers to make such a mistake again. One reason is that the FAA itself provides them with rules and procedures that, if strictly followed, can snarl traffic nearly as effectively as a strike. But such a rule-book slowdown seems heavy-handed, since possibilities abound for more subtle dissent. Renegade job actions in particular can be as spontaneous and creative as a controller's best work, and where the air space is already crowded, they require just a delicate lack of cooperation to produce big results.

With such renegade actions, which have already begun, individual controllers quietly gum up the works. One man described the technique to me this way: 'Slow down, speed up, slow down. Now turn right, turn left, stay up, go down.' With one airplane you can create a ripple that will last for hours. You can also require unusually large in-trail spacing, or you can simply put airplanes into holding patterns. The details hardly matter, but what they add up to is sabotage.

The pilots involved may not be aware of the reasons for their handling, but increasingly they have begun to question their clearances and to express dissatisfaction on the frequency. Civility is slowly disappearing. But from the controllers' point of view, the beauty of renegade job actions is that they can occur naturally and without premeditation in the political climate of the control rooms, and they are easily deniable, or defensible in the name of safety. The delays they cause are difficult to distinguish from other, ordinary delays. Flow Control can eventually figure out what is happening, and may try to intervene, but usually does so too late. Airline passengers are affected, of course, but that is beside the point.

Once again, the argument is in code. Renegade slowdowns deliver a clear threat within the agency, yet a threat so technical that it remains invisible to the outside world. The public has been frightened into submission. Neither the union nor the FAA will admit that an invisible war has broken out. Air traffic keeps growing, and everyone fears a loss of control.

# 6

## *Valujet 592*

On a muggy May afternoon in 1996, an emergency dispatcher in southern Florida got a call from a man on a cellular phone. The caller said, 'Yes. I am fishing at Everglades Holiday Park, and a large jet aircraft has just crashed out here. Large. Like airliner size.'

The dispatcher said, 'Wait a minute. Everglades Park?'

'Everglades Holiday Park along canal L-67. You need to get your choppers in the air. I'm a pilot. I have a GPS. I'll give you coordinates.'

'Okay sir. What kind of plane did you say? Is it a large plane?'

'A large aircraft similar to a 727 or a umm . . . I can't think of it.'

This lapse was unimportant. The caller was a born accident observer – a computer engineer and private pilot with a pride in his technical competence and a passion for detail. His name was Walton Little. When he first saw the airplane it was banked steeply to the right and flying low, just above the swamp. Later he filed an official report in which he wrote:

There was no smoke, no strange engine noise, no debris in the air, no dangling materials or control surfaces, no apparent deformation of the airframe, and no areas that appeared to have missing panels or surfaces . . . Sunlight was shining on the aircraft, and some surfaces were more reflective than others. I saw a difference in reflection of the wing skin in the area where I would expect the ailerons to be, as though they were not in neutral. In particular, the lower (outboard) portion of the right wing appeared less reflective as though the aileron was deflected upward.

A couple of nearby fishermen instinctively ducked into their boat for cover, but not Walton Little, who stood on his deck facing 'about

115 degrees,' and watched the airplane hit the water. The shock wave passed through his body: 'I was in disbelief that the crash had occurred. I stood there for just a moment to consider that it really did happen. I was already thinking that I needed to get my cellular phone out of the storage compartment and call 911, but I wanted to assure myself of what I was doing because it is against the law to make false calls to 911.'

He called within a minute. After reading off his latitude and longitude to the dispatcher, he said, 'I'm in a bass boat on the canal. I thought it was an aircraft from an air show or something, and—'

The dispatcher interrupted. 'What did you . . . Did you see flames and stuff come up, sir?'

'I heard the impact and I saw dirt and mud fly in the air. The plane was sideways before it went out of my sight on the horizon about a mile from me.'

'Yes sir. Okay. You said it looked like a 727 that went down?'

'Uh, it's that type aircraft. It has twin engines in the rear. It is larger than an executive jet, like a Learjet.'

'Yes sir.'

'It's much bigger than that. I won't tell you it's a 727, but it's that type aircraft. No engines on the wing, two engines in the rear. I do not see any smoke, but I saw a tremendous cloud of mud and dirt go into the sky when it hit.'

'Okay sir.'

'It was white with blue trim.'

'White with blue trim, sir?'

'It will not be in one piece.'

Walton Little was right. The airplane was a twin-engine DC-9 painted the colors of Valujet, an aggressive young discount airline based in Atlanta. When it hit the Everglades, it was banked vertically to the right and pointed nearly straight down. The airplane did not sink mysteriously into the swamp, as reports later suggested, but shattered against it with the full furious force of a fast dive.

By the time Walton Little felt the shock wave, everyone aboard was dead – the 2 pilots, 3 flight attendants, and 105 passengers. Their remains lay smothered within a shallow, watery crater and the liquid mud and grass that surrounded it. All that marked the surface was a fractured engine, a few dead fish, some jet fuel, and a scattering of personal papers, clothes, and twisted aluminum pieces – the stuff of tragedy. During those first few days some officials worried aloud about the accident's effect on nature, but the swamp was not so fragile as that and quickly resumed its usual life. The families of those who died have proved less resilient.

For the rest of us, though, the accident should be finished business. The official investigation ran its complete course, a 'cause' was found, contributing factors were acknowledged, and the Federal Aviation Administration wrote new regulations. Editorialists expressed their outrage, and individuals were held responsible. After a long suspension, Valujet returned to flight with a renewed commitment to safety. Other airlines promised to be more careful, too. And even the FAA went through a house-cleaning. By conventional standards, therefore, the reaction to the tragedy was admirable. And yes, we know anyway that flying is safe, that we are a winged species now, that the sky is ours for the taking. Certainly my own experience is that passengers do not need to cower around the exit rows, or carry emergency 'smoke hoods,' or avoid certain airlines and airplanes, or fear bad weather, or worry about some impending collapse of airline safety. Those are assertions made by aviation illiterates – the overly cautious people who can always gain an audience and who would smother us in their fear of violent death. The public, now a flying public, has the sense in the long run to ignore them. Nonetheless, the Valujet accident continues years later to raise a series of troubling questions – no longer about what happened but about why it happened and what is to keep similar accidents from happening again. As these questions lead into the complicated and human core of flight safety, they become increasingly difficult to answer.

Consider for simplicity that there are only three kinds of airplane accidents. The most common ones you might call 'procedural.' They are those old-fashioned accidents which result from single obvious mistakes, which can be immediately understood in simple terms, and which lead to simple resolutions. For pilots – do not fly into violent thunderstorms, or take off with ice on your wings, or descend prematurely, or let fear or boredom gain the upper hand. Do not make the mistake of trusting your sense of balance, or of feeling too at home in the sky. Mechanics, ramp agents, and air traffic controllers must observe equally simple rules. As practitioners, we have together learned many such painful lessons.

The second sort of accident could be called 'engineered.' It consists of those surprising material failures which should have been predicted by designers or discovered by test pilots but were not. Such failures at first defy understanding, but ultimately they submit to examination and result in tangible solutions. The American Eagle ATR turboprop dives into a frozen field in Roselawn, Indiana, because its deicing boots did not protect its wings from freezing rain – and as a result, new boots are designed and the entire testing process undergoes review. The USAir Boeing 737 crashes near Pittsburgh because of a rare hard-over rudder movement – and as a result a redesigned rudder control mechanism is installed on the whole fleet. The TWA Boeing 747 blows apart off New York because (whatever the source of ignition) the empty center tank contained an explosive mixture of fuel and air – and as a result explosive mixtures might in the future be avoided. Such tragic failures may seem all too familiar, but in fact they are rare, and they will grow rarer still as aeronautical engineering improves. You can regret the lives lost, and deplore the slowness with which officials respond, but in the long run there is reason to be optimistic. Our science will prevail.

But the Valujet accident is different. It represents the third and most elusive kind of disaster, a type of 'system accident' which lies beyond the reach of conventional solution and which a small group of thinkers inspired by Yale sociologist Charles Perrow has been exploring elsewhere – in power generation, chemical manufacturing, nuclear weapons control, and space flight. Perrow has coined the more loaded term 'normal accident' for such disasters because he believes they are normal for our time. His point is that these accidents are science's illegitimate children, bastards born of the confusion that lies within the complex organizations with which we manage our dangerous technologies. Perrow does not know much about airline flying – and what he says about it he often gets wrong – but his thinking applies to it nonetheless. In this case, the organization includes not only Valujet, the archetype of new-style airlines, but also the contractors who serve it, the government agencies that despite economic deregulation are expected to oversee it, and even the press and Congress, who also play important roles. Taken as a whole, the airline system is complex indeed.

It is also competitive, and if one of its purposes is to make money, the other is to move the public through thin air cheaply and at high speed. Safety is never first, nor can it be, but for obvious reasons it is a necessary companion to the venture. Risk is a companion, too, but on the everyday level of practical compromises and small decisions – the building blocks of this ambitious enterprise – the view of risk is usually obscured. The people involved do not consciously trade safety for money or convenience, but inevitably they do make a lot of bad little choices. They get away with those choices because, as Charles Perrow mentioned to me, Murphy's Law is wrong – what *can* go wrong usually goes *right*. But then one day, a few of the bad little choices combine, and circumstances take an airplane down. Who then really is to blame?

We can find fault among those directly involved – and we probably need to. But if our purpose is to attack the roots of such an accident, we may find them so entwined with the system that they are impossible to extract without bringing the whole structure down. The study of system accidents acts either to radicalize people or to force them to speak frankly. It requires most of us to admit that we do put a price on human life, and that the price, though incalculable, is probably not very high. In the case of Valujet it faces us with the possibility that we have come to depend on flight, that nothing we are willing to do can stop the occasional sacrifice, and that therefore we are all complicitous. Beyond such questions of blame, it requires us to consider the possibility that our solutions, by adding to the complexity and obscurity of the airline business, may actually increase the risk of accidents. System accident thinking does not demand that we accept our fate without a struggle, but it serves as an important caution.

The distinction between the three types of accidents – procedural, engineered, and system – is of course not absolute. Most accidents have a bit of all three to them. And even in the most extreme cases of system failure, the post-crash investigation has to work its way forward conventionally, usefully identifying those problems which can be fixed, before the remaining questions begin to force a still deeper examination. That was certainly the way with Valujet Flight 592.

It was headed from Miami to Atlanta, flown by Captain Candalyn Kubeck, age thirty-five, and her copilot Richard Hazen, age fifty-two. They represented the new generation of pilots, experienced not only in the cockpit but in the rough-and-tumble of the deregulated airline industry, where each had held a slew of low-paid flying jobs before settling on Valujet. It was no shock to them that Valujet was a nonunion operation or that it required them to pay for their own training. With 9,000 flight hours, over 2,000 in the DC-9, Candalyn Kubeck now earned what the free market said she was worth, about $40,000 a year, plus bonuses; her copilot Richard Hazen, ex-Air Force and with similar experience, earned about half as much. Valujet executives had convinced themselves that the low pay had a positive effect – that it allowed them to employ 'real pilots' who just wanted to fly.

But the pilots didn't think about it that way. They felt bruised and probably a little deflated. Sure they wanted to fly, but they worked for Valujet for lack of choice. And they were not the only ones; the flight attendants, ramp agents, and mechanics made a lot less than they would have for a more traditional airline. So much work was farmed out to temporary employees and independent contractors that Valujet was sometimes called a 'virtual airline.' But why not? FAA regulators had begun to worry that the company was moving too fast and not keeping up on the paperwork, but there was no evidence that the people involved were as individuals inadequate. Many of the pilots were refugees from the labor wars at the old Eastern Airlines, and they were generally as competent and experienced as their higher-paid friends at United, American, and Delta. Valujet was helping the entire industry understand just how far the cost-cutting could be pushed. Its flights were cheap and full, and its stock was strong on Wall Street.

But six minutes out of Miami, while climbing northwest through 11,000 feet, the copilot Richard Hazen radioed, 'Ah, 592 needs an immediate return to Miami.'

In the deliberate calm of pilot-talk, this was strong language. The time was thirty-two seconds after 2:10 in the afternoon, and the sun was shining. Something had gone wrong with the airplane.

The radar controller at Miami Departure answered immediately. Using Valujet's radio name 'Critter' (for the company's cartoonish tail-logo – a smiling airplane) he gave the flight a clearance to turn initially toward the west, away from Miami and conflicting traffic flows, and to begin a descent to the airport. 'Critter 592, ah roger, turn left heading two-seven-zero, descend and maintain seven thousand.'

Hazen said, 'Two-seven-zero, seven thousand, Critter 592.'

The controller was Jesse Fisher, age thirty-six, a seven-year veteran, who had twice handled the successful returns of airliners that had lost cabin pressurization. He had worked the night before and had gone home, fed his cat, and slept well. He felt alert and rested. He said, 'What kind of problem are you having?'

Hazen said, 'Ah, smoke in the cockpit. Smoke in the cabin.' His tone was urgent.

Fisher kept his own tone flat. He said, 'Roger.' Over his shoulder he called, 'I need a supervisor here!'

The supervisor plugged in beside him. Flight 592 tracked across Fisher's radar screen, dragging its data tag, which included the automatic readout of the airplane's altitude. Fisher noticed that the pilots had not yet started to turn and descend, and this surprised him. He gave them another heading, farther to the left, and cleared them down to 5,000 feet.

Aboard the airplane, Hazen acknowledged the new heading but misheard the altitude assignment. It didn't matter. Flight 592 was burning, and the situation in the cockpit was rapidly getting out of hand. One minute into the emergency, the pilots were still tracking away from Miami and had not begun their return.

Hazen said, 'Critter 592, we need the, ah, closest airport available.'

The transmission was garbled or blocked, or Fisher was distracted by competing voices within the radar room. For whatever reason, he did not hear Hazen's request. When investigators later asked him if in retrospect he would have done anything differently, he admitted that he kept asking himself the same question. Even without hearing

Hazen's request, he might have suggested some slightly closer airport. But from the airplane's position only twenty-five miles to the northwest of the big airport, Miami International still seemed like the best choice because of the emergency equipment there. In any case 'Miami' was the request he *had* heard, and he had intended to deliver it.

To Hazen he said, 'Critter 592, they're gonna be standing, standing by for you.' He meant the crash crews at Miami. 'You can plan Runway 12. When able, direct to Dolphin now.'

Hazen said, '. . . need radar vectors.' His transmission was garbled by loud background noises. Fisher thought he sounded 'shaky.'

Fisher answered, 'Critter 592, turn left heading one-four-zero.'

Hazen said, 'One-four-zero.' It was his last coherent response.

The flight had only now begun to move through a gradual left turn. Fisher watched the target on his screen as it tracked through the heading changes: The turn tightened, then slowed again. With each sweep of the radar beam, the altitude readouts showed a gradual descent – 8,800, 8,500, 8,100. Two minutes into the crisis, Fisher said, 'Critter 592, keep the turn around, heading one-two-zero.'

Flight 592 may have tried to respond – someone keyed a microphone and transmitted a 'carrier' only, without voice.

Fisher said, 'Critter 592, contact Miami Approach on – correction, no, you just keep on my frequency.'

Two and a half minutes had gone by. It was 2:13 in the afternoon. The airplane was passing through 7,500 feet when suddenly it tightened the left turn and entered a steep dive. Fisher's radar showed the turn and an altitude readout of XXX – code for such a rapid altitude change that the computer could not keep up. Investigators later calculated that the airplane rolled to a sixty-degree left bank and dived 6,400 feet in thirty-two seconds. During that loss of control, Fisher radioed mechanically, 'Critter 592, you can, uh, turn left, heading one-zero-zero, and join the Runway 12 localizer at Miami.' He also radioed, 'Critter 592, descend and maintain three-thousand.'

Then the incredible happened. The airplane rolled wings-level again and pulled sharply out of its spiral dive. Despite what McDonnell-Douglas later claimed about the amazing stability of the DC-9, the airplane would not have done this on its own. It is remotely possible that the autopilot kicked in, that having been disabled by shorting wires, it temporarily re-engaged itself, but it seems more likely from the vigor of the recovery that one of the pilots, having been incapacitated by smoke or defeated by melting control-cables, somehow momentarily regained control. Fisher watched the radar target straighten toward the southeast and again read out a nearly level altitude – however of now merely a thousand feet. The airplane's speed was nearly 500 miles an hour.

The frequency crackled with another unintelligible transmission. Shocked into the realization that the airplane would be unable to make Miami, Fisher said, 'Critter 592, Opa Locka Airport's about twelve o'clock at fifteen miles.'

Walton Little, in his bass boat, spotted the airplane then, as it rolled steeply to the right. The radar, too, noticed that last quick turn toward the south, just before the final noseover. On the next sweep of the radar, the flight's data block went into 'coast' on Fisher's screen, indicating that radar contact had been lost. The supervisor marked the spot electronically, and launched rescue procedures.

Fisher continued to work the other airplanes in his sector. Five minutes after the impact, another low-paid pilot, this one for American Eagle, radioed, 'Ah, how did Critter make out?' Fisher did not answer.

It was known from the start that fire took the airplane down. The federal investigation began within hours, with the arrival that evening of a National Transportation Safety Board team from Washington. The investigators set up shop in an airport hotel, which they began to refer to without embarrassment as the 'command center.' The English is important. Similar forms of linguistic stiffness, specifically of engineer-speak, ultimately proved to have been involved in the downing of Flight 592 – and this was a factor that the NTSB investigators, because of their own verbal awkwardness, were unable quite to recognize.

It is not reasonable to blame them for this, though. The NTSB is a technical agency, staffed by technicians, and though it makes much of its independence, it occupies a central position in the stilted world of aviation. Its job is to examine important accidents and to issue nonbinding safety recommendations – opinions, really – to industry and government. Because the investigators have no regulatory authority and must rely on persuasion to influence the turn of events, it may even be necessary for them to use impressive, official-sounding language. Even among its opponents, who often feel that its recommendations are impractical, the NTSB has a reputation as a branch of government done right. It is technically competent, and in a world built on compromise, it manages to play the old-fashioned unambiguous role of the public's defender.

The press has a classically symbiotic relationship with the NTSB, relying on the investigators for information while at the same time providing them with their only effective voice. Nonetheless, in times of crisis immediately after an accident, a tension exists between the two. Working under pressure to get the story right, investigators for their part resent the reporters' incessant demands during the difficult first days of an accident probe – the recovery of human remains and aiplane parts. By the time I got to Miami, nineteen hours after Flight 592 hit the swamp, the two camps were passing each other warily in the hotel lobby.

Twenty miles to the west, deep in the Everglades, the recovery operation was already under way. The NTSB had set up a staging area – a 'forward ops base,' one official called it – beside the Tamiami Trail, a two-lane highway that traverses the watery grasslands of southern Florida. Within two days this staging area blossomed into a chaotic encampment of excited officials – local, state, and federal – with their tents and air-conditioned trailers, their helicopters, their cars and flashing lights. I quit counting the agencies. The NTSB had politely excluded most of them from the actual accident site, which lay seven miles to the north, along a narrow levee road.

The press was excluded even from the staging area but was provided with two news conferences a day, during which the investigators warily doled out tidbits of information. One NTSB official said to me, 'We've got to feed them or we'll lose control.' But the reporters were well behaved and if anything a bit overcivilized. Beside the staging area they settled in to their own little town of television trucks, tents, and lawn chairs. For camera work the location gave them good Everglade backdrops and shots of alligators swimming by; the viewing public could not have guessed that they stood so far from the action. They acted cynical and impatient, but in truth this was not a bad assignment; at its peak their little town boasted pay phones and pizza delivery.

Maybe it was because of my obvious lack of deadlines that the investigators made an exception in my case. They slipped me into the front seat of a Florida Game helicopter whose pilot, in a frater- nal gesture, invited me to take the controls for the run out to the crash site. From the staging area, we skimmed north across the swamped grasslands, loosely following the levee road, until swinging wide to circle over the impact zone – a new pond defined by a ring of turned mud and surrounded by a larger area of grass and water and accident debris. Searchers in white protective suits waded line-abreast through the muck, piling pieces of people and airplane into flat-bottomed boats. It was hot and unpleasant work performed in a contained little hell, a place which one investigator later described to me as reeking of jet fuel, earth, and rotting flesh – the special smell of an airplane accident. We descended overhead to touch down on the levee, about 300 yards away from the crash site, where an American flag and a few tents and trucks constituted the recovery base.

The mood there was quiet and purposeful, with no sign among the workers of the emotional trauma that officials had been worriedly predicting since the operation began. The workers on break sat in the shade of an awning, sipping cold drinks and chatting. They were policemen and firemen – not heroes, but straightforward guys accus- tomed to confronting death as a matter of fact.

It was of course a somber place to be. Human remains lay bagged in a refrigerated truck for later transport to the morgue. A decon- tamination crew washed down torn and twisted pieces of airplane, none longer than a few feet. Investigators tagged the most promising wreckage to be trucked immediately to a hangar at an outlying Miami airport, where specialists could study it. Farther down the levee I came upon a soiled photograph of a young woman with a small-town face and a head of teased hair. A white-suited crew arrived on an airboat and clambered up the embankment to be washed down. Another crew set off. A boatload of muddy wreckage arrived. The next day, the families of the dead came out from Miami on buses, and laid flowers and cried. After they left, pieces of the airplane kept arriving for nearly another month.

Much was made of this recovery, which – prior to the offshore retrieval of TWA's Flight 800 – the NTSB called the most challenging in its history. The swamp did make the search slow and difficult, and the violence of the impact meant that meticulous work was required during the reconstruction of the critical forward cargo hold. However, in truth the Herculean physical part of the investigation served merely to confirm what a simple look at a shipping ticket had already shown – that Valujet Flight 592 burned and crashed not because the airplane failed but because the airline did.

For me the most impressive aspect of the investigation was the speed with which it worked through the false pursuit of an electrical fire – an explanation supported by my own experiences in flight, and made all the more plausible here because the Valujet DC-9 was old and had experienced a variety of electrical failures earlier the same day, including a tripped circuit breaker (for a redundant pump) that had resisted the attentions of a mechanic in Atlanta and then mysteriously had fixed itself. I was impressed also by the instincts of the reporters, who for all their technical ignorance seized upon the news that Flight 592 had been loaded with a potentially dangerous cargo of chemical oxygen generators – scores of little firebombs which could have caused this accident, and indeed did.

Flight 592 crashed on a Saturday afternoon. By Sunday the recovery teams were pulling up scorched and soot-stained pieces. On Monday a searcher happened to step on the flight data recorder, one of the 'black boxes' meant to help with accident investigations. The NTSB took the recorder to its Washington laboratory and found there that six minutes after Flight 592's takeoff there had been a blip in the flight data consistent with a momentary rise in air pressure. Immediately afterward the recorder began to fail intermittently, apparently because of electrical power interruptions. On Tuesday night at the hotel press conference, Robert Francis, the vice-chairman of the NTSB and the senior official on the scene, announced in a deliberate monotone, 'There could have been an explosion.' A hazardous materials team would be joining the investigation. The investigation was focusing on the airplane's forward cargo hold, which was located just below and behind the cockpit and was unequipped with fire detection or extinguishing systems. Routine paperwork indicated that the Miami ground crew had loaded it with homeward-bound Valujet 'company material,' a witch's brew of three mounted tires and five cardboard boxes of old oxygen generators.

Oxygen generators are safety devices. They are small steel canisters mounted in airplane ceilings and seatbacks and linked to the flimsy oxygen masks that dangle in front of the passengers when a cabin loses pressurization. To activate an oxygen flow, the passenger pulls a lanyard, which slides a retaining pin from a spring-loaded hammer, which falls on a minute explosive charge, which in turn sparks a chemical reaction that liberates the oxygen within the sodium chlorate core. This reaction produces heat, which may cause the surface temperature of the canister to rise to 500 degrees Fahrenheit when it is mounted correctly in a ventilated bracket and much higher if the canister is sealed into a box with other canisters, which may themselves be heating up. If the materials surrounding the canister catch fire, the presence of pure oxygen will cause them to burn furiously. If those materials are rubber tires, they will provide a particularly rich source of fuel. Was there an explosion? Perhaps. In any event, Flight 592 was blow-torched into the ground.

It is ironic that the airplane's own emergency oxygen system was different – a set of simple oxygen tanks, similar to those used in hospitals, that grow *colder* during use. The oxygen generators in Flight 592's forward cargo hold came from three MD-80s, a more modern kind of twin-jet, which Valujet had recently purchased and was having refurbished at a hanger across the airport in Miami. As was its practice for most of its maintenance, Valujet had hired an outside company to do the job, in this case a large firm called Sabretech, owned by Sabreliner of St Louis and licensed by the FAA to perform the often critical work. Sabretech, in turn, had hired other companies to supply contract mechanics on an as-needed basis. It later turned out that three-fourths of the people on the Valujet project were just such temporary outsiders. Many of them held second temporary jobs as well. After the accident, the vulnerability of American wage workers could be seen in their testimonies. They inhabited a world of boss-men and sudden firings, with few protections or guarantees for the future. As the Valujet deadline approached they worked in shifts, day and night, and sometimes through their weekends as well. It was their contribution to our cheap flying.

We will never know everyone at fault in this story. Valujet gave the order to replace the MD-80s' oxygen generators, which had come to the end of their licensed lifetimes. It provided Sabretech with explicit removal procedures and general warnings about the dangers of fire. Over several weeks Sebretech workers extracted the old oxygen generators and tied or cut off their lanyards before stacking them in five cardboard boxes that happened to be lying around the hangar. Apparently they believed that the securing of the lanyards would keep the generators from inadvertently firing off.

What they did *not* do was place the required plastic safety caps over the firing pins – a precaution spelled out on the second line of Valujet's written work order. The problem for Sabretech was that no one had such caps or cared much about finding them. Ultimately, the caps were forgotten or ignored. At the end of the job, in the rush to complete batches of paperwork on all three airplanes, two of the mechanics routinely 'pencil-whipped' the problem by fraudulently signing off the safety cap line along with the others certifying that the work had been done. Sabretech inspectors and supervisors signed off on the work, too, apparently without giving the caps much thought.

The timing is not clear. For weeks the five boxes stood on a parts cart beside the airplanes. Eventually a variety of mechanics lugged them over to Sabretech's shipping and receiving department, where they sat on the floor in the area designated for Valujet property. Several days before the accident, a Sabretech manager told the shipping clerk to clean up the area and get all the boxes off the floor in preparation for an upcoming inspection by Continental Airlines, a potential customer. The boxes were unmarked, and the manager did not ask what was in them.

The shipping clerk then did what shipping clerks do and prepared to send the oxygen generators home to Valujet headquarters in Atlanta. He redistributed them equally between the five boxes, laying the canisters horizontally end to end and packing bubble wrap on top. After sealing the boxes he applied address labels and Valujet company-material stickers and wrote 'aircraft parts.' As part of the load he included two large main tires, mounted on wheels, and a smaller nose tire. The next day, he asked a co-worker, the receiving clerk, to make out a shipping ticket and to write *Oxygen Canisters – Empty* on it. The receiving clerk wrote *Oxy Canisters*, and then put *Empty* between quotation marks, as if he did not believe it. He also listed the tires.

The cargo stood for another couple of days until May 11, when the company driver had time to deliver them across the airport to Flight 592. There, the Valujet ramp agent accepted the material, though federal regulations forbade him to, even if the generators were empty, because Valujet was not licensed to carry any such officially designated hazardous materials. He discussed the cargo's weight with the copilot, Richard Hazen, who also should have known better. Together they decided to place the load in the forward hold, where Valujet workers laid one of the big main tires flat, placed the nose tire at the center of it, and stacked the five boxes on top of it around the outer edge, in a loose ring. They leaned the other main tire against a bulkhead. It was an unstable arrangement. No one knows exactly what happened then, but it seems likely that the first oxygen generator ignited during the loading, or during the taxiing or on takeoff, as the airplane climbed skyward.

Two weeks later and halfway through the recovery of the scorched and shattered parts, a worker finally found the airplane's cockpit-voice recorder, the second 'black box' sought by the investigators. It had recorded normal sounds and conversation up to the same moment – six minutes after takeoff – when the flight data recorder registered a pulse of high pressure. The pulse may have been one of the tires exploding. In the cockpit it sounded like a chirp and a simultaneous beep on the public address system. The captain, Candalyn Kubeck, asked, 'What was that?'

Hazen said, 'I don't know.'

They scanned the airplane's instruments and found sudden indications of electrical failure. It was not the cause but a symptom of the inferno in the hold – the wires and electrical panels were probably melting and burning – but the pilots' first thought was that the airplane was up to its circuit-breaking tricks again. The recording here is garbled. Candalyn Kubeck appears to have asked, 'About to lose a bus?' Then more clearly she said, 'We've got some electrical problem.'

Hazen said, 'Yeah. That battery charger's kickin' in. Oooh, we gotta—'

'We're losing everything,' Kubeck said. 'We need, we need to go back to Miami.'

Twenty seconds had passed since the strange chirp in the cockpit. A total electrical failure, though serious, was not in those sunny conditions a life-threatening emergency. But suddenly now there was incoherent shouting from the passenger cabin, and women and men screaming, 'Fire!' The shouting continued for thirteen seconds and subsided.

Kubeck said, 'To Miami,' and Hazen put in the call to Jesse Fisher, the air traffic controller who the night before had fed his cat and slept well. When Fisher asked, 'What kind of problem are you having?' Kubeck answered off radio, 'Fire,' and Hazen transmitted his urgent, 'Smoke in the cockpit, smoke in the cabin.'

Investigators now presume that the smoke was black and thick and perhaps poisonous. The recorder picked up the sound of the cockpit door opening and the voice of the chief flight attendant who said, 'Okay, we need oxygen, we can't get oxygen back there.' Did she mean that people could not breathe, or that the airplane's cabin masks had not dropped, or that they had dropped and were not working? We will never know. But if the smoke was poisonous, the masks might not have helped much anyway, since by design they mix cabin air into the oxygen flow. The pilots were equipped with better isolating-type masks and with goggles but may not have had the time to put them on. Only a minute had passed since the first strange chirp. Now just before it failed, the voice recorder captured the sound of renewed shouting from the cabin. In the cockpit the flight attendant said, 'Completely on fire.'

The recording was of little use to the NTSB's technical investigation, but because it showed that the passengers had died in agony, it added emotional weight to a political reaction that was already spreading beyond the details of the accident and that had begun to call the entire airline industry into question. The public, it seemed, would not be placated this time by standard reassurances and the discovery of a culprit or two. The press and the NTSB had set aside their on-site antagonism and had joined forces in a natural coalition with Congress. The questioning was motivated not by the immediate fear of unsafe skies (despite the warnings of Mary Schiavo, a federal whistle-blower who stepped forward to claim special insight) but rather by a more nuanced suspicion that competition in the open sky had gone too far and that the FAA, the agency charged with protecting the flying public, had fallen into the hands of industry insiders.

The FAA's administrator then was a one-time airline boss named David Hinson, the sort of glib and self-assured executive who does well in closed circles of like-minded men. Now, however, he would have to address a diverse and skeptical audience. The day after the Valujet accident he had flown to Miami and made the incredible assertion that Valujet was a safe airline – when for 110 people lying dead in a nearby swamp it very obviously was not. He also said, 'I would fly on it,' as if he believed he had to reassure a nation of children. It was an insulting performance, and it was taken as further evidence of the FAA's isolation and its betrayal of the public's trust.

After a good night's sleep Hinson might have tried to repair the damage. Instead he appeared two days later at a Senate hearing in Washington sounding like an unrepentant Prussian: 'We have a very professional, highly dedicated, organized, and efficient work force that do their job day in and day out. And when we say an airline is safe to fly, it is safe to fly. There is no gray area.'

His colleagues must have winced. Aviation safety is nothing but a gray area, and the regulation of it is an indirect process involving negotiation and maneuver. The FAA can affect safety by establishing standards and enforcing them through inspections and paperwork, but it cannot throw the switches in the cockpits or turn the wrenches in the hangars, or in this case supervise the disposal of old oxygen generators. Safety is ultimately in the hands of the operators, the pilots and mechanics and their managers, because it involves a blizzard of small judgments. Hinson might have admitted this, but instead, inexplicably, he chose to link the FAA's reputation to that of Valujet. This placed the agency in an impossible position. It would now inevitably be found to blame.

Within days evidence emerged that certain inspectors at the FAA had been worried about Valujet for years and had included their concerns in their reports. Their consensus was that the airline was expanding too fast (from two to fifty-two airplanes over two and a half years) and that it had neither the procedures nor the people in place to maintain standards of safety. The FAA tried to keep pace, but because of its other commitments – including countering the threat of terrorism – it could assign a crew of only three furiously overloaded inspectors to the entire airline. At the time of the accident they had run 1,471 routine checks on Valujet operations, and 2 additional eleven-day inspections in both 1994 and 1995. Despite the burden it placed on the individual inspectors, this level of scrutiny was, at least on paper, about normal for an airline of this size. But by early 1996, concern had grown within the FAA about the airline's disproportionate number of infractions and its string of small bang-ups. The agency began to move more aggressively. An aircraft maintenance group found such serious problems in both the FAA's field-level surveillance and the airline's operations that it wrote an internal report recommending that Valujet be 'recertified' immediately – meaning that it be grounded and started all over again. The report was sent to Washington, where for unexplained reasons it lay buried until after the accident. Meanwhile, on February 22, 1996, headquarters launched a 120-day 'special emphasis' inspection, which after the first week issued a preliminary report suggesting a wide range of problems. The special emphasis inspection was ongoing when, on May 11, Flight 592 went down.

As this record of official concern emerged, the questions changed from why Hinson had insisted on calling Valujet 'safe' after the accident to why he had not shut down the airline *before* the accident. Trapped by his earlier simplistic formulations, he could provide no convincing answer. The press and Congress jeered. The FAA now launched an exhaustive thirty-day review of Valujet, the most concentrated airline inspection in U.S. aviation history, assigning sixty inspectors to perform in one month the equivalent of four years' work. Lewis Jordan, the founder and president of Valujet, complained that Hinson was playing to the mob and conducting a witch hunt that no airline could withstand. Jordan had been trying shamelessly to shift the blame for the deaths onto his own cut-rate contractor, Sabretech, and he received little sympathy now. But he was right about the witch hunt. Even when Valujet did things right under the pressure of the inspection, the results were compared to earlier statistics to demonstrate that when the inspectors were not present Valujet normally did things wrong. Five weeks after the accident, it was a surprise to no one when Valujet was indefinitely grounded.

Here now was the proof that the FAA had earlier neglected its duties. The agency's chief regulator, Anthony Broderick, was the first to lose his job. Broderick was an expert technocrat, disliked by safety crusaders because of his cautious approach to regulation and respected by aviation insiders for the same reason. Hinson pushed him out in front, knowing that he was a man of integrity and would accept responsibility for the FAA's poor performance. But if Hinson thought that he himself could escape with this sacrifice, he was wrong. Broderick's airline friends now joined the critics in disgust, and the jeering grew so loud that Hinson was forced from office.

In that sense the system worked. One year after the accident it was possible to conclude that the tragedy had perhaps had some positive consequences – primarily because the NTSB had done an even better job than usual, not only of pinpointing the source and history of the fire but of recognizing some of its larger implications. With a well-timed series of press feedings and public hearings, the accident team had kept the difficult organizational issues alive and had managed to stretch the soul-searching through the end of the year and beyond. By shaking up the FAA, the team had reminded the agency of its original responsibilities – prodding it perhaps into a renewed commitment to inspections and a resolution to impose greater responsibility on the airlines for their actions, including the performance of outside shops.

For the airlines, the investigation served as a necessary reminder of the possible consequences of cost cutting and complacency. Among airline executives smart enough to notice, it may also have served as a warning about the public's growing distrust of their motivations and about widespread anger with the whole business – anger that may have as much to do with the way passengers are handled as with their fears of dying. However you wanted to read it, the Valujet turmoil marked the limits of the public's tolerance. The airlines were cowed, and they submitted eagerly to the banning of oxygen generators as cargo on passenger flights. Having lost their friend Broderick, they then rushed ahead of the FAA with a $400 million promise (not yet fulfilled) to install fire detectors and extinguishers in all cargo holds. As it had before, the discussion of hidden cargo hazards ran up against the practical difficulties of inspection. Nonetheless, after the accident the ground crews could be counted on for a while to watch what they loaded into airplanes and what they took out and threw away.

And the guilty companies? They were sued, of course, and lost money. After firing the two mechanics who had fraudulently signed the work orders, Sabretech tried to put its house in order. Nonetheless, its customers fled and did not return. The Miami operation dropped from 650 to 135 employees and in January 1997 was forced to close its doors. Soon afterward, as the result of a three-month FAA investigation, Sabretech's new Orlando facility was forced to close as well. Valujet survived its grounding and under intense FAA scrutiny returned to the sky toward the end of 1996, with a reduced and standardized fleet of DC-9s. Because of continuing public worries it changed its name to Airtran, and for a while it was probably the safest airline in the country. What then explains the feeling, particular to this case, that so little has in reality been achieved?

Charles Perrow came unintentionally to his theories about 'normal accidents' after studying the failings of large organizations. His point is not that some technologies are riskier than others, which is obvious, but that the control and operation of some of the riskiest technologies like nuclear power generation and some chemical manufacturing require organizations so complex that serious failures are virtually guaranteed to occur. Those failures will occasionally combine in unforeseeable ways, and if they induce further failures in an operating environment of tightly interrelated processes, the failures will spin out of control, defeating all interventions. The resulting accidents are inevitable, Perrow observes, because they emerge from the very heart of the ventures. You cannot eliminate one without killing the other.

Perrow's insight has the power of an authentic observation. It tends to impose its logic across pre-existing ideological lines and in unanticipated ways. Perrow himself has run up against it: He is a moralist with an urge to blame elites for the failings of their organizations, and in examining some of the more notorious modern cases he has drawn back from what his own theory coolly suggests – that good and evil were not ultimately at play.

I went to see Perrow one rainy day in New Haven and suggested to him that his observations could be used to excuse the bad decisions of big business. He stood up and began pacing his brick-walled office, exclaiming that this of course was not what he had intended. I pursued the subject. After a while he seemed delighted to claim that I had stumped him.

At sixty-two, Perrow is a burly and disheveled man with a fleshy face and the dust of old rebellions about him. He is affable, excitable, physically restless, strong, and no doubt a bit reckless. I got the impression that his students must enjoy him. As a teacher he is at his best as a generalist, heated and irrepressible, spinning off new ideas, acknowledging his errors, and confidently moving on. He is also a storyteller, and accidents are his passion; even in print he wanders into their unimportant details and loses track of his larger subjects. During our conversation about Valujet he diverged into an irrelevant description of a barge collision and then apologized with a self-deprecating smile, calling himself 'an accident maven.'

Beneath his affability, however, I saw a seriousness in his eyes and in the unexpected soberings of his facial expressions. I won't link this directly to his professional contemplation of catastrophe, because like most of us Perrow must deal with horror in the abstract; his sudden soberings may be related simply to his intelligence or his age. Nonetheless, I got the impression that he rarely loses sight of the human suffering contained within his musings. When a reporter from the *New York Times* called, fishing for a quote on an accident, Perrow grew angry and hung up on him abruptly, after snapping, 'The people I talk to are graduate students. The *New York Times* lacks the sophistication.' I thought this was unfair, since the *New York Times* had just proved itself with that phone call. Perrow is precisely the man who can explain why the-news-that's-fit-to-print is so regularly the news of disaster.

In fact it seemed to me, sitting in his office, that Perrow had just hung up on one of his natural allies. His natural opponents are people like me – at least in the general sense. Pilots are safety practitioners, steeped in a can-do attitude toward survival, fluent in the language of collective learning, confident in their own skills, trained to 'fly the airplane' to the end. My secret emotion at the Valujet crash site was not compassion or sadness but annoyance with the dead crew. So what if they had a fire, I thought – they still should not have lost control. If that reaction seems too severe, for an active pilot it is nonetheless probably healthy. As a child of the sky, before I first soloed, I was taken aside by my pilot-father, who rather than talking about the risks that lay ahead simply said, 'If you are crossing the street at a crosswalk, and some drunk driver runs you over, then it is your own fault for being there in the first place.' And I understood even then that he was right. Pilots have to take their fate firmly into their own hands. Airplanes speak to them through their controls, but they remain inanimate machines and mindlessly unforgiving. I took a job with a great Texas airman named Fritz Kahl, who upon seeing 'God Is My Copilot' stenciled below a pilot's window once remarked to me, 'Any son of a bitch who needs God to fly beside him oughta stay on the goddamned ground.' And he was right, too. Pilots are not paid to wonder.

The basis for such an attitude is the idea that man-made accidents must by definition lie within human control. The strongest proponents of this approach are a group of Berkeley professors – notably the political scientist Todd La Porte – who study 'high-reliability organizations,' meaning those with good track records at handling apparently risky technologies – aircraft carriers, air traffic control centers, certain power companies. They search for elements which might explain the high levels of safety already achieved and which might be extended to produce perfect safety.

These high-reliability theorists object to being called 'optimistic,' which sounds to them like 'naive.' They say they accept the inevitability of human error and mechanical failure, and they deny that they use a 'closed' organizational model – one that simplistically assumes that civilian organizations might, like military units, be isolated from the confusions of the larger society. Nonetheless, they work with the idea that organizations can be made superior to the sum of their parts, that redundancies count, that decision making and formal responsibilities can be centralized or decentralized according to need, that organizations are rational beings which learn from past mistakes and can tailor themselves to achieve new objectives, and that if the right steps are taken, accidents can be avoided. A zero-accident rate, they say, is a theoretical possibility.

Perrow studied at Berkeley and once worked with some of the high-reliability theorists, but his thinking grew up beside theirs, not in reaction to it. It has close but unacknowledged ties to the idea of chaos in the natural world – the disorder discovered by Edward Lorenz that frustrates forecasts and limits practical science. More explicitly, Perrow's accident theory grows from a skeptical view of large organizations as overly rigid, internally divided, and inherently unfocused systems – collectives that resist learning, gloss over failures, suffer from internal conflicts and confusion, and defy rational plans.

This approach was refined in the 1970s by sociologist James March, who wrote about 'organized anarchies,' and coined the term 'garbage can' to characterize their internal functioning – a bewildering mix of solutions looking for problems, inconsistent and ill-defined goals, fluid and uninformed participation in decision making, changes in the outside world, and pure chance as well. Of course, organizations do succeed in producing products, including services like safe airline flying. The garbage can model explains the reasons only for their difficulties, but it does so with a ring of truth among executives long frustrated by their lack of direct control.

Perrow uses the garbage can model to explain why institutional failures are unavoidable, even 'normal,' and why when organizations are required to handle dangerous technologies safely, they regularly do not. By necessity these are the very organizations that claim, often sincerely, to put safety first. Their routine failures sometimes become Perrow's 'normal accidents' and may blossom as they did for the FAA and Valujet into true catastrophes.

Perrow's seminal book, *Normal Accidents: Living with High Risk Technologies* (1984), is a hodgepodge of story-telling and exhortation, weakened by contradiction and factual error, out of which however this new way of thinking has risen. His central device is an organizational scale against which to measure the likelihood of serious 'system' accidents. He does not assign a numerical index to the scale but uses a set of general risk indicators. On the low end stand the processes – like those of most manufacturing – that are simple, slow, linear, and visible, and in which the operators experience failures as isolated and containable events. At the other end stand the opaque and tangled processes characterized by a combination of what Perrow calls 'interactive complexity' and 'close coupling.'

By 'interactive complexity' he means not simply that there are many elements involved but that those elements are linked to one another in multiple and often unpredictable ways. The failure of one part – whether material, psychological, or organizational – may coincide with the failure of an entirely different part, and this unforeseeable combination will cause the failure of other parts, and so on. If the system is large, the combinations are practically infinite. Such unravelings seem to have an intelligence of their own; they expose hidden connections, neutralize redundancies, bypass 'firewalls,' and exploit chance circumstances which no engineer could have anticipated. When the operating system is also inherently quick (like a chemical process, an automated response to missile attack, or a jet airliner in flight), the cascading failures will accelerate out of control, confounding the human operators and denying them a chance to jerry-rig a recovery. That lack of slack is Perrow's 'close coupling.' Then the only difference between an accident and a human tragedy may be a question, as in chemical plants, of which way the wind blows.

I ran across this thinking by chance, a year before the Valujet crash, when I picked up a copy of Scott D. Sagan's book, *The Limits of Safety: Organizations, Accidents, and Nuclear Weapons* (1993). Sagan is a Stanford political scientist, as fastidious and contained a man as Perrow is not. He is a generation younger, the sort of deliberate careerist who moves carefully between posts in academia and the Pentagon. Unlike Perrow, he seems drawn to safety for personal as well as public reasons. Perrow needed such an ally. Sagan is the most persuasive of his interpreters, and with *The Limits of Safety* he has solidified system accident thinking, focusing it more clearly than Perrow was able to. The book starts by opposing high-reliability and normal-accident theories, then tests them against a laboriously researched and previously secret history of failures within U.S. nuclear weapons operations. The test is a transparent artifice, but it serves to define the opposing theories. Sagan's obvious bias does not diminish his work.

Strategic weapons pose an especially difficult problem for system-accident thinking for two reasons: First, there has never been an accidental nuclear detonation, let alone an accidental nuclear war; and second, if a real possibility of such an apocalyptic failure exists, it threatens the very logic of nuclear deterrence – the expectation of rational behavior on which we continue to base our arsenals. Once again the pursuit of system accidents leads to uncomfortable ends. Sagan is not a man to advocate disarmament, and he shies away from it here, observing realistically that nuclear weapons are here to stay. Nonetheless, once he has defined 'accidents' as less than nuclear explosions – as false warnings, near launches, and other unanticipated breakdowns in this ultimate 'high-reliability' system – Sagan discovers a pattern of such accidents, some of which were contained only by chance. The reader is hardly surprised when Sagan concludes that the accidents were inevitable.

The book interested me not because of the catastrophic potential of such accidents but because of the quirkiness of the circumstances that underlay so many of them. It was a quirkiness which seemed uncomfortably familiar to me. Though it represented possibilities that I as a pilot had categorically rejected, this new perspective required me to face the wild side of my own experience with the sky. I had to admit that some of my friends had died in crazy and unlucky ways, that some flights had gone uncontrollably wrong, and that perhaps not even the pilots were to blame. What is more, I had to admit that no matter how carefully I checked my own airplanes and how deliberately now I flew them, the same could happen to me.

That is where we stand now as a society with Valujet, and it explains our continuing discomfort with the accident. Flight 592 burned because of its cargo of oxygen generators, yes, but more fundamentally because of a tangle of confusions which the next time will take some entirely different form. It is frustrating to fight such a phenomenon. At each succeeding level of inquiry we seize upon the evidence of wrongdoing, only to find after reflection that our outrage has slipped away. Flight's greatest gift is to let us look around, to explore the inner world of sky, but also in the end to bring us back down again, and leave us facing ourselves.

Take, for example, the case against the two Sabretech mechanics who removed the oxygen canisters from the Valujet MD-80s, ignored the written work orders to install the safety caps, stacked the dangerous canisters improperly in the cardboard boxes, and finished by fraudulently signing off on a job well done. They will probably suffer much of their lives for their negligence, as perhaps they should. But here is what really happened. Nearly 600 people logged work time against the three Valujet airplanes in Sabretech's Miami hangar; of them, 72 workers logged 910 hours across several weeks against the job of replacing the 'expired' oxygen generators – those at the end of their approved lives. According to the supplied Valujet work card 0069, the second step of the seven-step removal process was: *If generator has not been expended, install shipping cap on the firing pin.*

This required a gang of hard-pressed mechanics to draw a distinction between canisters that *were* 'expired,' meaning the ones they were removing, and canisters that were *not* 'expended,' meaning the same ones, loaded and ready to fire, on which they were now expected to put nonexistent caps. Also involved were canisters which were expired and expended, and others which were not expired but were expended. And then, of course, there was the simpler thing – a set of new replacement canisters, which were both unexpended and unexpired.

If this language seems confusing, do not waste your time trying to sort it out. The Sabretech mechanics certainly did not, nor should they have been expected to. The NTSB later suggested that one problem at Sabretech's Miami facility was the large number of Spanish-speaking immigrants on the work force, but quite obviously the language problem lay on the other side – with Valujet and the narrowly educated English-speaking engineers who wrote work orders and technical manuals as if they were writing to themselves.

Eleven days after the accident, one of the hapless mechanics who had signed off on the work still seemed unclear about basic distinctions between the canisters. An NTSB agent asked him about a batch of old oxygen generators, removed from the MD-80s, that the mechanic had placed in a box.

AGENT: Okay. Where were they?

MECHANIC: On the table.

AGENT: On the table?

MECHANIC: Yes.

AGENT: And there were only how many left to do? (He meant old oxygen generators to be replaced, remaining in the airplane.)

MECHANIC: How many left?

AGENT: Yeah. You said you did how many?

MECHANIC: Was like eight or twelve, something like that.

AGENT: Eight or twelve left?

MECHANIC: The rest were already back in the airplane.

AGENT: The new ones?

MECHANIC: Yes.

AGENT: What about the old ones?

MECHANIC: The old ones?

AGENT: Yeah. Yeah, that's the one we're worried about, the old ones.

MECHANIC: You're worried about the old ones?

AGENT: Yeah.

But that was after the accident. Before the accident, the worry was not about old parts but about new ones – the safe refurbishing of the MD-80s in time to meet the Valujet deadline. The mechanics quickly removed the oxygen canisters from the brackets and wired green tags to most of them. The green tags meant 'repairable,' which these canisters were not. It is not clear how many of the seventy-two workers were aware that the canisters could not be used again, since the replacement of oxygen generators is a rare operation, though most claimed after the accident to have known at least why the canisters had to be removed. But here, too, there is evidence of confusion. After the accident, two tagged canisters were found still lying in the Sabretech hangar. On one of the tags under 'Reason for removal' someone had written, 'Out of date.' On the other tag someone had written, 'Generators have been fired.'

Yes, a perfect mechanic might have found his way past the Valujet work card, and into the massive MD-80 Maintenance Manual, to chapter 35-22-01, within which line 'h' would have instructed him to 'store or dispose of oxygen generator.' By diligently pursuing these two options, he could eventually have found his way to a different part of the manual and learned that 'all serviceable and unserviceable (unexpended) oxygen generators (canisters) are to be stored in an area that ensures each unit is not exposed to high temperatures or possible damage.' By pondering the structure of that sentence he might have deduced that 'unexpended' canisters are also 'unserviceable' canisters, and therefore perhaps should be taken to a safe area and 'initiated' according to the procedures provided in section 2.D.

To 'initiate' an oxygen generator is, of course, to fire it off, triggering the chemical reaction that produces oxygen and leaves a mildly toxic residue within the canister, which then is classified as a hazardous waste. Section 2.D ends with the admonition that 'an expended oxygen generator (canister) contains both barium oxide and asbestos fibers and must be disposed of in accordance with local regulatory compliances and using authorized procedures.' No wonder the mechanics stuck the old generators in boxes.

The supervisors and inspectors failed miserably here, though after the accident they proved clever at ducking responsibility. At the least they should have supplied the required safety caps and verified that those caps were being used. If they had – despite all the other errors that were made – Flight 592 would not have burned. For larger reasons, too, their failure is an essential part of this story. It represents not the avarice of profit takers but rather something more insidious, the sort of collective relaxation of technical standards that Boston College sociologist Diane Vaughan has called 'the normalization of deviance' and that she believes existed at NASA in the years leading to the 1986 explosion of the space shuttle *Challenger*. The leaking o-ring that caused the catastrophic blow-through of rocket fuel was a well-known design weakness, and it had been the subject of worried memos and conferences up to the eve of the launch. Afterward it was widely claimed that the decision to launch anyway had been made because of political pressure from the top – the agency was drifting, its budget was threatened, and the leadership from the White House down wanted to avoid the embarrassment of an expensive delay. But after an exhaustive exploration of NASA's closed and technical world, Vaughan concluded that the real problems were more cultural than political and that the error had actually come from below. Simply put, NASA had proceeded with the launch despite its o-ring worries largely because it had gotten away with launching the o-ring before. What can go wrong usually goes right – and people just naturally draw the wrong conclusions. In a general way, this is what happened at Sabretech. Some mechanics now claim to have expressed their concerns about the safety caps, but if they did they were not heard. The operation had grown used to taking shortcuts.

But let's be honest. Mechanics who are too careful will never get the job done. Whether in flight or on the ground, the airline system requires the people involved to compromise, to improvise, and some-times even to gamble. The Sabretech crews went astray – but not far astray – by allowing themselves quite naturally not to worry about discarded parts.

A fire hazard? Sure. The mechanics tied off the lanyards and shoved the canisters a little farther away from the airplanes they were work-ing on. The canisters had warnings about heat on them, but none of the standard hazardous material placards. It probably would not have mattered anyway because the work area was crowded with placards and officially designated hazardous materials, and people had learned not to take them too seriously. Out of curiosity, a few of the mechanics fired off some canisters and listened to the oxygen come out – it went *pssst*. Oh yeah, the things got hot, too. No one even considered the possibility that the canisters might accidentally be shipped. The mechanics did finally carry the five cardboard boxes over to the shipping department, but only because that was where Valujet property was stored – an arrangement that itself made sense.

The shipping clerk was a regular fellow. When he got to work the next morning, he found the boxes without explanation on the floor of the Valujet area. The boxes were innocent-looking, and he left them alone until he was told to tidy up. Sending them to Atlanta seemed like the best way to do that. He had shipped off 'company material' before without Valujet's specific approval, and he had heard no complaints. He knew he was dealing now with oxygen canisters but apparently did not understand the difference between oxygen storage tanks and chemical generators designed to fire off. When he prepared the boxes for shipping, he noticed the green 'repairable' tags mistakenly placed on the canisters by the mechanics, and he misunderstood them to signify 'unserviceable' or 'out of service,' as he variably said after the accident. He also drew the unpredictable conclusion that the canisters were therefore empty. He asked the receiving clerk to fill out a shipping ticket.

The receiving clerk did as he was instructed, listing the tires and canisters, but he put quotation marks around the word 'empty.' Later, when asked why, he replied, 'No reason. I always put like, when I put my check, I put "Carlos" in quotations. No reason I put that.'

The reason was, it was his habit. On the shipping ticket he also wrote '5 boxes' between quotation marks – a nonsensical use of punctuation which in context now can be taken to mean not that Carlos suspected there were fewer boxes or more but by implication that he too believed the oxygen canisters were empty.

Two days later, over by Flight 592 the Valujet ramp agent who signed for the cargo did not care about such subtleties anyway. Valujet was not authorized to carry hazardous cargoes of any sort, and it seems obvious now that a shipping ticket listing inflated tires and oxygen canisters (whether 'empty' or not) should have aroused the ramp agent's suspicions. No one would have complained had he opened the boxes or summarily rejected the load. There was no 'hazardous material' paperwork associated with it, but he had been formally trained in the recognition of unmarked hazards. His Valujet Station Operations Manual specifically warned that 'cargo may be declared under a general description that may have hazards which are not apparent, that the shipper may not be aware of this. You must be conscious of the fact that these items have caused serious incidents, and in fact, endangered the safety of the aircraft and personnel involved.' It also warned:

Your responsibility in recognizing hazardous materials is dependent on your ability to: 1. Be Alert! 2. Take time to ask questions! 3. Look for labels . . . Ramp agents should be alert whenever handling luggage or boxes. Any item that might be considered hazardous should be brought to the attention of your supervisor or pilot, and brought to the immediate attention of Flight Control and, if required, the FAA. REMEMBER: SAFETY OF PASSENGERS AND FELLOW EMPLOYEES DEPENDS ON YOU!

It is possible that the ramp agent was lulled by the company-material labels. Would the Sabretech workers, aviation insiders, ship him a hazardous cargo of his own material without letting him know? His conversation with the copilot, Richard Hazen, about the weight of the load may have lulled him as well. Hazen, too, had been formally trained to spot hazardous materials, and he would have understood better than the ramp agent the dangerous nature of oxygen canisters, but he said nothing. It was a routine moment in a routine day. The morning's pesky electrical problems had perhaps been resolved. The crew was calmly and rationally preparing the airplane for the next flight. As a result, the passengers' last line of defense folded.

What are we to make of this tangle of circumstance and error? One suspicion is that its causes may lie in the market forces of a deregulated airline industry and that in order to keep such accidents from happening again we might consider the possibility of re-regulation – a return to the old system of limited competition, union work forces, higher salaries, and expensive tickets. There are calls, of course, to do just that. The improvement in safety would come from slowing things down and allowing a few anointed airlines the leisure to discover their mistakes and to act on them. The effects on society, however, would be inflationary and anti-egalitarian – a return to a constricted system that most people could not afford to use. Moreover, aviation history would argue against it. Despite the obvious chaos of the business and the apparent regularity of airline accidents, air travel has become safer under deregulation. Much of that improvement comes from technical advances that would have occurred anyway – those that have resulted in the continued reduction of 'procedural' and 'engineered' accidents.

The other way to regulate the airline industry is not economic but operational – detailed governmental oversight of all the technical aspects of flight. This is the approach we have taken since the birth of the airlines in the 1920s, and it is what we expect of the FAA today. Strictly applied standards are all the more important in a free market, in which unchecked competition would eventually force the airlines to cut costs to the point of operating unsafely, until accidents forced each in turn out of business. An airline should not overload its airplanes or fly them with worn-out parts, but it also cannot compete effectively against other airlines that do. Day to day, airline executives may resent the intrusion of government, but in their more reflective moments they must also realize that they *need* this regulation in order to survive. The friendship that has grown up between the two sides – between the regulators and the regulated – is an expression of this fact which no amount of self-reform at the FAA can change. When after the Valujet crash David Hinson of the FAA reacted to accusations of cronyism by going to Congress and humbly requesting that the agency's 'dual mandate' be eliminated, so that it would no longer be required by law to promote the airlines, he was engaged in a particularly hollow form of political theater.

The critics had real points to make. The FAA had become too worried about the reactions of its friends in the airline industry, and it needed to try harder to enforce the existing regulations. Perhaps it needed even to write some new regulations. And like NASA before, it needed to listen to the opinions and worries of its own lower-level employees. But there are limits to all this, too. The dream of a zero-accident future is about as realistic as the old Valujet promise to put safety first. When at a post-crash press conference in Miami a reporter asked Robert Francis of the NTSB, 'Shouldn't the government protect us against this kind of thing?' the honest answer would have been, 'It cannot, and never will.'

The truth helps because in our frustration with such accidents we are tempted to invent solutions that, by adding to the obscurity and complexity of the system, may aggravate just those characteristics which led to the accidents in the first place. This argument for a theoretical point of *diminishing* safety is a central part of Perrow's thinking, and it seems to be borne out in practice. In his exploration of the North American early warning system, Sagan found that it was failures of safeties and redundancies that gave the most dangerous false indications of missile attack – the kind that could have triggered a response. The radiation accidents at both the Chernobyl and the Three Mile Island power plants were induced by failures in the safety systems. Remember also that the Valujet oxygen generators were safety devices, that they were redundant, and that they were removed from the MD-80s because of regulations limiting their useful lives. This is not an argument against such devices but a reminder that elaboration comes at a price.

Human reactions add to the problem. Administrators can think up impressive chains of command and control and impose complex double-checks and procedures on an operating system, and they can load the structure with redundancies, but there comes a point – in the privacy of a cockpit or a hangar or an office or a house – beyond which people will rebel. These rebellions are commonplace, and they result in unpredictable and apparently arbitrary actions, all the more so because in the modern insecure workplace they remain undeclared. The one thing that always gets done right is the required paperwork.

The paperwork is a necessary and inevitable part of the system, but it, too, introduces dangers. The problem is not just its wastefulness but the deception that it breeds. In the Sabretech hangar the two unfortunate mechanics who signed the lines about the nonexistent safety caps just happened to be the slowest to slip away when the supervisors needed signatures. The other mechanics almost certainly would have signed, too, as did the inspectors. Their good old-fashioned pencil whipping is the most widespread form of Vaughan's 'normalization of deviance.'

The fraud they committed was a small part of a much larger deception – the creation of fully formed pretend realities that include unworkable chains of command, unlearnable training programs, unreadable manuals, and the fiction of regulations, checks, and controls. Such pretend realities are familiar to all of us. They extend even into the most self-consciously progressive organizations, with their attempts to formalize informality, deregulate the workplace, share profits and responsibilities, respect the integrity and initiative of the individual. The systems work in principle, and usually in practice as well, but the two may have little to do with each other.

No one is to blame for this divergence, and there may be no way to avoid it, but we might now begin to see how the pretend realities lie falsely within our new world like the old-fashioned parks of a formal landscape. We can hide for a while in our fantasies of agreement and control, but ultimately we cannot escape the vernacular terrain – the cockpits and hangars and auto body shops, the lonely lit farmhouses sailing backward through the night – where we continue to struggle through life on the face of a planet.

We have come to a point in history not of an orderly existence but of something less expected: the possibility of seeing ourselves reflected perfectly in the turbulence and confusion that exists inside the sky. This gives me hope. It means that the sky is not some separate place but a vast new extension of our human earth, and that I as a pilot have perhaps not wasted my time there. Flight's greatest gift is to let us look around, and when we do we discover that the world is larger than we have been told and that our wings have helped to make it so.

# 7

## *The Crash of EgyptAir 990*

I remember first hearing about the accident early in the morning after the airplane went down. It was October 31, 1999, Halloween morning. I was in my office when a fellow pilot, a former flying companion, phoned with the news: It was EgyptAir Flight 990, a giant twin-engine Boeing 767 on the way from New York to Cairo, with 217 people aboard. It had taken off from Kennedy Airport in the middle of the night, climbed to 33,000 feet, and flown normally for half an hour before mysteriously plummeting into the Atlantic Ocean sixty miles south of Nantucket. Rumor had it that the crew had said nothing to airtraffic control, that the flight had simply dropped off the New York radar screens. Soon afterward an outbound Air France flight had swung over the area and had reported no fires in sight – only a dim and empty ocean far below. It was remotely possible that Flight 990 was still in the air some-where, diverting toward a safe landing. But sometime around daybreak a Merchant Marine training ship spotted debris floating on the waves – aluminum scraps, cushions and clothing, some human remains. The midshipmen on board gagged from the stench of jet fuel – a planeload of unburned kerosene rising from shattered tanks on the ocean floor, about 250 feet below. By the time rescue ships and helicopters arrived, it was obvious that there would be no survivors. I remember reacting to the news with regret for the dead, followed by a thought for the complexity of the investigation that now lay ahead. This accident had the markings of a tough case. The problem was not so much the scale of the carnage – a terrible consequence of the 767's size – but, rather, the still-sketchy profile of the upset that preceded it, this bewildering fall out of the sky on a calm night, without explanation, during an utterly uncritical phase of the flight.

I don't fly the 767, or any other airliner. In fact, I no longer fly for a living. But I know through long experience with flight that such machines are usually docile, and that steering them does not require the steady nerves and quick reflexes that passengers may imagine. Indeed, as we saw on September 11, 2001, steering them may not even require much in the way of training – the merest student-pilot level is probably enough. It's not hard to understand why. At their core airplanes are very simple devices – winged things that belong in the air. They are designed to be flyable, and they are. Specifically, the 767 has ordinary mechanical and hydraulic flight controls that provide the pilot with smooth and conventional responses; it is normally operated on autopilot, but can easily be flown by hand; if you remove your hands from the controls entirely, the airplane sails on as before, until it perhaps wanders a bit, dips a wing, and starts into a gentle descent; if you pull the nose up or push it down (within reason) and then fold your arms, the airplane returns unassisted to steady flight; if you idle the engines, or shut them off entirely, the airplane becomes a rather well-behaved glider. It has excellent forward visibility, through big windshields. It has a minimalist cockpit that may look complicated to the untrained eye but is a masterpiece of clean design. It can easily be managed by the standard two-person crew, or even by one pilot alone. The biggest problem in flying the airplane on a routine basis is boredom. Settled into the deep sky at 33,000 feet, above the weather and far from any obstacle, the 767 simply makes very few demands.

Not that it's idiot-proof, or necessarily always benign. As with any fast and heavy airplane, operating a 767 safely even under ordinary circumstances requires anticipation, mental clarity, and a practical understanding of the various systems. Furthermore, when circumstances are not ordinary – for example, during an engine failure just after takeoff or an encounter with unexpected wind shear during an approach to landing – a wilder side to the airplane's personality suddenly emerges. Maintaining control then requires firm action and sometimes a strong arm. There's nothing surprising about this: all airplanes misbehave on occasion, and have to be disciplined. 'Kicking the dog,' I called it in the ornery old cargo crates I flew when I was in college – it was a regular part of survival. In the cockpits of modern jets it is rarely necessary. Nonetheless, when trouble occurs in a machine as massive and aerodynamically slick as the 767, if it is not quickly suppressed the consequences can blossom out of control. During a full-blown upset like that experienced by the Egyptian crew, the airplane may dive so far past its tested limits that it exceeds the very scale of known engineering data – falling off the graphs as well as out of the sky. Afterward the profile can possibly be reconstructed mathematically by aerodynamicists and their like, but it cannot be even approximated by pilots in flight if they expect to come home alive.

I got a feel for the 767's dangerous side last summer, after following the accident's trail from Washington, D.C., to Cairo to the airplane's birthplace, in Seattle, where Boeing engineers let me fly a specially rigged 767 simulator through a series of relevant upsets and recoveries along with some sobering replays of Flight 990's final moments. These simulations had been flown by investigators more than a year before and had been reported on in detail in the publicly released files. Boeing's argument was not that the 767 is a flawless design but, more narrowly, that none of the imaginable failures of its flight-control systems could explain the known facts of this accident.

But that's getting ahead of the story. Back on October 31, 1999, with the first news of the crash, it was hard to imagine any form of pilot error that could have condemned the airplane to such a sustained and precipitous dive. What switch could the crew have thrown, what lever? Nothing came to mind. And why had they perished so silently, without a single distress call on the radio? A total electrical failure was very unlikely, and would not explain the loss of control. A fire would have given them time to talk. One thing was certain: the pilots were either extremely busy or incapacitated from the start. Of course there was always the possibility of a terrorist attack – a simple if frightening solution. But otherwise something had gone terribly wrong with the airplane itself, and that could be just as bad. There are more than 800 Boeing 767s in the world's airline fleet, and they account for more transatlantic flights than all other airplanes combined. They are also very similar in design to the smaller and equally numerous Boeing 757s. So there was plenty of reason for alarm.

One of the world's really important divides lies between nations that react well to accidents and nations that do not. This is as true for a confined and technical event like the crash of a single flight as it is for political or military disasters. The first requirement is a matter of national will, and never a sure thing: it is the intention to get the story right, wherever the blame may lie. The second requirement follows immediately upon the first, and is probably easier to achieve: it is the need for people in the aftermath to maintain even tempers and open minds. The path they follow may not be simple, but it can provide for at least the possibility of effective resolutions.

In the case of EgyptAir Flight 990 the only information available at first was external. The airplane had arrived in New York late on a flight from Los Angeles, and had paused to refuel, take on passengers, and swap crews. Because of the scheduled duration of the flight to Cairo, two cockpit crews had been assigned to the ocean crossing – an 'active crew,' including the aircraft commander, to handle the first and last hours of the flight; and a 'cruise crew,' whose role was essentially to monitor the autopilot during the long, sleepy mid-Atlantic stretch. Just before midnight these four pilots rode out to the airport on a shuttle bus from Manhattan's Pennsylvania Hotel, a large establishment where EgyptAir retained rooms for the use of its personnel. The pilots had been there for several days and, as usual, were well rested. Also in the bus was one of the most senior of EgyptAir's captains, the company's chief 767 pilot, who was not scheduled to fly but would be 'deadheading' home to Cairo. An EgyptAir dispatcher rode out on the bus with them, and subsequently reported that the crew members looked and sounded normal. At the airport he gave them a standard briefing and an update on the New York surface weather, which was stagnant under a low, thin overcast, with light winds and thickening haze.

Flight 990 pushed back from the gate and taxied toward the active runway at 1:12 AM. Because there was little other traffic at the airport, communications with the control tower were noticeably relaxed. At 1:20 Flight 990 lifted off. It topped the clouds at 1,000 feet and turned out over the ocean toward a half moon rising above the horizon. The airplane was identified and tracked by air traffic control radar as it climbed through the various New York departure sectors and entered the larger airspace belonging to the en-route controllers of New York Center; its transponder target and data block moved steadily across the controllers' computer-generated displays, and its radio transmissions sounded perhaps a little awkward, but routine. At 1:44 it leveled off at the assigned 33,000 feet.

The en-route controller working the flight was a woman named Ann Brennan, a private pilot with eight years on the job. She had the swagger of a good controller, a real pro. Later she characterized the air traffic that night as slow, which it was – during the critical hour she had handled only three other flights. The offshore military-exercise zones, known as warning areas, were inactive. The sky was sleeping.

At 1:47 Brennan said, 'EgyptAir nine-ninety, change to my frequency one-two-five-point-niner-two.'

EgyptAir acknowledged the request with a friendly 'Good day,' and after a pause checked in on the new frequency: 'New York, EgyptAir nine-nine-zero heavy, good morning.' Brennan answered, 'EgyptAir nine-ninety, roger.'

That was the last exchange. Brennan noticed that the flight still had about fifteen minutes to go before leaving her sector. Wearing her headset, she stood up and walked six feet away to sort some paperwork. A few minutes later she approved a request by Washington Center to steer an Air France 747 through a corner of her airspace. She chatted for a while with her supervisor, a man named Ray Redhead. In total she spent maybe six minutes away from her station, a reasonable interval on such a night. It was just unlucky that while her back was turned Flight 990 went down.

A computer captured what she would have seen – a strangely abstract death no more dramatic than a video game. About two minutes after the final radio call, at 1:49:53 in the morning, the radar swept across EgyptAir's transponder at 33,000 feet. Afterward, at successive twelve-second intervals, the radar read 31,500, 25,400, and 18,300 feet – a descent rate so great that the air traffic control computers interpreted the information as false, and showed 'XXXX' for the altitude on Brennan's display. With the next sweep the radar lost the transponder entirely, and picked up only an unenhanced 'primary' blip, a return from the airplane's metal mass. The surprise is that the radar continued to receive such returns (which show only location, and not altitude) for nearly another minute and a half, indicating that the dive must have dramatically slowed or stopped, and that the 767 remained airborne, however tenuously, during that interval. A minute and a half is a long time. As the Boeing simulations later showed, it must have been a strange and dreamlike period for the pilots, hurtling through the night with no chance of awakening.

When radar contact was lost, the display for EgyptAir 990 began to 'coast,' indicating that the computers could no longer find a correlation between the stored flight plan and the radar view of the sky. When Brennan noticed, she stayed cool. She said, 'EgyptAir nine-ninety, radar contact lost, recycle transponder, squawk one-seven-one-two.' EgyptAir did not answer, so she tried again at unhurried intervals over the following ten minutes. She advised Ray Redhead of the problem, and he passed the word along. She called an air-defense radar facility, and other air traffic control centers as far away as Canada, to see if by any chance someone was in contact with the flight. She asked a Lufthansa crew to try transmitting to EgyptAir from up high. Eventually she brought in Air France for the overflight. The prognosis was of course increasingly grim, but she maintained her professional calm. She continued to handle normal operations in her sector while simultaneously setting the search-and-rescue forces in motion. Half an hour into the process, when a controller at Boston Center called and asked, 'Any luck with the EgyptAir?' she answered simply, 'No.'

Among the dead were one hundred Americans, eighty-nine Egyptians (including thirty-three army officers), twenty-two Canadians, and a few people of other nationalities. As the news of the disaster spread, hundreds of frantic friends and relatives gathered at the airports in Los Angeles, New York, and Cairo. EgyptAir officials struggled to meet people's needs – which were largely, of course, for the sort of information that no one yet had. Most of the bodies remained in and around the wreckage at the bottom of the sea. Decisions now had to be made, and fast, about the recovery operation and the related problem of an investigation. Because the airplane had crashed in international waters, Egypt had the right to lead the show. Realistically, though, it did not have the resources to salvage a heavy airplane in waters 250 feet deep and 5,000 miles away.

The solution was obvious, and it came in the form of a call to the White House from Egyptian President Hosni Mubarak, an experienced military pilot with close ties to EgyptAir, requesting that the investigation be taken over by the U.S. government. The White House in turn called Jim Hall, the chairman of the National Transportation Safety Board. Hall, a Tennessee lawyer and friend of the Gores, had in the aftermath of the TWA Flight 800 explosion parlayed his position into one of considerable visibility. The Egyptians produced a letter formally signing over the investigation to the United States, an option accorded under international convention, which would place them in a greatly diminished role (as 'accredited representatives') but would also save them trouble and money. Mubarak is said to have regretted the move ever since.

In retrospect it seems inevitable that the two sides would have trouble getting along. The NTSB is a puritanical construct, a small federal agency without regulatory power whose sole purpose is to investigate accidents and issue safety recommendations that might add to the public discourse. Established in 1967 as an 'independent' unit of the Washington bureaucracy, and shielded by design from the political currents of that city, the agency represents the most progressive American thinking on the role and character of good government. On call twenty-four hours a day, with technical teams ready to travel at a moment's notice, it operates on an annual baseline budget of merely $62 million or so, and employs only about 420 people, most of whom work at the headquarters on four floors of

Washington's bright and modern Loews L'Enfant Plaza Hotel. In part because the NTSB seems so lean, and in part because by its very definition it advocates for the 'right' causes, it receives almost universally positive press coverage. The NTSB is technocratic. It is clean. It is Government Lite.

EgyptAir, in contrast, is Government Heavy – a state-owned airline with about six hundred pilots and a mixed fleet of about forty Boeings and Airbuses that serves more than eighty destinations worldwide and employs 22,000 people. It operates out of dusty Stalinist-style office buildings at the Cairo airport, under the supervision of the Ministry of Transport, from which it is often practically indistinguishable. It is probably a safe airline, but passengers dislike it for its delays and shoddy service. They call it Air Misère, probably a play on the airline's former name, Misr Air ('Misr' is Arabic for 'Egypt'). It has been treated as a fiefdom for years by Mubarak's old and unassailable air-force friends, and particularly by the company's chairman, a man named Mohamed Fahim Rayan, who fights off all attempts at reform or privatization. This is hardly a secret. In parliamentary testimony six months before the crash of Flight 990, Rayan said, 'My market is like a water pond which I developed over the years. It is quite unreasonable for alien people to come and seek to catch fish in my pond.' His critics answer that the pond is stagnant and stinks of corruption – but this, too, is nothing new. The greatest pyramids in Egypt are made not of stone but of people: they are the vast bureaucracies that constitute society's core, and they function not necessarily to get the 'job' done but to reward the personal loyalty of those at the bottom to those at the top. Once you understand that, much of the rest begins to make sense. The bureaucracies serve mostly to shelter their workers and give them something like a decent life. They also help to define Cairo. It is a great capital city, as worldly as Washington, D.C., and culturally very far away.

An official delegation traveled from Cairo to the United States and ended up staying for more than a year. It was led by two EgyptAir pilots, Mohsen al-Missiry, an experienced accident investigator on temporary assignment to the Egyptian Civil Aviation Authority for this case, and Shaker Kelada, who had retired from active flying to become a flight-operations manager and eventually vice-president for safety and quality assurance. These men were smart and tough, and managed a team primarily of EgyptAir engineers, many of whom were very sharp.

The U.S. Navy was given the job of salvage, and it in turn hired a contractor named Oceaneering, which arrived with a ship and grapples and remote-controlled submarines. The debris was plotted by sonar, and found to lie in two clusters: the small 'west field,' which included the left engine; and, 1,200 feet beyond it in the direction of flight, the 'east field,' where most of the airplane lay. From what was known of the radar profile and from the tight concentration of the debris, it began to seem unlikely that an in-flight explosion was to blame. The NTSB said nothing. Nine days after the accident the flight-data recorder – the 'black box' that records flight and systems data – was retrieved and sent to the NTSB laboratory in Washington. The NTSB stated tersely that there was preliminary evidence that the initial dive may have been a 'controlled descent.' Five days later, on Sunday, 14 November, a senior official at the Egyptian Transportation Ministry – an air-force general and a former EgyptAir pilot – held a news conference in Cairo and, with Rayan at his side, announced that the evidence from the flight-data recorder had been inconclusive but the dive could be explained only by a bomb in the cockpit or in the lavatory directly behind it. It was an odd assertion to make, but of little importance, because the second black box, the cockpit voice recorder, had been salvaged the night before and was sent on Sunday to the NTSB. The tape was cleaned and processed, and a small group that included a translator (who was not Egyptian) gathered in a listening room at L'Enfant Plaza to hear it through.

Listening to cockpit recordings is a tough and voyeuristic duty, restricted to the principal investigators and people with specific knowledge of the airplane or the pilots, who might help to prepare an accurate transcript. Experienced investigators grow accustomed to the job, but I talked to several who had heard the EgyptAir tape, and they admitted that they had been taken aback. Black boxes are such pitiless, unblinking devices. When the information they contained from Flight 990 was combined with the radar profile and the first, sketchy information on the crew, this was the story it seemed to tell:

The flight lasted thirty-one minutes. During the departure from New York it was captained, as required, by the aircraft commander, a portly senior pilot named Ahmad al-Habashi, fifty-seven, who had flown thirty-six years for the airline. Habashi of course sat in the left seat. In the right seat was the most junior member of the crew, a thirty-six-year-old copilot who was progressing well in his career and looking forward to getting married. Before takeoff the copilot advised the flight attendants by saying, in Arabic, 'In the name of God, the merciful, the compassionate. Cabin crew takeoff position.' This was not unusual.

After takeoff the autopilot did the flying. Habashi and the copilot kept watch, talked to air traffic control, and gossiped about their work. The cockpit door was unlocked, which was fairly standard on Egypt-Air flights. Various flight attendants came in and left; for a while the chief pilot, the man who was deadheading back to Cairo, stopped by the cockpit to chat. Then, twenty minutes into the flight, the 'cruise' copilot, Gameel al-Batouti, arrived. Batouti was a big, friendly guy with a reputation for telling jokes and enjoying life. Three months short of sixty, and mandatory retirement, he was unusually old for a copilot. He had joined the airline in his mid-forties, after a career as a flight instructor for the Air Force, and had rejected several opportunities for command. His lack of ambition was odd but not unheard of: his English was poor and might have given him trouble on the necessary exams; moreover, as the company's senior 767 copilot, he made adequate money and had his pick of long-distance flights. Now he used his seniority to urge the junior copilot to cede the right seat ahead of the scheduled crew change. When the junior man resisted, Batouti said, 'You mean you're not going to get up? You will get up. Go and get some rest and come back.' The junior copilot stayed in his seat a bit longer and then left the cockpit. Batouti took the seat and buckled in.

Batouti was married and had five children. Four of them were grown and doing well. His fifth child was a girl, age ten, who was sick with lupus but responding to treatment that he had arranged for her to receive in Los Angeles. Batouti had a nice house in Cairo. He had a vacation house on the beach. He did not drink heavily. He was moderately religious. He had his retirement planned. He had acquired an automobile tire in New Jersey the day before, and was bringing it home in the cargo hold. He had also picked up some free samples of Viagra, to distribute as gifts.

Captain Habashi was more religious, and was known to pray some-times in the cockpit. He and Batouti were old friends. Using Batouti's nickname, he said, in Arabic, 'How are you, Jimmy?' They groused to each other about the chief pilot and about a clique of young and arrogant 'kids,' junior EgyptAir pilots who were likewise catching a ride back to the Cairo base. One of those pilots came into the cockpit dressed in street clothes. Habashi said, 'What's with you? Why did you get all dressed in red like that?' Presumably the man then left. Batouti had a meal. A female flight attendant came in and offered more. Batouti said pleasantly, 'No, thank you, it was marvelous.' She took his tray.

At 1:47 AM the last calls came in from air traffic control, from Ann Brennan, far off in the night at her display. Captain Habashi handled the calls. He said, 'New York, EgyptAir nine-nine-zero heavy, good morning,' and she answered with her final 'EgyptAir nine-ninety, roger.'

At 1:48 Batouti found the junior copilot's pen and handed it across to Habashi. He said, 'Look, here's the new first officer's pen. Give it to him, please. God spare you.' He added, 'To make sure it doesn't get lost.' Habashi said, 'Excuse me, Jimmy, while I take a quick trip to the toilet.' He ran his electric seat back with a whir. There was the sound of the cockpit door moving. Batouti said, 'Go ahead, please.' Habashi said, 'Before it gets crowded. While they are eating. And I'll be back to you.' Again the cockpit door moved. There was a clunk. There was a clink. It seems that Batouti was now alone in the cockpit. The 767 was at 33,000 feet, cruising peacefully eastward at .79 Mach.

At 1:48:30 a strange, word-like sound was uttered, three syllables with emphasis on the second, perhaps more English than Arabic, and variously heard on the tape as 'control it,' 'hydraulic,' or something unintelligible. The NTSB ran extensive speech and sound-spectrum studies on it, and was never able to assign it conclusively to Batouti or to anyone else. But what is clear is that Batouti then softly said, *'Tawakkalt ala Allah,'* which proved difficult to translate, and was at first rendered incorrectly, but essentially means 'I rely on God.' An electric seat whirred. The autopilot disengaged, and the airplane sailed on as before for another four seconds. Again Batouti said, 'I rely on God.' Then two things happened almost simultaneously, according to the flight-data recorder: the throttles in the cockpit moved back fast to minimum idle, and a second later, back at the tail, the airplane's massive elevators (the pitch-control surfaces) dropped to a three-degrees-down position. When the elevators drop, the tail goes up; and when the tail goes up, the nose points down. Apparently Batouti had chopped the power and pushed the control yoke forward.

The effect was dramatic. The airplane began to dive steeply, dropping its nose so quickly that the environment inside plunged to nearly zero gs, the weightless condition of space. Six times in quick succession Batouti repeated 'I rely on God.' His tone was calm. There was a loud thump. As the nose continued to pitch downward, the airplane went into the negative-G range, nudging loose objects against the ceiling. The elevators moved even farther down. Batouti said, 'I rely on God.'

Somehow, in the midst of this, now sixteen seconds into the dive, Captain Habashi made his way back from the toilet. He yelled, 'What's happening? What's happening?' Batouti said, 'I rely on God.' The wind outside was roaring. The airplane was dropping through 30,800 feet, and accelerating beyond its maximum operating speed of .86 Mach. In the cockpit the altimeters were spinning like cartoon clocks. Warning horns were sounding, warning lights were flashing – low oil pressure on the left engine, and then on the right. The master alarm went off, a loud high-to-low warble. For the last time Batouti said, 'I rely on God.'

Again Habashi shouted, 'What's happening?' By then he must have reached the left control yoke. The negative Gs ended as he countered the pitch-over, slowing the rate at which the nose was dropping. But the 767 was still angled down steeply, 40 degrees below the horizon, and it was accelerating. The rate of descent hit 39,000 feet a minute. 'What's happening, Gameel? What's happening?'

Habashi was clearly pulling very hard on his control yoke, trying desperately to raise the nose. Even so, thirty seconds into the dive, at 22,200 feet, the airplane hit the speed of sound, at which it was certainly not meant to fly. Many things happened in quick succession in the cockpit. Batouti reached over and shut off the fuel, killing both engines. Habashi screamed, 'What is this? What is this? Did you shut the engines?' The throttles were pushed full forward – for no obvious reason, since the engines were dead. The speed-brake handle was then pulled, deploying drag devices on the wings.

At the same time, there was an unusual occurrence back at the tail: the right-side and left-side elevators, which normally move together to control the airplane's pitch, began to 'split,' or move in opposite directions. Specifically: the elevator on the right remained down, while the left-side elevator moved up to a healthy recovery position. That this could happen at all was the result of a design feature meant to allow either pilot to overpower a mechanical jam and control the airplane with only one elevator. The details are complex, but the essence in this case seemed to be that the right elevator was being pushed down by Batouti while the left elevator was being pulled up by the captain. The NTSB concluded that a 'force fight' had broken out in the cockpit.

Words were failing Habashi. He yelled, 'Get away in the engines!' And then, incredulously, '. . . shut the engines!' Batouti said calmly, 'It's shut.'

Habashi did not have time to make sense of the happenings. He probably did not have time to get into his seat and slide it forward. He must have been standing in the cockpit, leaning over the seatback and hauling on the controls. The commotion was horrendous. He was reacting instinctively as a pilot, yelling, 'Pull!' and then, 'Pull with me! Pull with me! Pull with me!'

It was the last instant captured by the on-board flight recorders. The elevators were split, with the one on the right side, Batouti's side, still pushed into a nose-down position. The ailerons on both wings had assumed a strange upswept position, normally never seen on an airplane. The 767 was at 16,416 feet, doing 527 miles an hour, and pulling a moderately heavy 2.4 Gs, indicating that the nose, though still below the horizon, was rising fast, and that Habashi's efforts on the left side were having an effect. A belated recovery was under way. At that point, because the engines had been cut, all non-essential electrical devices were lost, blacking out not only the recorders, which rely on primary power, but also most of the instrument displays and lights. The pilots were left to the darkness of the sky, whether to work together or to fight. I've often wondered what happened between those two men during the 114 seconds that remained of their lives. We'll never know. Radar reconstruction showed that the 767 recovered from the dive at 16,000 feet and, like a great wounded glider, soared steeply back to 24,000 feet, turned to the southeast while beginning to break apart, and shed its useless left engine and some of its skin before giving up for good and diving to its death at high speed.

When this evidence emerged at the NTSB, the American investigators were shocked but also relieved by the obvious conclusion. There was no bomb here. Despite initial fears, there was nothing wrong with the airplane. The apparent cause was pilot error at its extreme: Batouti had gone haywire. Every detail that emerged from the two flight recorders fit that scenario: the sequence of the switches and controls that were moved, the responses of the airplane, and the words that were spoken, however cryptic and incomplete. Batouti had waited to be alone in the cockpit, and had intentionally pushed the airplane to its death. He had even fought the captain's valiant attempt at recovery. Why? Professionally, the NTSB didn't need to care. It was up to the criminal investigators at the FBI to discover if this was a political act, or the result of a plot. Even at the time, just weeks after the airplane went down, it was hard to imagine that Batouti had any terrorist connections, and indeed, the FBI never found any such evidence. But in pure aviation terms it didn't really matter why Batouti did it, and pure aviation is what the NTSB is all about. So this was easy – Crash Investigation 101. The guy to blame was dead. The NTSB wouldn't have to go after Boeing – a necessary task on occasion, but never a pleasant prospect. The wreckage, which was still being pulled out of the ocean, would not require tedious inspection. The report could be written quickly and filed away, and the NTSB could move on to the backlog of work that might actually affect the future safety of the flying public.

When Jim Hall, the NTSB chairman, held a news conference to address the initial findings, on November 19, 1999, he was culturally sensitive, responsible, and very strict about the need to maintain an open mind. There had been leaks to the press about the content of the cockpit voice recorder. It was being said that Batouti's behavior had been strange during the dive and that he had recited Muslim prayers. Hall scolded the assembled reporters for using unofficial information and exciting the public's emotions. He made a show of being careful with his own choice of words. He said that the accident 'might, and I emphasize might, be the result of a deliberate act.' He did not say 'suicide' or 'Arab' or 'Muslim.' He did not even say 'Batouti.' He said, 'No one wants to get to the bottom of this mystery quicker than those investigating this accident, both here and in Egypt, but we won't get there on a road paved with leaks, supposition, speculation, and spin. That road does not lead to the truth, and the truth is what both the American people and the Egyptian people seek.' It was standard stuff, a prelude to a quick wrapping up of the investigation. The Egyptian delegation, which had moved into rooms at the Loews L'Enfant Plaza Hotel, might have felt grateful to have such a man at the NTSB to guide them through these difficult times. Instead the Egyptians were outraged.

At the NTSB this came as a surprise. Looking back, it's possible to see signs of a disconnect, especially the Egyptian government's baffling speculation about a bomb in the forward lavatory; but just the day before Hall's press conference the Egyptian ambassador had heaped praise on the NTSB and the investigation. Now, suddenly and with startling vigor, the Egyptian delegation went on the offensive. The leader of the charge, Shaker Kelada, later told me about running across one of the American investigators in the halls of the NTSB. When the investigator mentioned with satisfaction that the work might wrap up within a few weeks, Kelada brought him up short with the news that he'd better change his plans – because far from being over, the investigation had hardly begun.

First the Egyptians had to prepare the ground: the delegation started to loudly criticize the performance and intentions of Boeing, the FBI, and the entire NTSB. Kelada said that Batouti was the scapegoat, and that this was happening because it was an Egyptian airliner that had gone down. It did not escape Kelada's attention that the legendary head of aviation investigations at the NTSB – a brilliant and abrasive engineer named Bernard Loeb, who was overseeing the Flight 990 inquiry – was Jewish and something of a Zionist.

Loeb retired last spring; Kelada implied to me last summer that this was a deception, and that Loeb continued to pull the strings. Loeb laughed when I mentioned it to him afterward. He was looking forward to spending time with his grandchildren. But at the same time, he was angry that Egypt, after receiving $1.3 billion in American assistance every year, would have used any of its budget to cause the United States unnecessary expense by prolonging an investigation that for the NTSB alone had so far cost $17 million. As to Zionism, Loeb did seem bothered by aspects of the Egyptian culture. I got the feeling, though, that his opinion was fresh – that it stemmed from his contacts with EgyptAir, rather than from experiences that had preceded them.

But it didn't really matter who at the NTSB was in charge of the investigation. In faraway Cairo, inevitably, it was seen as unfair. From the day that Flight 990's recorder tape was transcribed and word of its contents began to leak out, the feeling in Egypt was that all Arabs were under attack, and that the assault had been planned. More than a year after the crash I met a sharp young reporter in Cairo who continued to seethe about it. He said, 'For many Egyptians it was a big example of this business of dictating the reality. What made many people question the authenticity of the U.S. claims was the rush to conclusions . . . The rush, the interpretation of a few words, it left no chance. The whole thing seemed to apply within a framework of an American sort of soap opera, one of those movies you make. You know – this is a fanatic, he comes from the Middle East, he utters a few religious words, he brings the plane down.' But what if Batouti really had brought the plane down – where did the reporter's reaction leave Egypt? Earlier the reporter had written critically about the corruption at EgyptAir, but he refused even to think critically about it anymore.

The reporter's anger was similar, at least superficially, to the anger that was seething through Shaker Kelada and the rest of the Egyptian delegation in November of 1999. For Jim Hall, Bernard Loeb, and others at the NTSB, the source of the problem seemed at first to be the media coverage, which was typically overeager. Rumors of suicide had circulated in the press almost since the airplane hit the water, but it was only after the voice recorder was recovered that the reports began to make uninformed reference to Muslim prayers. Three days before Hall's press conference the *Washington Post* ran a headline saying, 'PILOT PRAYED, THEN SHUT OFF JET'S AUTOPILOT.' Television stations speculated that the 'prayer' was the shahada ('There is no god but God; Muhammad is the messenger of God'), as if this were what one might say before slaughtering infidels. When the actual Arabic words – *Tawakkalt ala Allah* – became public, some news outlets gave the following translation: 'I have made my decision. I put my fate in God's hands.' This was reported so widely that the NTSB took the unusual step of announcing that 'I have made my decision' had never been spoken. By implication, 'I put my fate . . .' had.

When NTSB investigators explained their lack of control over the American press, the Egyptians scoffed and pointed out – correctly – that the reporters' sources were people inside the investigation. And anyway, the Egyptians added, what Batouti had said was not 'I put my fate in God's hands' – as the NTSB's interpreter had claimed – but, rather, 'I rely on God.' The investigators blinked at the subtlety of this distinction, and made the necessary changes to the transcript. Then the Egyptians produced a letter from an Islamic scholar in Cairo who certified that the meaning of *Tawakkalt ala Allah* is 'I depend in my daily affairs on the omnipotent Allah alone.' The Egyptians wanted the letter inserted into the record, but were willing to allow 'I rely on God' to remain in the transcript. Again, the investigators blinked. This was not the sort of thing they normally dealt with. They tried sometimes to bridge the gap as they might have with Americans, with a nudge and a smile, but it got them nowhere.

In essence the Egyptians were making two intertwined arguments: first, that it was culturally impossible for Batouti to have done what the NTSB believed; second, that the NTSB lacked the cultural sensitivity to understand what was on the cockpit voice recorder. With those arguments as a starting point, the Egyptians tore into the complexities of the evidence, disputing any assumptions or conclusions the NTSB put forward and raising new questions at every possible turn – a process that continues to this day. They were tenacious. For example (and this is just a small sample of the Egyptians' arguments): When Batouti said *'Tawakkalt ala Allah,'* he was not preparing to die but responding in surprise to something wrong with the flight. He said it quietly, yes, but with emotion that the Americans lacked the cultural sensitivity to hear. When he started the dive, he was trying to avoid a plane or a missile outside. If not that, then the airplane went into the dive on its own. When he idled the engines, it was to keep from gaining speed. When he cut the engines, he was going through the required restart procedure, because he erroneously believed – on the basis of the low-oil-pressure warning light that flashed in the cockpit – that the engines had flamed out. Apparently Habashi made the same mistake, which is why he discussed engine cuts. When Habashi called 'Pull with me!', Batouti did exactly that. The split elevators were like the upswept ailerons – either an aerodynamic anomaly, resulting from the unknown pressures of ultra-high-speed flight on the 767, or, more simply, an error in the flight-data recorder. Whichever way, the Egyptians argued that expensive wind-tunnel testing was necessary at high Mach numbers near the speed of sound.

Meanwhile, most of the wreckage had been recovered and spread out in a hangar in Rhode Island. A second salvage operation was mounted in the spring to coincide with a state visit by Mubarak to Washington. It went to the west debris field and brought up the left engine and a boatload of worthless scraps. At the NTSB a story circulated about Al Gore, who was said to have angered Mubarak by making a casual reference to 'the suicide flight.' There was a short flap about that. The investigation continued. The documentation grew. The possibilities multiplied and ran off in a hundred directions. An airline pilot observing the scene said to me, 'It could have been this, it could have been that. Bottom line is, it could have been anything except their guy.'

While the Egyptians were proposing theory after theory to absolve Batouti, the FBI was conducting a criminal investigation, collecting evidence that provided for his possible motive. Mostly through interviews with employees of the Pennsylvania Hotel, the FBI found that Batouti had a reputation for sexual impropriety – and not merely by the prudish standards of America. It was reported that on multiple occasions over the previous two years he had been suspected of exposing himself to teenage girls, masturbating in public, following female guests to their rooms, and listening at their doors. Some of the maids, it was said, were afraid of him, and the hotel security guards had once brought him in for questioning and a warning. Apparently the hotel had considered banning him. The FBI learned that EgyptAir was aware of these problems and had warned Batouti to control his behavior. He was not considered to be a dangerous man – and certainly he was more sad than bad. In fact, there was a good side to Batouti that came out in these interviews as well. He was very human. Many people were fond of him, even at the hotel. But a story soon surfaced that an altercation may have occurred during the New York layover before the fatal departure. The FBI was told that there had been trouble, and possibly an argument with the chief pilot, who was also staying at the hotel. It was hypothesized that the chief pilot might have threatened disciplinary action upon arrival back in Cairo – despite the public humiliation that would entail. Was that perhaps Batouti's motive? Did the killing of 217 people result from a simple act of vengeance against one man? The evidence was shaky at best. Then, in February of 2000, an EgyptAir pilot named Hamdi Hanafi Taha, forty-nine, landed in England and requested political asylum, claiming that he had information on the accident. FBI and NTSB investigators flew immediately to interview him, hoping that he would provide the answers they needed. They were disappointed. Taha told a story that seemed to confirm that Batouti had been confronted by the chief pilot, and he added some new details, but he turned out to be an informant of questionable utility – a radical Muslim who, along with others in the ranks of EgyptAir pilots, had forced the airline to ban the serving of alcohol, and who now went on at length about corruption at EgyptAir, and also what he claimed was rampant alcoholism and drug use among his secular peers. The request for asylum was itself a little flaky. The American investigators flew home without solid information. Most of this came out in the press when the story of Batouti's sexual improprieties was leaked, further angering the Egyptians. They countered, eventually producing a Boeing 777 captain named Mohamed Badrawi, who had been with the other pilots in New York on the fateful night, and who testified at length that they were like a band of brothers – that Batouti and the chief pilot got along well and had had no direct confrontations. Rather, Badrawi said, he had acted at times as a 'mediator' between the two men, cautioning Batouti on behalf of the chief pilot to 'grow up' in order to avoid legal problems in the United States.

With that on the record, assigning a motive to Batouti became all the more difficult. For a variety of reasons, Bernard Loeb thought the FBI was wasting everyone's time. He did not really oppose the search for a motive, but he was against entering such speculative and easily countered discussions into the NTSB's public record. Privately he believed in the story of the fight. But as he later emphasized to me, 'We just didn't need to go there.'

Loeb thought the same about much of the investigation. Month after month, as the NTSB chased down the theories that EgyptAir kept proposing, Loeb worried about all the other projects that were being put aside. He tried to keep a sense of distance from the work, driving from suburban Maryland to his office dressed in a sports jacket and tie, just like any other Washingtonian with a quiet job. But it was a hopeless ambition. Most mornings the Egyptian delegation was there too. Later Loeb said to me, his voice strangled with frustration, 'You had to be there! You had to live through this! Day in and day out! It was as if these people would go back to their rooms at night and then identify some kind of reason . . . And then it would start all over again. It was insane! It was just insane!'

To bolster their arguments the Egyptians had hired some former accident investigators and also the retired NTSB chairman Carl Vogt, whose willingness to legitimize the Egyptian campaign was seen by many within the NTSB as a betrayal. The Egyptians also turned to the American pilots' union – in principle to improve their communication with the NTSB, but in practice probably just to add weight to their side. In the spring of 2000 the union sent to Washington a man named Jim Walters, a U.S. airline pilot with long experience in accident investigations. Walters thought he could patch things up. Later he said to me, 'The Egyptians appeared to be listening to me. But as it turned out, they weren't.' Then he said, 'I thought I was there to give them advice . . .' It was a disappointment. He liked the Egyptians personally, and remained sympathetic to their side even after he left.

I asked him to describe the scene in Washington. He said, 'The NTSB isn't terribly tolerant of people who don't follow good investigative procedure. And they weren't used to dealing with a group like this, right in their back yard, with offices in the same building, there every day. I thought, The first thing we have to do is calm everybody down. I thought I could explain to the Egyptians, "This is how the NTSB operates," and explain to Jim Hall, "Hey, these guys are Egyptians. You've got to understand who these guys are, and why they're doing things the way they are, and maybe we can all just kiss and make up and get along from here."'

But it didn't work out that way. Walters was naive. Kiss and make up? The Egyptians no more needed his advice about investigative procedure than they had needed the NTSB's opinions about the nature of a free press.

A small war had broken out between Egypt and the United States on a battlefield called Loews L'Enfant Plaza Hotel. On one side stood Shaker Kelada and his men, fighting for the honor of their nation against the mysterious forces of American hegemony, and specifically against an agency whose famed independence they believed had been compromised. On the other side stood Bernard Loeb and his people, fighting just as hard – but to set a schedule, write the report, and disengage. Jim Hall was scurrying in between. And Boeing was off in Seattle, not quite out of range, trying unsuccessfully to look small.

The irony is that Loeb, too, thought the agency's independence had been compromised, though for the opposite reason: there were meetings at the White House, and phone calls to Jim Hall, in which concern was expressed about accommodating the Egyptian view, and in which it was implied that there should be no rush to finish a report that inevitably would offend Mubarak. Loeb was disgusted and typically vocal about his opinion. When I asked him if the influence was necessarily so wrong, he said, 'Next they ask you to change the report – to say Batouti didn't do it.' He added, however, that no one had ever suggested such a change – and it was a good thing, too.

By late last May the fight had slowed, and Shaker Kelada was able to spend most of his time back home in Cairo. The NTSB had just issued a draft report, and Egypt was preparing an opposing response. I found Kelada in his expansive new office at the Cairo airport, where we talked several times over the course of a week. These were not good conversations. Kelada insisted on repeating the official Egyptian positions, and would go no further. At one point he began to attack the New York air traffic controllers, and specifically Ann Brennan, for having walked away from her display. He implied that her absence had a bearing on the accident, or perhaps sparked a subsequent cover-up by the American government. He said, 'It was very sloppy air-traffic control, and not what the U.S. wants to show. They're number one at everything, and they don't want anyone to know that they have a sloppy operation in New York.'

I tried to reach him as one pilot to another. I said, 'Come on, I think of that as being a normal operation, don't you?'

He said, 'Well, if it is, I don't want to fly in the New York area!'

It was nonsense. And in aviation terms, a lot of what he said to me was equally unconvincing. Eventually I stopped taking notes. Even when he was being reasonable, the party line kept showing through. He said, 'I cannot say it's a mechanical failure. I don't have enough

evidence, but I cannot dismiss the possibility of a mechanical failure
. . . if I want to be careful.'

I said, 'On the other hand, you do have enough evidence to dismiss
the human factor?'

He said, 'Yes.'

'To dismiss the intentional act?'

'Yes.' He paused. He said, 'We search for the truth.'

It was late in the day. Kelada sat behind his desk – a man in a big
office with jets outside, a smart man, a careful man. I thought of the
question that had plagued me all along: not whether the Egyptians
were right or wrong but whether they really believed their own words.
Loeb had said to me, 'Do they believe it? I believe they believe in fear.'

I went downtown, to an old coffeehouse near the Nile, and spent
a few hours with Hani Shukrallah, a columnist and one of the more
thoughtful observers of the Egyptian scene. Shukrallah is a small,
nervous man, and a heavy smoker. He said, 'I know that as far as the
Egyptian government was concerned, the point that this was not pilot
error, and that the Egyptian pilot did not bring it down – this was
decided before the investigation began. It had to do with Egypt's
image in the outside world . . . The government would have viewed
this exactly as it would, for example, an Islamic terrorist act in Luxor
– something that we should cover up. So it got politicized immediately.
And this became an official line: You are out there to prove that
EgyptAir is not responsible. It became a national duty. It was us versus
the West. And all the history played into it, from Bonaparte's campaign
until now.' In the minds even of people on the street, Shukrallah said,
it became 'an all-out war.'

If so, the United States was in such a strong position that it could lose
the struggle only by defeating itself. This is why from the very start
of the difficult process it was all the more important for the NTSB
to consider the evidence fairly and keep an open mind. The problem
was that so many of the scenarios the Egyptians posited were patently
absurd – stray missiles, ghost airplanes, strange weather, and the like.
Yet that didn't mean that everything they said was wrong. As long as
Batouti's motive could not be conclusively shown, the possibility

remained that the dive of Flight 990 was unintentional, just as Kelada maintained. And in the background the Egyptians had some very smart engineers looking into the various theories.

The 767's elevator movements are powered by three redundant hydraulic circuits, driving a total of six control mechanisms called 'actuators,' which normally operate in unison. Given the various linkages and cross-connections, the system is complex. The Egyptians thought it through and realized that if two of the six actuators were to fail on the same side of the airplane, they would drive both elevators down, forcing the 767 to pitch into a dive that might match the profile that had emerged from EgyptAir 990's flight-data recorder. Furthermore, if such a failure happened and either pilot tried to right it, that could conceivably explain the 'splitting' of the elevators that occurred during 990's attempted recovery.

As might be expected, the discussion about dual actuator failures grew complicated. It also grew political. The NTSB had salvaged most of the actuators from the ocean floor and had found no clear evidence of failure, but with perceptions of public safety at stake, the agency asked Boeing for further information. Boeing engineers calculated that a dual actuator failure would not have deflected the elevators far enough down to equal the known elevator deflections of Flight 990, and that such a failure therefore would not have caused as steep a dive. To explore the question they performed a series of ground tests of a 767 elevator, inducing dual actuator failures and 'splits' on a parked airplane in Seattle. After adjusting the measured effects for the theoretical aerodynamic pressures of flight, they found – as they had expected – poor correlation with the known record of Flight 990 elevator positions. They believed in any case that either pilot could quickly have recovered from a dual actuator failure by doing what comes naturally at such moments – pulling back hard on the controls.

The NTSB was satisfied; the Egyptians were not. They poked holes in the conclusions and requested basic and costly aerodynamic research, at speeds well beyond the 767's limits, toward Mach 1. The question was, of course, To what end? But for Boeing this was a delicate thing, because Egypt kept buying expensive airplanes and was influential in the Arab world. A bit of additional research would perhaps be in order.

Meanwhile, the company's engineers had moved on to flight simulations of the accident, a series of dives set up to be flown in Boeing's highly programmable 767 engineering simulator – a 'fixed cab' without motion, capable of handling extremes. These were the profiles that I flew when I went to Seattle last summer. On that same trip I went to Everett, Washington, where the airplanes are made, and in a cockpit with a company test pilot split the elevators in a powered-up 767, as the Egyptian crew presumably had. In order to do this we needed to break the connection between the left and right control yokes, which are mechanically joined under the floorboards, and usually move together. He pushed on his, I pulled on mine, and at fifty pounds of pressure between us the controls were suddenly no longer working in tandem. Far behind us, at the tail, the elevators separated smoothly. On a cockpit display we watched each elevator go its own way. The airplane shuddered from the movement of the heavy control surfaces. We played with variations. Toward the end the pilot laughed and said I was compressing his bones.

But when I got to the simulations, they felt too real to be a game. The simulator was a surrogate cockpit already in flight – humming and warm, with all the controls and familiar displays, and a view outside of an indistinct twilight. It was headed east at 33,000 feet and .79 Mach – just as Flight 990 had been. The first set of profiles were 'back-driven' duplications of the fatal dive, generated directly from Flight 990's flight-data recorder. Another Boeing test pilot sat in Batouti's seat, and the engineers clustered around behind. I let the simulation run on automatic the first few times, resting one hand on the controls to feel the beast die – the sudden pitch and shockingly fast dive, the clicking of a wildly unwinding altimeter, the warbling alarm, the loss of most displays at the bottom after the engines were gone, and the dark, steep, soaring climb up to 24,000 feet, the control yoke rattling its warning of an aerodynamic stall, the airplane rolling southeast to its end. I watched this several times and then flew the same thing by hand, matching the pressure I put on the control yoke to a specially rigged indicator, which, after the elevators' split had occurred, allowed me to match the force required to achieve Habashi's 'pull' and Batouti's 'push' as captured by the flight-data recorder. First I stood and flew Habashi's 'Pull with me!' from behind the seat – up to ninety pounds of force, which under those conditions seemed like not very much. It was the other intention, the pushing, that was dramatic. What was required was not only pushing but then pushing harder. The idea that someone would do that in an airplane full of passengers shocked me as a pilot. If that's what Batouti did, I will never understand what was going on in his mind.

The second set of simulations were easier to fly. These were the dual actuator failures, which EgyptAir proposed might have overcome Batouti when he was alone in the cockpit. The purpose was to test the difficulty or ease of recovery from such an upset. Again the simulations began at 33,000 feet and .79 Mach. I flew by hand from the start. The airplane pitched down strongly and without warning. I hauled back on the controls and lost 800 feet. It was an easy recovery, but not fair – I had been ready. The engineers then made me wait before reacting, as they had made other pilots – requiring delays of five, ten, and finally fifteen seconds before I began the recovery. Fifteen seconds seems like an eternity in a 767 going out of control. Even so, by hauling hard on the yoke and throttling back, I managed to pull out after losing only 12,000 feet; and though I went to the maximum allowable dive speed, the airplane survived. This was not unusual. Airplanes are meant to be flown. During the original simulation sessions done for the NTSB every pilot with a dual actuator failure was able to recover, and probably better than I. So what was wrong with Batouti? The simplest explanation is that he was trying to crash the airplane. But if he wasn't, if the Egyptians were right that he couldn't recover from a dual actuator failure, what was wrong with him as an aviator?

I posed the question to Jim Walters, the airline pilot who despite his disappointment remained sympathetic to the Egyptians' position. He had a ready answer. He called Batouti 'the world's worst airline pilot.'

But how good do you have to be?

Bernard Loeb would have none of it. He said, 'Sure. In the end they were willing to sell him down the river. They said, "He panicked!" Bottom line is, if the actuator drops the nose, you can pull it up. They know that. They admit it. Pulling the nose up is the most intuitive, reflexive thing you can do in an airplane. So when you start hearing arguments like that, you know people are blowing smoke.

'Look, first we sit through this cockpit voice recording in which . . .' He shook his head. 'How many cockpit voice recordings have I heard? Hundreds? Thousands? When someone has a problem with an airplane, you know it. One of our investigators used to say to me, "These damned pilots, they don't tell us what's happening. Why don't they say, 'It's the rudder!'" They don't do that. But I'll tell you what they do say. They make it clear as hell that there's something really wrong. "What the hell's going on? What is that?" Every single one of them. When there's a control problem of some sort, it is so crystal clear that they are trying desperately to diagnose what is going on. Right to when the recorder quits. They are fighting for their lives.

'But this guy is sitting there saying the same thing in a slow, measured way, indicating no stress. The captain comes in and asks what's going on, and he doesn't answer! That's what you start with. Now you take the dual actuator failure that doesn't match the flight profile, and is also fully recoverable. Where do you want to go after that?'

The NTSB's final report on Flight 990 was expected for the fall of 2001, and it was widely presumed in aviation circles that the report would find no mechanical failure or external cause for the crash. It also seemed likely that the report would at least implicitly blame Batouti for the disaster – a conclusion that would, of course, be unacceptable within Egypt. Nonetheless, when I met him in Cairo, Shaker Kelada was looking pleased, and I later found out why. His engineers had gotten busy again, and had come up with new concerns – certain combinations of tail-control failures that might require further testing. Now Boeing had come to town for a quiet talk with its customers, and had agreed to do the tests. Boeing was going to inform the NTSB of the new work, and the end would again be delayed.

Sitting in his office, Kelada could not help gloating. He said, 'Jim Hall told me, "I've learned a very good lesson. When you deal with a foreign carrier in an investigation, before you go anywhere with it, you have to study the history and culture of the country." These were his own words to me! He said, "I knew nothing about Egypt or its culture before we got into EgyptAir 990."'

I said, 'What would he have learned?'

'Not to underestimate people. To think that he's way up there, and everybody's way down here.'

Fair enough. But in the end there was the question of the objective truth – and there was the inclination not to seek real answers for even such a simple event as a single accident nearly two years before.

I knew that at the start of the investigation the Egyptian delegation had included a man named Mamdouh Heshmat, a high official in civil aviation. When the cockpit voice recording first arrived at L'Enfant Plaza, Heshmat was there, and he heard it through with a headset on. According to several investigators who listened alongside him, he came out of the room looking badly shaken, and made it clear he knew that Batouti had done something wrong. He may have called Cairo with that news. The next day he flew home, never to reappear in Washington. When NTSB investigators went to Cairo, they could not find him, though it was said that he was still working for the government. I knew I wouldn't find him either, but I wanted to see how Kelada would react to the mention of him. Kelada and I had come to the end. I said I had heard about a man who had been one of the first to listen to the tape – who could it have been? Kelada looked straight at me and said, 'I don't recall his name.' There was no reason to continue, from his perspective or mine.

# 8

# Columbia's Last Flight

Space flight is known to be a risky business, but during the minutes before dawn on February 1, 2003, as the doomed shuttle *Columbia* began to descend into the upper atmosphere over the Pacific Ocean, only a handful of people – a few engineers deep inside of NASA – worried that the vehicle and its seven souls might actually come to grief. It was the responsibility of NASA's managers to hear those suspicions, and from top to bottom they failed. After the fact, that's easy to see. But in fairness to those whose reputations have now been sacrificed, seventeen years and eighty-nine shuttle flights had passed since the *Challenger* explosion, and within the agency a new generation had risen that was smart, perhaps, but also unwise – confined by NASA's walls and routines, and vulnerable to the self-satisfaction that inevitably had set in.

Moreover, this mission was a yawn – a low-priority 'science' flight forced onto NASA by Congress and postponed for two years because of a more pressing schedule of construction deliveries to the International Space Station. The truth is, it had finally been launched as much to clear the books as to add to human knowledge, and it had gone nowhere except into low Earth orbit, around the globe every ninety minutes for sixteen days, carrying the first Israeli astronaut, and performing a string of experiments, many of which, like the shuttle program itself, seemed to suffer from something of a make-work character – the examination of dust in the Middle East (by the Israeli, of course); the ever popular ozone study; experiments designed by schoolchildren in six countries to observe the effect of weightlessness on spiders, silkworms, and other creatures; an exercise in 'astroculture' involving the extraction of essential oils from rose and rice flowers, which was said to hold promise for new perfumes; and so forth. No doubt some good science was done too – particularly pertaining to space flight itself – though none of it was so urgent that it could not have been performed later, under better circumstances, in the under-booked International Space Station. The astronauts aboard the shuttle were smart and accomplished people, and they were deeply committed to human space flight and exploration. They were also team players, by intense selection, and nothing if not wise to the game. From orbit one of them had radioed, 'The science we're doing here is great, and it's fantastic. It's leading-edge.' Others had dutifully reported that the planet seems beautiful, fragile, and border-less when seen from such altitudes, and they had expressed their hopes in English and Hebrew for world peace. It was Miracle Whip on Wonder Bread, standard NASA fare. On the ground so little attention was being paid that even the radars that could have been directed upward to track the *Columbia*'s re-entry into the atmosphere – from Vandenberg Air Force Base, or White Sands Missile Range – were sleeping. As a result, no radar record of the breakup exists – only of the metal rain that drifted down over East Texas, and eventually came into the view of air-traffic control.

Along the route, however, stood small numbers of shuttle enthu-siasts, who had gotten up early with their video cameras and had arrayed themselves on hills or away from city lights to record the spectacle of what promised to be a beautiful display. The shuttle came into view, on track and on schedule, just after 5:53 Pacific time, cross-ing the California coast at about 15,000 mph in the super-thin air 230,000 feet above the Russian River, northwest of San Francisco. It was first picked up on video by a Lockheed engineer in suburban Fairfield, who recorded a bright meteor passing almost directly over-head, not the shuttle itself but the sheath of hot gases around it, and the long, luminous tail of ionized air known as plasma. Only later, after the engineer heard about the accident on television, did he check his tape and realize that he had recorded what appeared to be two pieces coming off the *Columbia* in quick succession, like little flares in its wake. Those pieces were recorded by others as well, along with the third, fourth, and fifth 'debris events' that are known to have occurred during the sixty seconds that it took the shuttle to cross California. From the top of Mount Hamilton, southeast of San Francisco, another engineer, the former president of the Peninsula Astronomical Society, caught all five events on tape but, again, did not realize it until afterward. He later said, 'I'd seen four re-entries before this one. When we saw it, we did note that it was a little brighter and a little bit whiter in color than it normally is. It's normally a pink-magenta color. But you know, it wasn't so different that it really flagged us as something wrong. With the naked eye we didn't see the particles coming off.'

One minute after the *Columbia* left California, as it neared southwestern Utah, the trouble was becoming more obvious to observers on the ground. There had been a bright flash earlier over Nevada, and now debris came off that was large enough to cause multiple secondary plasma trails. North of the Grand Canyon, in Saint George, Utah, a man and his grown son climbed onto a ridge above the county hospital, hoping for the sort of view they had seen several years before, of a fireball going by. It was a sight they remembered as 'really neat.' This time was different, though. The son, who was videotaping, started yelling, 'Jesus, Dad, there's stuff falling off!' and the father saw it too, with his naked eyes.

The *Columbia* was flying on autopilot, as is usual, and though it continued to lay flares in its wake, the astronauts aboard remained blissfully unaware of the trouble they were in. They passed smoothly into dawn above the Arizona border, and sailed across the Navajo reservation and on over Albuquerque, before coming to the Texas Panhandle on a perfect descent profile, slowing through 13,400 mph at 210,000 feet five minutes after having crossed the California coastline. Nineteen seconds later, at 7:58:38 central time, they got the first sign of something being a little out of the ordinary: it was a cockpit indication of low tire pressures on the left main landing gear. This was not quite a trivial matter. A blown or deflated main tire would pose serious risks during the rollout after landing, including loss of lateral control and the possibility that the nose would slam down, conceivably leading to a catastrophic breakup on the ground. These scenarios were known, and had been simulated and debated in the inner world of NASA, leading some to believe that the best of the imperfect choices in such a case might be for the crew to bail out – an alternative available only below 30,000 feet and 220 mph of dynamic airspeed.

Nonetheless, for *Columbia*'s pilots it was reasonable to assume for the moment that the indication of low pressure was due to a problem with the sensors rather than with the tires themselves, and that the teams of Mission Control engineers at NASA's Johnson Space Center, in Houston, would be able to sort through the mass of automatically transmitted data – the so-called telemetry, which was far more complete than what was available in the cockpit – and to draw the correct conclusion. The reverse side of failures in a machine as complex as the shuttle is that most of them can be worked around, or turn out to be small. In other words, there was no reason for alarm. After a short delay the *Columbia*'s commander, Rick Husband, calmly radioed to Mission Control, 'And, ah, Houston . . .' Sheathed in hot atmospheric gases, the shuttle was slowing through 13,100 mph at 205,000 feet.

Houston did not clearly hear the call.

With the scheduled touchdown now only about fifteen minutes ahead, it was a busy time at Mission Control. Weather reports were coming in from the landing site at the Kennedy Space Center, in Florida. Radar tracking of the shuttle, like the final accurate ground-based navigation, had not yet begun. Sitting at their specialized positions, and monitoring the numbers displayed on the consoles, a few of the flight controllers had begun to sense, just barely, that something was going seriously wrong. The worry was not quite coherent yet. One of the controllers later told me that it amounted to an inexplicable bad feeling in his gut. But it was undeniable nonetheless. For the previous few minutes, since about the time when the shuttle had passed from California to Nevada, Jeff Kling, an engineer who was working the mechanical-systems position known as MMACS (pronounced Macs), had witnessed a swarm of erratic indications and sensor failures. The pattern was disconcerting because of the lack of common circuitry that could easily explain the failures – a single box that could be blamed.

Kling had been bantering good-naturedly on an intercom with one of his team, a technician sitting in an adjoining back room and monitoring the telemetry, when the technician noted a strange failure of temperature transducers on a hydraulic return line. The technician said, 'We've had some hydraulic 'ducers go off-scale low.'

Kling had seen the same indications. He said, 'Well, I guess!'

The technician said, 'What in the world?'

Kling said, 'This is not funny. On the left side.'

The technician confirmed, 'On the left side . . .'

Now Kling got onto the main control-room intercom to the lead controller on duty, known as the flight director, a man named Leroy Cain. In the jargon-laced language of the control room Kling said, 'Flight, Macs.'

Cain said, 'Go ahead, Macs.'

'FYI, I've just lost four separate temperature transducers on the left side of the vehicle, hydraulic return temperatures. Two of them on system one, and one in each of systems two and three.'

Cain said, 'Four hyd return temps?'

Kling answered, 'To the left outboard and left inboard elevon.'

'Okay, is there anything common to them? DSC or MDM or anything? I mean, you're telling me you lost them all at exactly the same time?'

'No, not exactly. They were within probably four or five seconds of each other.'

Cain struggled to assess the meaning. 'Okay, where are those . . . where is that instrumentation located?'

Kling continued to hear from his back-room team. He said, 'All four of them are located in the aft part of the left wing, right in front of the elevons . . . elevon actuators. And there is no commonality.'

Cain repeated, 'No commonality.'

But all the failing instruments were in the left wing. The possible significance of this was not lost on Cain: during the launch a piece of solid foam had broken off from the shuttle's external fuel tank, and at high speed had smashed into the left wing; after minimal consideration the shuttle program managers (who stood above Mission Control in the NASA hierarchy) had dismissed the incident as essentially unthreatening. Like almost everyone else at NASA, Cain had taken the managers at their word – and he still did. Nonetheless, the strange cluster of left-wing failures was an ominous development. Kling had more specific reasons for concern. In a wonkish, engineering way he had discussed with his team the telemetry they might observe if a hole allowed hot gases into the wing during re-entry, and he had come up with a profile eerily close to what was happening now. Still, he maintained the expected detachment.

Cain continued to worry the problem. He asked for reassurance from his 'guidance, navigation, and control' man, Mike Sarafin. 'Everything look good to you, control and rates and everything is nominal, right?'

Sarafin said, 'Control's been stable through the rolls that we've done so far, Flight. We have good trims. I don't see anything out of the ordinary.'

Cain directed his attention back to Kling: 'All other indications for your hydraulic systems are good?'

'They're all good. We've had good quantities all the way across.'

Cain said, 'And the other temps are normal?'

'The other temps are normal, yes, sir.' He meant only those that the telemetry allowed him to see.

Cain said, 'And when you say you lost these, are you saying they went to zero . . .'

'All four of them are off-scale low.'

'. . . or off-scale low?'

Kling said, 'And they were all staggered. They were, like I said, within several seconds of each other.'

Cain said, 'Okay.'

But it wasn't okay. Within seconds the *Columbia* had crossed into Texas and the left tire-pressure indications were dropping, as observed also by the cockpit crew. Kling's informal model of catastrophe had predicted just such indications, whether from blown tires or wire breaks. The end was now coming very fast.

Kling said, 'Flight, Macs.'

Cain said, 'Go.'

'We just lost tire pressure on the left outboard and left inboard, both tires.'

Cain said, 'Copy.'

At that moment, twenty-three seconds after 7:59 local time, the Mission Control consoles stopped receiving telemetry updates, for reasons unknown. The astronaut sitting beside Cain, and serving as the Mission Control communicator, radioed, 'And *Columbia*, Houston, we see your tire-pressure messages, and we did not copy your last call.'

At the same time, on the control-room intercom, Cain was talking again to Kling. He said, 'Is it instrumentation, Macs? Gotta be.'

Kling said, 'Flight, Macs, those are also off-scale low.'

From the speeding shuttle Rick Husband – Air Force test pilot, religious, good family man, always wanted to be an astronaut – began to answer the communicator. He said, 'Roger, ah,' and was cut off on a word that began with 'buh . . .'

It turned out to be the *Columbia*'s last voice transmission. Brief communication breaks, however, are not abnormal during re-entries, and this one raised no immediate concern in Houston.

People on the ground in Dallas suddenly knew more than the flight controllers in Houston. Four seconds after 8:00 they saw a large piece leave the orbiter and fall away. The shuttle was starting to come apart. It continued intermittently to send telemetry, which though not immediately displayed at Mission Control was captured by NASA computers and later discovered; the story it told was that multiple systems were failing. In quick succession two additional chunks fell off.

Down in the control room Cain said, 'And there's no commonality between all these tire-pressure instrumentations and the hydraulic return instrumentations?'

High in the sky near Dallas the *Columbia*'s main body began to break up. It crackled and boomed, and made a loud rumble.

Kling said, 'No, sir, there's not. We've also lost the nose-gear down talkback, and right-main-gear down talkback.'

'Nose-gear and right-main-gear down talkbacks?'

'Yes, sir.'

At Fort Hood, Texas, two Dutch military pilots who were training in an Apache attack helicopter locked on to the breakup with their optics and videotaped three bright objects – the main rocket engines

– flying eastward in formation, among other, smaller pieces and their contrails.

Referring to the loss of communications, one minute after the main-body breakup, Laura Hoppe, the flight controller responsible for the communications systems, said to Cain, 'I didn't expect, uh, this bad of a hit on comm.'

Cain asked another controller about a planned switchover to a ground-based radio ahead, 'How far are we from UHF? Is that two-minute clock good?'

Kling, also, was hanging on to hope. He said. 'Flight, Macs.'

Cain said, 'Macs?'

Kling said, 'On the tire pressures, we did see them go erratic for a little bit before they went away, so I do believe it's instrumentation.'

'Okay.'

At about that time the debris began to hit the ground. It fell in thousands of pieces along a swath ten miles wide and 300 miles long, across East Texas and into Louisiana. There were many stories later. Some of the debris whistled down through the leaves of trees and smacked into a pond where a man was fishing. Another piece went right through a backyard trampoline, evoking a mother's lament: 'Those damned kids . . .' Still another piece hit the window of a moving car, startling the driver. The heaviest parts flew the farthest. An 800-pound piece of engine hit the ground in Fort Polk, Louisiana, doing 1,400 mph. A 600-pound piece landed nearby. Thousands of people began to call in, swamping the 911 dispatchers with reports of sonic booms and metal falling out of the sky. No one, however, was hit. This would be surprising were it not for the fact, so visible from above, that the world is still a sparsely populated place.

In Houston the controllers maintained discipline, and continued preparing for the landing, even as they received word that the Merritt Island radar, in Florida, which should by now have started tracking the inbound craft, was picking up only false targets. Shuttles arrive on time or they don't arrive at all. But, repeatedly, the communicator radioed, 'Columbia, Houston, UHF comm check,' as if he might still hear a reply. Then, at thirteen minutes past the hour, precisely when the Columbia should have been passing overhead the runway before circling down for a landing at the Kennedy Space Center, a phone call came in from an off-duty controller who had just seen a video broadcast by a Dallas television station of multiple contrails in the sky. When Cain heard the news, he paused, and then put the contingency plan into effect. To the ground-control officer he said, 'GC, Flight.'

'Flight, GC.'

'Lock the doors.'

'Copy.'

The controllers were stunned, but lacked the time to contemplate the horror of what had just happened. Under Cain's direction they set about collecting numbers, writing notes, and closing out their logs, for the investigation that was certain to follow. The mood in the room was somber and focused. Only the most basic facts were known: the *Columbia* had broken up at 200,000 feet doing 12,738 mph, and the crew could not possibly have survived. Ron Dittemore, the shuttle program manager, would be talking to reporters later that day, and he needed numbers and information. At some point sandwiches were brought in and consumed. Like the priests who harvest faith at the bedsides of the dying, grief counselors showed up too, but they were not much used.

Cain insisted on control-room discipline. He said, 'No phone calls off site outside of this room. Our discussions are on these loops – the recorded DVIS loops only. No data, no phone calls, no transmissions anywhere, into or out.'

Later this was taken by some critics to be a typical NASA reaction – insular, furtive, overcontrolling. And it may indeed have reflected certain aspects of what had become of the agency's culture. But it was also, more simply, a rule-book procedure meant to stabilize and preserve the crucial last data. The room was being frozen as a crime scene might be. Somewhere inside NASA something had obviously gone very wrong – and it made sense to start looking for the evidence here and now.

Less than an hour later, at 10:00 AM eastern time, a retired four-star admiral named Hal Gehman met his brother at a lawyer's office in Williamsburg, Virginia. At the age of sixty, Gehman was a tall, slim, silver-haired man with an unlined face and soft eyes. Dressed in civilian clothes, standing straight but not stiffly so, he had an accessible, unassuming manner that contrasted with the rank and power he had achieved. After an inauspicious start as a mediocre engineering student in the Penn State Naval ROTC program ('Top four fifths of the class,' he liked to say), he had skippered a patrol boat through the thick of the Vietnam War and gone on to become an experienced sea captain, the commander of a carrier battle group, vice-chief of the Navy, and finally NATO Atlantic commander and head of the U.S. Joint Forces Command. Upon his retirement, in 2000, from the sixth-ranked position in the U.S. military, he had given all that up with apparent ease. He had enjoyed a good career in the Navy, but he enjoyed his civilian life now too. He was a rare sort of man – startlingly intelligent beneath his guileless exterior, personally satisfied, and quite genuinely untroubled. He lived in Norfolk in a pleasant house that he had recently remodeled; he loved his wife, his grown children, his mother and father, and all his siblings. He had an old Volkswagen bug convertible, robin's-egg blue, that he had bought from another admiral. He had a modest thirty-four-foot sloop, which he enjoyed sailing in the Chesapeake, though its sails were worn out and he wanted to replace its icebox with a twelve-volt refrigeration unit. He was a patriot, of course, but not a reactionary. He called himself a fiscal conservative and a social moderate. His life as he described it was the product of convention. It was also the product of a strict personal code. He chose not to work with any company doing business with the Department of Defense. He liked power, but understood its limitations. He did not care to be famous or rich. He represented the American establishment at its best.

In the lawyer's office in Williamsburg his brother told him that the *Columbia* had been lost. Gehman had driven there with his radio off and so he had not heard. He asked a few questions, and absorbed the information without much reaction. He did not follow the space program and, like most Americans, had not been aware that a mission was under way. He spent an hour with the lawyer on routine family business. When he emerged, he saw that messages had been left on his cell phone, but because the coverage was poor, he could not retrieve them; only later, while driving home on the interstate, was he finally able to connect. To his surprise, among mundane messages he found an urgent request to call the deputy administrator of NASA, a man he had not heard of before, named Fred Gregory. Like a good American, Gehman made the call while speeding down the highway. Gregory, a former shuttle commander, said, 'Have you heard the news?'

Gehman said, 'Only secondhand.'

Gregory filled him in on what little was known, and explained that part of NASA's contingency plan, instituted after the *Challenger* disaster of 1986, was the activation of a standing 'interagency' investigation board. By original design the board consisted of seven high-ranking civilian and military officials who were pre-selected mechanically on the basis of job titles – the institutional slots that they filled. For the *Columbia*, the names were now known: the board would consist of three Air Force generals, John Barry, Kenneth Hess, and Duane Deal; a Navy admiral, Stephen Turcotte; a NASA research director, G. Scott Hubbard; and two senior civil aviation officials, James Hallock and Steven Wallace. Though only two of these men knew much about NASA or the space shuttle, in various ways each of them was familiar with the complexities of large-scale, high-risk activities. Most of them also had strong personalities. To be effective they would require even stronger management. Gregory said that it was NASA's administrator, Sean O'Keefe, who wanted Gehman to come in as chairman to lead the work. Gehman was not immune to the compliment, but he was cautious. He had met O'Keefe briefly years before, but did not know him. He wanted to make sure he wasn't being suckered into a NASA sideshow.

O'Keefe was an able member of Washington's revolving-door caste, a former congressional staffer and budget specialist – and a longtime protégé of Vice President Dick Cheney – who through the force of his competence and Republican connections had briefly landed the position of Secretary of the Navy in the early 1990s. He had suffered academic banishment through the Clinton era, but under the current administration had re-emerged as a deputy at the Office of Management and Budget, where he had been assigned to tackle the difficult problem of NASA's cost overruns and lack of delivery, particularly in the Space Station program. It is hard to know what he thought when he was handed the treacherous position of NASA administrator. Inside Washington, NASA's reputation had sunk so low that some of O'Keefe's former congressional colleagues snickered that Cheney was trying to kill his own man off. But O'Keefe was not a space crusader, as some earlier NASA administrators had been, and he was not about to pick up the fallen banners of the visionaries and try to lead the way forward; he was a tough, level-headed money man, grounded in the realities of Washington, D.C., and sent in on a mission to bring discipline to NASA's budget and performance before moving on. NASA's true believers called him a carpetbagger and resented the schedule pressures that he brought to bear, but in fairness he was a professional manager, and NASA needed one.

O'Keefe had been at NASA for just over a year when the *Columbia* self-destructed. He was in Florida standing at the landing site beside one of his deputies, a former shuttle commander named William Readdy. At 9:05 eastern time, ten minutes before the scheduled landing, Readdy got word that communications with the shuttle had been lost; O'Keefe noticed that Readdy's face went blank. At 9:10 Readdy opened a book to check a time sequence. He said, 'We should have heard the sonic booms by now. There's something really wrong.' By 9:29 O'Keefe had activated the full-blown contingency plan. When word got to the White House, the executive staff ducked quickly into defensive positions: President Bush would grieve alongside the families and say the right things about carrying on, but rather than involving himself by appointing an independent presidential commission, as Ronald Reagan had in response to the *Challenger* accident, he would keep his distance by expressing faith in NASA's ability to find the cause. In other words, this baby was going to be dropped squarely onto O'Keefe's lap. The White House approved Gehman's appointment to lead what would essentially be NASA's investigation – but O'Keefe could expect little further communication. There was a chance that the President would not even want to receive the final report directly but would ask that it be deposited more discreetly in the White House in-box. He had problems bigger than space on his mind.

Nonetheless, that morning in his car Gehman realized that even with a lukewarm White House endorsement, the position that NASA was offering, if handled correctly, would allow for a significant inquiry into the accident. Gregory made it clear that Gehman would have the full support of NASA's engineers and technical resources in unraveling the physical mysteries of the accident – what actually had happened to the *Columbia* out there in its sheath of fire at 200,000 feet. Moreover, Gehman was confident that if the investigation had to go further, into why this accident had occurred, he had the experience necessary to sort through the human complexities of NASA and emerge with useful answers that might result in reform. This may have been overconfident of him, and to some extent utopian, but it was not entirely blind: he had been through big investigations before, most recently two years earlier, just after leaving the Navy, when he and a retired Army general named William Crouch had led an inquiry into the loss of seventeen sailors aboard the USS *Cole*, the destroyer that was attacked and nearly sunk by suicide terrorists in Yemen in October of 2000. Their report found fundamental errors in the functioning of the military command structure, and issued recommendations (largely classified) that are in effect today. The success of the *Cole* investigation was one of the arguments that Gregory used on him now. Gehman did not disagree, but he wanted to be very clear. He said, 'I know you've got a piece of paper in front of you. Does it say that I'm not an aviator?'

Gregory said, 'We don't need an aviator here. We need an investigator.'

And so, driving down the highway to Norfolk, Gehman accepted the job. When he got home, he told his wife that he was a federal employee again and that there wouldn't be much sailing in the spring. That afternoon and evening, as the faxes and phone calls came in, he began to exercise control of the process, if only in his own mind, concluding that the board's charter as originally written by NASA would have to be strengthened and expanded, and that its name should immediately be changed from the absurd International Space Station and Space Shuttle Mishap Interagency Investigations Board (the ISSSSMIIB) to the more workable *Columbia* Accident Investigation Board, or CAIB, which could be pronounced in one syllable, as Cabe.

NASA initially did not resist any of his suggestions. Gregory advised Gehman to head to Barksdale Air Force Base, in Shreveport, Louisiana, where the wreckage was being collected. As Gehman began to explore airline connections, word came that a NASA executive jet, a Gulfstream, would be dispatched to carry him, along with several other board members, directly to Barksdale. The jet arrived in Norfolk on Sunday afternoon, the day after the accident. One of the members already aboard was Steven Wallace, the head of accident investigations for the FAA. Wallace is a second-generation pilot, an athletic, tightly wound man with wide experience in government and a skeptical view of the powerful. He later told me that when Gehman got on the airplane, he was dressed in a business suit, and that, having introduced himself, he explained that they might run into the press. He said if they did, he would handle things. This raised some questions about Gehman's motivations (and indeed Gehman turned out to enjoy the limelight), but as Wallace soon discovered, grandstanding was not what Gehman was about. As the Gulfstream proceeded toward Louisiana, Gehman rolled up his sleeves and, sitting at the table in the back of the airplane, began to ask for the thoughts and perspectives of the board members there – not about what might have happened to the *Columbia* but about how best to find out. It was the start of what would become an intense seven-month relationship. It was obvious that Gehman was truly listening to the ideas, and that he was capable of integrating them quickly and productively into his own thoughts. By the end of the flight even Wallace was growing impressed.

But Gehman was in some ways also naive, formed as he had been by investigative experience within the military, in which much of the work proceeds behind closed doors, and conflict of interest is not a big concern. The *Columbia* investigation, he discovered, was going to be a very different thing. Attacks against the CAIB began on the second day, and by midweek, as the board moved from Shreveport to Houston to set up shop, they showed no signs of easing. Congress in particular was thundering that Gehman was a captive investigator, that his report would be a whitewash, and that the White House should replace the CAIB with a *Challenger*-style presidential commission. This came as a surprise to Gehman, who had assumed that he could just go about his business but who now realized that he would have to accommodate these concerns if the final report was to have any credibility at all. Later he said to me, 'I didn't go in thinking about it, but as I began to hear the independence thing – "You can't have a panel appointed by NASA investigating itself!" – I realized I'd better deal with Congress.' He did this at first mainly by listening on the phone. 'They told me what I had to do to build my credibility. I didn't invent it – they told me. They also said, "We hate NASA. We don't trust them. Their culture is no good. And their cost accounting is no good." And I said, "Okay."'

More than that, Gehman came to realize that it was the elected representatives in Congress – and neither O'Keefe nor NASA – who constituted the CAIB's real constituency, and that their concerns were legitimate. As a result of this, along with a growing understanding of the depth and complexity of the work at hand, he forced through a series of changes, establishing a congressional-liaison office, gaining an independent budget (ultimately of about $20 million), wresting the report from O'Keefe's control, re-writing the stated mission to include the finding of 'root causes and circumstances,' and hiring an additional five board members, all civilians of unimpeachable reputation: the retired Electric Boat boss Roger Tetrault, the former astronaut Sally Ride, the Nobel-laureate physicist Douglas Osheroff, the aerodynamicist and former Air Force Secretary Sheila Widnall, and the historian and space-policy expert John Logsdon. Afterward, the loudest criticism faded away. Still, Gehman's political judgment was not perfect. He allowed the new civilian members to be brought on through the NASA payroll (at pro-rated annual salaries of $134,000) – a strange lapse under the circumstances, and one that led to superficial accusations that the CAIB remained captive. The *Orlando Sentinel* ran a story about the lack of public access to the CAIB's interviews under the ambiguous headline 'Board Paid to Ensure Secrecy.' The idea evoked laughter among some of the investigators, who knew the inquiry's direction. But unnecessary damage was done.

Equally unnecessary was Gehman's habit of referring to O'Keefe as 'Sean,' a clubbish mannerism that led people to conclude, erroneously, that the two men were friends. In fact their relationship was strained, if polite. Gehman told me that he had never asked for the full story behind his selection on the morning of the accident – maybe because it would have been impossible to know the unvarnished truth. Certainly, though, O'Keefe had had little opportunity to contemplate his choice. By quick view Gehman was a steady hand and a good establishment man who could lend the gravitas of his four stars to this occasion; he was also, of course, one of the men behind the *Cole* investigation. O'Keefe later told me that he had read the *Cole* report during his stint as a professor, but that he remembered it best as the subject of a case study presented by one of his academic colleagues as an example of a narrowly focused investigation that, correctly, had not widened beyond its original mandate. This was true, but a poor predictor of Gehman as a man. His *Cole* investigation had not widened (for instance, into assigning individual blame) for the simple reason that other investigations, by the Navy and the FBI, were already covering that ground. Instead, Gehman and Crouch had gone deep, and relentlessly so. The result was a document that bluntly questioned current American dogma, identified arrogance in the command structure, and critiqued U.S. military assumptions about the terrorist threat. The tone was frank. For example, while expressing understanding of the diplomatic utility of labeling terrorists as 'criminals,' the report warned against buying into that language, or into the parallel idea that these terrorists were 'cowards.' When, later, I expressed my surprise at his freedom of expression, Gehman did not deny that people have recently been decried as traitors for less. But freedom of expression was clearly his habit: he spoke to me just as openly about the failures of his cherished Navy, of Congress, and increasingly of NASA.

When I mentioned this character trait to one of the new board members, Sheila Widnall, she laughed and said she'd seen it before inside the Pentagon. She said that people just didn't understand the highest level of the U.S. military: these officers are indeed the establishment, but they are so convinced of the greatness of the American construct that they will willingly tear at its components in the belief that its failures can be squarely addressed. Almost all of the current generation of senior leaders have also been through the soul-searching that followed the defeat in Vietnam.

O'Keefe had his own understanding of the establishment, and it was probably sophisticated, but he clearly did not anticipate Gehman's rebellion. By the end of the second week, as Gehman established an independent relationship with Congress and began to break through the boundaries initially drawn by NASA, it became clear that O'Keefe was losing control. He maintained a brave front of wanting a thorough inquiry, but it was said that privately he was angry. The tensions came to the surface toward the end of February, at about the same time that Gehman insisted, over O'Keefe's resistance, that the full report ultimately be made available to the public. The CAIB was expanding to a staff of about 120 people, many of them professional accident investigators and technical experts who could support the core board members. They were working seven days a week out of temporary office space in the sprawling wasteland of South Houston, just off the property of the Johnson Space Center. One morning several of the board members came in to see Gehman, and warned him that the CAIB was headed for a 'shipwreck.'

Gehman knew what they meant. In the days following the accident O'Keefe had established an internal Mishap Investigation Team, whose job was to work closely with the CAIB, essentially as staff, and whose members – bizarrely – included some of the decision-makers most closely involved with the *Columbia*'s final flight. The team was led by Linda Ham, a razor-sharp manager in the shuttle program, whose actions during the flight would eventually be singled out as an egregious example of NASA's failings. Gehman did not know that yet, but it dawned on him that Ham was in a position to filter the inbound NASA reports, and he remembered a recent three-hour briefing that she had run with an iron hand, allowing little room for spontaneous exploration. He realized that she and the others would have to leave the CAIB, and he wrote a careful letter to O'Keefe in Washington, requesting their immediate removal. It is a measure of the insularity at the Johnson Space Center that NASA did not gracefully acquiesce. Ham and another manager, Ralph Roe, in particular reacted badly. In Gehman's office, alternately in anger and tears, they refused to leave, accusing Gehman of impugning their integrity and asking him how they were supposed to explain their dismissal to others. Gehman suggested to them what Congress had insisted to him – that people simply cannot investigate themselves. Civics 101. Once stated, it seems like an obvious principle.

O'Keefe had a master's degree in public administration, but he disagreed. It was odd. He had not been with the agency long enough to be infected by its insularity, and as he later promised Congress, he was willing – no, eager – to identify and punish any of his NASA subordinates who could be held responsible for the accident. Nonetheless, he decided to defy Gehman, and he announced that his people would remain in place. It was an ill-considered move. Gehman simply went public with his letter, posting it on the CAIB Website. Gehman understood that O'Keefe felt betrayed – 'stabbed in the back' was the word going around – but NASA had left him no choice. O'Keefe surrendered. Ham and the others were reassigned, and the Mishap Investigation Team was disbanded, replaced by NASA staffers who had not been involved in the *Columbia*'s flight and would be more likely to cooperate with the CAIB's investigators. The board was never able to overcome completely the whiff of collusion that had accompanied its birth, but Gehman had won a significant fight, even if it meant that he and 'Sean' would not be friends.

The space shuttle is the most audacious flying machine ever built, an engineering fantasy made real. Before each flight it stands vertically on the launch pad at the Kennedy Space Center, as the core component of a rocket assembly 184 feet tall. The shuttle itself, which is also known as the orbiter, is a winged vehicle roughly the size of a DC-9, with three main rocket engines in the tail, a large unpressurized cargo bay in the midsection, and a cramped two-level crew compartment in the nose. It is attached to a huge external tank containing liquid fuel for the three main engines. That tank in turn is attached to two solid-fuel rockets, known as boosters, which flank the assembly and bear its full weight on the launch pad. Just before the launch, the weight is about 4.5 million pounds, 90 percent of which is fuel. It is a dramatic time, ripe with anticipation; the shuttle vents vapors like a breathing thing; the ground crews pull away until finally no one is left; the air seems unusually quiet. Typically there are seven astronauts aboard. Four of them sit in the cockpit, and three on the lower level, in the living quarters known as the mid-deck. Because of the shuttle's vertical position, their seats are effectively rotated backward 90 degrees, so they are sitting on their backs, feeling their own weight in a way that tends to emphasize gravity's pull. At the front of the cockpit, positioned closer to the instrument panel than is necessary for the typical astronaut's six-foot frame, the commander and the pilot can look straight ahead into space. They are highly trained. They know exactly what they are getting into. Sometimes they have waited years for this moment to arrive.

The launch window may be just a few minutes wide. It is ruled by orbital mechanics, and defined by the track and position of the destination – usually now the unfinished International Space Station. Six seconds before liftoff the three main engines are ignited and throttled up to 100 percent power, producing more than a million pounds of thrust. The shuttle responds with what is known as 'the twang,' swaying several feet in the direction of the external tank and then swaying back. This is felt in the cockpit. The noise inside is not very loud. If the computers show that the main engines are operating correctly, the solid rocket boosters ignite. The boosters are ferocious devices – the same sort of monsters that upon failure blew the *Challenger* apart. Each of them produces three million pounds of thrust. Once ignited, they cannot be shut off or throttled back. The shuttle lifts off. It accelerates fast enough to clear the launch tower doing about 100 mph, though it is so large that seen from the outside, it appears to be climbing slowly.

The flying is done entirely by autopilot unless something goes wrong. Within seconds the assembly rotates and aims on course, tilting slightly off the vertical and rolling so that the orbiter is inverted beneath the external tank. Although the vibrations are heavy enough to blur the instruments, the acceleration amounts to only about 2.5 Gs – a mild sensation of heaviness pressing the astronauts back into their seats. After about forty seconds the shuttle accelerates through Mach 1, 760 mph, at about 17,000 feet, climbing nearly straight up. Eighty seconds later, with the shuttle doing about 3,400 mph and approaching 150,000 feet, the crew can feel the thrust from the solid rocket boosters begin to tail off. Just afterward, with a bright flash and a loud explosion heard inside the orbiter, the rocket boosters separate from the main tank; they continue to travel upward on a ballistic path to 220,000 feet before falling back and parachuting into the sea. Now powered by the main engines alone, the ride turns smooth, and the forces settle down to about 1 G.

One pilot described the sensations to me on the simplest level. He said, 'First it's like, "Hey, this is a rough ride!" and then, "Hey, I'm on an electric train!" and then, "Hey, this train's starting to go pretty darned fast!"' Speed is the ultimate goal of the launch sequence. Having climbed steeply into ultra-thin air, the shuttle gently pitches over until it is flying nearly parallel to earth, inverted under the external tank, and thrusting at full power. Six minutes after launch, at about 356,000 feet, the shuttle is doing around 9,200 mph, which is fast, but only about half the speed required to sustain an orbit. It therefore begins a shallow dive, during which it gains speed at the rate of 1,000 mph every twenty seconds – an acceleration so fast that it presses the shuttle against its 3 G limit, and the engines have to be briefly throttled back. At 10,300 mph the shuttle rolls to a head-up position. Passing through 15,000 mph, it begins to climb again, still accelerating at 3 Gs, until seconds later, in the near vacuum of space, it achieves orbital velocity, or 17,500 mph. The plumes from the main engines wrap forward and dance across the cockpit windows, making light at night like that of Saint Elmo's fire. Only eight and a half minutes have passed since the launch. The main engines are extinguished, and the external tank is jettisoned. The shuttle is in orbit. After further maneuvering it assumes its standard attitude, flying inverted in relation to earth and tail first as it proceeds around the globe.

For the astronauts aboard, the uphill flight would amount to little more than an interesting ride were it not for the possibility of failures. That possibility, however, is very real, and as a result the launch is a critical and complicated operation, demanding close teamwork, tight coordination with Mission Control, and above all extreme concentration – a quality often confused with coolness under fire. I was given a taste of this by an active shuttle commander named Michael Bloomfield, who had me strap in beside him in NASA's full-motion simulator in Houston, and take a realistic run from the launch pad into space. Bloomfield is a former Air Force test pilot who has flown three shuttle missions. He had been assigned to assist the CAIB, and had been watching the investigation with mixed emotions – hopeful that some effects might be positive, but concerned as well that the inquiry might veer into formalism without sufficiently taking into account the radical nature of space flight, or the basic truth that every layer of procedure and equipment comes at a cost, often unpredictable. Bloomfield called this the 'risk versus risk' tradeoff, and made it real not by defending NASA against specific criticisms but by immersing me, a pilot myself, in the challenges of normal operations.

Much of what he showed me was of the what-if variety, the essence not only of simulator work but also of the crew's real-world thinking. For instance, during the launch, as the shuttle rockets upward on autopilot, the pilots and flight controllers pass through a succession of mental gates, related to various combinations of main-engine failures, at various altitudes and speeds. The options and resulting maneuvers are complicated, ranging from a quick return to the launch site, to a series of tight arrivals at select runways up the eastern seaboard, to transatlantic glides, and finally even an 'abort into orbit' – an escape route used by a *Challenger* crew in 1985 after a single main-engine failure. Such failures allow little time to make the right decision. As Bloomfield and I climbed away from earth, tilted onto our backs, he occasionally asked the operators to freeze the simulation so that he could unfold his thoughts to me. Though the choices were clear, the relative risks were rarely so obvious. It was a deep view into the most intense sort of flying.

After we arrived in space, we continued to talk. One of the gates for engine failure during the climb to the Space Station stands at Mach 21.8 (14,900 mph), the last point allowed for a 'high energy' arrival into Gander, Newfoundland, and the start of the emergency transatlantic track for Shannon, Ireland. An abort at that point provides no easy solution. The problem with Gander is how to bleed off excess energy before the landing (Bloomfield called this 'a take-all-your-brain-cells type of flying'), whereas the problem with Shannon is just the opposite – how to stretch the glide. Bloomfield told me that immediately before his last space flight, in the spring of 2002, his crew and a Mission Control team had gone through a full-dress simulation during which the orbiter had lost all three engines by Mach 21.7 (less than 100 mph from the decision speed). Confident in his ability to fly the more difficult Canadian arrival, Bloomfield, from the cockpit of the simulator, radioed, 'We're going high-energy into Gander.'

Mission Control answered, 'Negative,' and called for Shannon instead.

Bloomfield looked over at his right-seat pilot and said, 'I think we oughta go to Gander. What do you think?'

'Yeah.'

Bloomfield radioed back: 'No, we think we oughta go to Gander.'

Mission Control was emphatic. 'Negative. We see you having enough energy to make Shannon.'

As commander, Bloomfield had formal authority for the decision, but Mission Control, with its expert teams and wealth of data, was expressing a strong opinion, so he acquiesced. Acquiescence is standard in such cases, and usually it works out for the best. Bloomfield had enormous respect for the expertise and competence of Mission Control. He was also well aware of errors he had made in the past, despite superior advice or instructions from the flight controllers. This time, however, it turned out that two of the flight controllers had not communicated correctly with each other, and that the judgment of Mission Control therefore was wrong. Lacking the energy to reach Shannon, the simulator went into the ocean well short of the airport. The incident caused a disturbance inside the Johnson Space Center, particularly because of the long-standing struggle for the possession of data (and ultimately control) between the pilots in flight and the engineers at their consoles. Nevertheless, the two groups worked together, hammered out the problems, and the next day flew the same simulator profile successfully. But that was not the point of Bloomfield's story. Rather, it was that these calls are hard to make, and that mistakes – whether his or the controllers' – may become obvious only after it is too late.

For all its realism, the simulator cannot duplicate the gravity load of the climb, or the lack of it at the top. The transition to weightlessness is abrupt, and all the more dramatic because it occurs at the end of the 3 G acceleration: when the main engines cut off, the crew gets the impression of going over an edge and suddenly dropping into a free fall. That impression is completely accurate. In fact the term zero gravity (0 G), which is loosely used to describe the orbital environment, refers to physical acceleration, and does not mean that earth's gravitational pull has somehow gone away. Far from it: the diminution of gravitational pull that comes with distance is small at these low-orbit altitudes (perhaps 200 miles above the surface), and the shuttle is indeed now falling – about like a stone dropped off a cliff. The fall does not, of course, diminish the shuttle's mass (if it bumps the Space Station, it does so with tremendous force), but it does make the vehicle and everything inside it very nearly weightless. The orbital part of the trick is that though the shuttle is dropping like a stone, it is also progressing across earth's surface so fast (17,500 mph) that its path matches (roughly) the curvature of the globe. In other words, as it plummets toward the ground, the ground keeps getting out of its way. Like the orbits of all other satellites, and of the Space Station, and of the Moon as well, its flight is nothing but an unrestricted free fall around and around the world. To help the astronauts adapt to weightlessness, the quarters are designed with a conventional floor-down orientation. This isn't quite so obvious as it might seem, since the shuttle flies inverted in orbit. 'Down' therefore is toward outer space – and the view from the cockpit windows just happens to be of earth sliding by from behind and overhead. The crews are encouraged to live and work with their heads 'up' nonetheless. It is even recommended that they use the ladder while passing through the hatch between the two levels, and that they 'descend' from the cockpit to the mid-deck feet first. Those sorts of cautions rarely prevail against the temptations of weightlessness. After Bloomfield's last flight one of his crew commented that they had all been swimming around 'like eels in a can.' Or like superhumans, as the case may be. It's true that there are frustrations: if you try to throw a switch without first anchoring your body, the switch will throw you. On the other hand, once you are anchored, you can shift multi-ton masses with your fingertips. You can also fly without wings, perform unlimited flips, or simply float for a while, resting in midair. Weightlessness is bad for the bones, but good for the soul. I asked Bloomfield how it had felt to experience gravity again. He said he remembered the first time, after coming to a stop on the runway in Florida, when he picked up a small plastic checklist in the cockpit and thought, 'Man, this is so heavy!' He looked at me and said, 'Gravity sucks.'

And orbital flight clearly does not. The ride is smooth. When the cabin ventilation is turned off, as it must be once a day to exchange the carbon dioxide scrubbers, the silence is absolute. The smell inside the shuttle is distinctly metallic, unless someone has just come in from a spacewalk, after which the quarters are permeated for a while with 'the smell of space,' a pungent burned odor that some compare to that of seared meat, and that Bloomfield describes as closer to the smell of a torch on steel. The dominant sensation, other than weightlessness, is of the speed across the ground. Bloomfield said, 'From California to New York in ten minutes, around the world once in ninety minutes – I mean, we're moving.' He told me that he took to loitering in the cockpit at the end of the workdays, just for the view. By floating forward above the instrument panel and wrapping his legs around one of the pilot seats, he could position his face so close to the front windshield that the structure of the shuttle would seem to disappear.

The view from there was etched into his memory as a continuous loop. In brief, he said, It's night and you're coming up on California, with that clearly defined coastline, and you can see all the lights all the way from Tijuana to San Francisco, and then it's behind you, and you spot Las Vegas and its neon-lit Strip, which you barely have time to identify before you move across the Rockies, with their helter-skelter of towns, and then across the Plains, with its monotony of look-alike wheels and spokes of light, until you come to Chicago and its lakefront, from which point you can see past Detroit and Cleveland all the way to New York. These are big cities, you think. And because you grew up on a farm in Michigan, played football there in high school, and still know it like a home, you pick out Ann Arbor and Flint, and the place where I-75 joins U.S. Highway 23, and you get down to within a couple of miles of your house before zip, you're gone. Zip goes Cleveland, and zip New York, and then you're out over the Atlantic beyond Maine, looking back down the eastern seaboard all the way past Washington, D.C. Ten minutes later you come up on Europe, and you hardly have time to think that London is a sprawl, France is an orderly display, the Alps are the Rockies again, and Italy is indeed a boot. Over Sicily you peer down into Etna's crater, into the glow of molten rock on earth's inside, and then you are crossing Africa, where the few lights you see are not yellow but orange, like open flames. Past the Equator and beyond Madagascar you come to a zone of gray between the blackness of the night and the bright blue of the day. At the center of that zone is a narrow pink slice, which is the atmospheric dawn as seen from above. Daylight is for the oceans – first the Indian and then the Pacific, which is very, very large. Atolls appear with coral reefs and turquoise lagoons, but mostly what you see is cloud and open water. Then the pink slice of sunset passes below, night arrives, and soon afterward you come again to California, though at another point on the coast, because ninety minutes have passed since you were last here, and during that time the world has revolved beneath you.

Ultimately the shuttle must return to earth and land. The problem then is what to do with the vast amount of physical energy that has been invested in it – almost all the calories once contained in the nearly four million pounds of rocket fuel that was used to shove the shuttle into orbit. Some of that energy now resides in the vehicle's altitude, but most resides in its speed. The re-entry is a descent to a landing, yes, but primarily it is a giant deceleration, during which atmospheric resistance is used to convert velocity into heat, and to slow the shuttle by roughly 17,000 mph, so that it finally passes overhead the runway in Florida at airline speeds, and circles down to touch the ground at a well tamed 224 mph or less. Once the shuttle is on the runway, the drag chute and brakes take care of the rest.

The re-entry is a one-way ride that cannot be stopped once it has begun. The opening move occurs while the shuttle is still proceeding tail first and inverted, halfway around the world from the runway, high above the Indian Ocean. It is a simple thing, a brief burn by the twin orbital maneuvering rockets against the direction of flight, which slows the shuttle by perhaps 200 mph. That reduction is enough. The shuttle continues to free-fall as it has in orbit, but it now lacks the speed to match the curvature of earth, so the ground no longer gets out of its way. By the time it reaches the start of the atmosphere, the 'entry interface' at 400,000 feet, it has gently flipped itself around so that it is right-side up and pointed for Florida, but with its nose held 40 degrees higher than the angle of the descent path. The effect of this so-called angle of attack (which technically refers to the wings, not the nose) is to create drag, and to shield the shuttle's internal structures from the intense re-entry heat by cocking the vehicle up to greet the atmosphere with leading edges made of heat-resistant carbon-composite panels, and with 24,305 insulating surface tiles, each one unique, which are glued primarily to the vehicle's underside. To regulate the sink and drag (and to control the heating), the shuttle goes through a program of sweeping S-turns, banking as steeply as 80 degrees to one side and then the other, tilting its lift vector and digging into the atmosphere. The thinking is done by redundant computers, which use onboard inertial sensing systems to gauge the shuttle's position, altitude, descent rate, and speed. The flying is done by autopilot. The cockpit crews and mission controllers play the role of observers, albeit extremely interested ones who are ready to intervene should something go wrong. In a basic sense, therefore, the re-entry is a mirror image of the launch and climb, decompressed to forty-five minutes instead of eight, but with the added complication that it will finish with the need for a landing.

Bloomfield took me through it in simulation, the two of us sitting in the cockpit to watch while an experienced flight crew and full Mission Control team brought the shuttle in from the de-orbit burn to the touchdown, dealing with a complexity of cascading system failures. Of course, in reality the automation usually performs faultlessly, and the shuttle proceeds to Florida right on track, and down the center of the desired descent profile. Bloomfield expressed surprise at how well the magic had worked on his own flights. Because he had launched on high-inclination orbits to the Russian station Mir and the International Space Station, he had not flown a *Columbia*-style re-entry over the United States, but had descended across Central America instead. He said, 'You look down over Central America, and you're so low that you can see the forests! You think, "There's no way we're going to make it to Florida!" Then you cross the west coast of Florida, and you look inside, and you're still doing Mach 5, and you think, "There's no way we're going to slow in time!"' But you do. Mach 5 is 3,500 mph. At that point the shuttle is at 117,000 feet, about 140 miles out. At Mach 2.5, or 1,650 mph, it is at 81,000 feet, about sixty miles out. At that point the crew activates the head-up displays, which project see-through flight guidance into the field of vision through the windshield. When the shuttle slows below the speed of sound, it shudders as the shock waves shift. By tradition if not necessity, the commander then takes over from the autopilot, and flies the rest of the arrival manually, using the control stick.

Bloomfield invited me to fly some simulated arrivals myself, and prompted me while I staggered around for a few landings – overhead the Kennedy Space Center at 30,000 feet with the runway and the coastal estuaries in sight below, banking left into a tight, plunging energy-management turn, rolling out onto final approach at 11,000 feet, following an extraordinarily steep, 18-degree glide slope at 345 mph, speed brakes on, pitching up through a 'preflare' at 2,000 feet to flatten the descent, landing gear out at 300 feet, touching down on the main wheels with some skips and bumps, then drag chute out, nose gear gently down, and brakes on. My efforts were crude, and greatly assisted by Bloomfield, but they gave me an impression of the shuttle as a solid, beautifully balanced flying machine that in thick air, at the end, is responsive and not difficult to handle – if everything goes just right. Bloomfield agreed. Moreover, years have passed in which everything did go just right – leaving the pilots to work on the finesse of their touchdowns, whether they were two knots fast, or 100 feet long. Bloomfield said, 'When you come back and you land, the engineers will pull out their charts and they'll say things like "The boundary layer tripped on the left wing before the right one. Did you feel anything?" And the answer is always "Well . . . no. It was an incredibly smooth ride all the way down."' But then, on the morning of February 1, something went really wrong – something too radical for simulation, that offered the pilots no chance to fly – and the *Columbia* lay scattered for 300 miles across the ground.

The foam did it. That much was suspected from the start, and all the evidence converged on it as the CAIB's investigation proceeded through the months that followed. The foam was dense and dry; it was the brownish-orange coating applied to the outside of the shuttle's large external tank to insulate the extreme cold of the rocket fuel inside from the warmth and moisture of the air. Eighty-two seconds after liftoff, as the *Columbia* was accelerating through 1,500 mph, a piece of that foam – about nineteen inches long by eleven inches wide, weighing about 1.7 pounds – broke off from the external tank and collided with the left wing at about 545 mph. Cameras near the launch site recorded the event – though the images when viewed the following day provided insufficient detail to know the exact impact point, or the consequences. The CAIB's investigation ultimately found that a gaping hole about ten inches across had been punched into the wing's leading edge, and that sixteen days later the hole allowed the hot gases of the re-entry to penetrate the wing and consume it from the inside. Through enormous effort this would be discovered and verified beyond doubt. It was important nonetheless to explore the alternatives. In an effort closely supervised by the CAIB, groups of NASA engineers created several thousand flow charts, one for each scenario that could conceivably have led to the re-entry breakup. The thinking was rigorous. For a scenario to be 'closed,' meaning set aside, absolute proof had to be found (usually physical or mathematical) that this particular explanation did not apply: there was no cockpit fire, no flight-control malfunction, no act of terrorism or sabotage that had taken the shuttle down. Unexpected vulnerabilities were found during this process, and even after the investigation was formally concluded, in late August, more than a hundred scenarios remained technically open, because they could not positively be closed. For lack of evidence to the contrary, for instance, neither bird strikes nor micrometeorite impacts could be completely ruled out.

But for all their willingness to explore less likely alternatives, many of NASA's managers remained stubbornly closed-minded on the subject of foam. From the earliest telemetric data it was known that intense heat inside the left wing had destroyed the *Columbia*, and that such heat could have gotten there only through a hole. The connection between the hole and the foam strike was loosely circumstantial at first, but it required serious consideration nonetheless. NASA balked at going down that road. Its reasons were not rational and scientific but, rather, complex and cultural, and they turned out to be closely related to the errors that had led to the accident in the first place: simply put, it had become a matter of faith within NASA that foam strikes – which were a known problem – could not cause mortal damage to the shuttle. Sean O'Keefe, who was badly advised by his NASA lieutenants, made unwise public statements deriding the 'foamologists'; and even Ron Dittemore, NASA's technically expert shuttle program manager, joined in with categorical denials.

At the CAIB, Gehman, who was not unsympathetic to NASA, watched these reactions with growing skepticism and a sense of *déjà vu*. Over his years in the Navy, and as a result of the *Cole* inquiry, he had become something of a student of large organizations under stress. To me he said, 'It has been scorched into my mind that bureaucracies will do anything to defend themselves. It's not evil – it's just a natural reaction of bureaucracies, and since NASA is a bureaucracy, I expect the same out of them. As we go through the investigation, I've been looking for signs where the system is trying to defend itself.' Of those signs the most obvious was this display of blind faith by an organization dependent on its engineering cool; NASA, in its absolute certainty, was unintentionally signaling the very problem that it had. Gehman had seen such certainty proved wrong too many times, and he told me that he was not about to get 'rolled by the system,' as he had been rolled before. He said, 'Now when I hear NASA telling me things like "Gotta be true!" or "We know this to be true!" all my alarm bells go off . . . Without hurting anybody's feelings, or squashing people's egos, we're having to say, "We're sorry, but we're not accepting that answer."'

That was the form that the physical investigation took on, with hundreds of NASA engineers and technicians doing most of the detailed work, and the CAIB watching closely and increasingly stepping in. Despite what Gehman said, it was inevitable that feelings got hurt and egos squashed – and indeed that serious damage to people's lives and careers was inflicted. At the NASA facilities dedicated to shuttle operations (Alabama for rockets, Florida for launch and landing, Texas for management and mission control) the CAIB investigators were seen as invaders of sorts, unwelcome strangers arriving to pass judgment on people's good-faith efforts. On the ground level, where the detailed analysis was being done, there was active resistance at first, with some NASA engineers openly refusing to cooperate, or to allow access to records and technical documents that had not been pre-approved for release. Gehman had to intervene. One of the toughest and most experienced of the CAIB investigators later told me he had a gut sense that NASA continued to hide relevant information, and that it does so to this day. But cooperation between the two groups gradually improved as friendships were made, and the intellectual challenges posed by the inquiry began to predominate over fears about what had happened or what might follow. As so often occurs, it was on an informal basis that information flowed best, and that much of the truth was discovered.

Board member Steven Wallace described the investigation not as a linear path but as a picture that gradually filled in. Or as a jigsaw puzzle. The search for debris began the first day, and soon swelled to include more than 25,000 people, at a cost of well over $300 million. NASA received 1,459 debris reports, including some from nearly every state in the union, and also from Canada, Jamaica, and the Bahamas. Discounting the geographic extremes, there was still a lot to follow up on. Though the amateur videos showed pieces separating from the shuttle along the entire path over the United States, and though search parties backtracked all the way to the Pacific coast in the hope of finding evidence of the breakup's triggering mechanism, the westernmost piece found on the ground was a left-wing tile that landed near a town called Littlefield, in the Texas Panhandle. Not surprisingly, the bulk of the wreckage lay under the main breakup, from south of Dallas eastward across the rugged, snake-infested brushland of East Texas and into Louisiana; and that is where most of the search took place. The best work was done on foot, by tough and dedicated crews who walked in tight lines across several thousand square miles. Their effort became something of a close sampling of the American landscape, turning up all sorts of odds and ends, including a few apparent murder victims, plenty of junked cars, and the occasional clandestine meth lab. More to the point, it also turned up crew remains and more than 84,000 pieces of the *Columbia*, which, at 84,900 pounds, accounted for 38 percent of the vehicle's dry weight. Certain pieces that had splashed into the murky waters of lakes and reservoirs were never found. It was presumed that most if not all the remaining pieces had been vaporized by the heat of re-entry, either before or after the breakup.

Some of the shuttle's contents survived intact. For instance, a vacuum cleaner still worked, as did some computers and printers and a Medtronic Tono-Pen, used to measure ocular pressure. A group of worms from one of the science experiments not only survived but continued to multiply. Most of the debris, however, was a twisted mess. The recovered pieces were meticulously plotted and tagged, and transported to a hangar at the Kennedy Space Center, where the wing remnants were laid out in correct position on the floor, and what had been found of the left wing's reinforced carbon-carbon (RCC) leading edge was reconstructed in a transparent Plexiglas mold – though with large gaps where pieces were missing. The hangar was a quiet, poignant, intensely focused place, with many of the same NASA technicians who had prepared the *Columbia* for flight now involved in the sad task of handling its ruins. The assembly and analysis went on through the spring. One of the principal CAIB agents there was an affable Air Force pilot named Patrick Goodman, an experienced accident investigator who had made both friends and enemies at NASA for the directness of his approach. When I first met him, outside the hangar on a typically warm and sunny Florida day, he explained some of the details that I had just seen on the inside – heat-eroded tiles, burned skin and structure, and aluminum slag that had emerged in molten form from inside the left wing, and had been deposited onto the aft rocket pods. The evidence was complicated because it resulted from combinations of heat, physical forces, and wildly varying airflows that had occurred before, during, and after the main-body breakup, but for Goodman it was beginning to read like a map. He had faith. He said, 'We know what we have on the ground. It's the truth. The debris is the truth, if we can only figure out what it's saying. It's not a theoretical model. It exists.' Equally important was the debris that did not exist, most significantly large parts of the left wing, including the lower part of a section of the RCC leading edge, a point known as Panel Eight, which was approximately where the launch cameras showed that the foam had hit. Goodman said, 'We look at what we don't have. What we do have. What's on what we have. We start from there, and try to work backward up the timeline, always trying to see the previous significant event.' He called this 'looking uphill.' It was like a movie run in reverse, with the found pieces springing off the ground and flying upward to a point of reassembly above Dallas, and then the *Columbia*, looking nearly whole, flying tail-first toward California, picking up the Littlefield tile as it goes, and then higher again, through entry interface over the Pacific, through orbits flown in reverse, inverted but nose first, and then back down toward earth, picking up the external tank and the solid rocket boosters during the descent, and settling tail-first with rockets roaring, until just before a vertical touchdown a spray of pulverized foam appears below, pulls together at the left-wing leading edge, and rises to lodge itself firmly on the side of the external tank.

The foam did it.

There was plenty of other evidence, too. After the accident the Air Force dug up routine radar surveillance tapes that upon close inspection showed a small object floating alongside the *Columbia* on the second day of its mission. The object slowly drifted away and disappeared from view. Subsequent testing of radar profiles and ballistic coefficients for a multitude of objects found a match for only one – a fragment of RCC panel of at least 140 square inches. The match never quite passed muster as proof, but investigators presumed that the object was a piece of the leading edge, that it had been shoved into the inside of the wing by the impact of the foam, and that during maneuvering in orbit it had floated free. The picture by now was rapidly filling in.

But the best evidence was numerical. It so happened that because the *Columbia* was the first of the operational shuttles, it was equipped with hundreds of additional engineering sensors that fed into an onboard data-collection device, a box known as a modular auxiliary data system, or MADS recorder, that was normally used for post-flight analysis of the vehicle's performance. During the initial debris search this box was not found, but such was its potential importance that after careful calculation of its likely ballistic path, another search was mounted, and on March 19 it was discovered – lying in full view on ground that had been gone over before. The really surprising thing was its condition. Though the recorder was not designed to be crash-proof, and used Mylar tape that was vulnerable to heat, it had survived the breakup and fall completely intact, as had the data that it contained, the most interesting of which pertained to heat rises and sequential sensor failures inside the left wing. When combined with the telemetric data that already existed, and with calculations of the size and location of the sort of hole that might have been punched through the leading edge by the foam, the new data allowed for a good fit with computational models of the theoretical airflow and heat propagation inside the left wing, and it steered the investigation to an inevitable conclusion that the breach must have been in the RCC at panel eight.

By early summer the picture was clear. Though strictly speaking the case was circumstantial, the evidence against the foam was so persuasive that there remained no reasonable doubt about the physical cause of the accident. As a result, Gehman gave serious consideration to NASA's request to call off a planned test of the launch incident, during which a piece of foam would be carefully fired at a fully rigged RCC Panel Eight. NASA's argument against the test had some merit: the leading-edge panels (forty-four per shuttle) are custom-made, $700,000 components, each one different from the others, and the testing would require the use of the last spare panel eight in the entire fleet. NASA said that it couldn't afford the waste, and Gehman was inclined to agree, precisely because he felt that breaking the panel would prove nothing that hadn't already been amply proved. By a twist of fate it was the sole NASA member of the CAIB, the quiet, cerebral, earnestly scientific Scott Hubbard, who insisted that the test proceed. Hubbard was one of the original seven board members. At the time of the accident he had just become the director of NASA's Ames Research Center, in California. Months later now, in the wake of Gehman's rebellion, and with the CAIB aggressively moving beyond the physical causes and into the organizational ones, he found himself in the tricky position of collaborating with a group that many of his own people at NASA saw as the enemy. Hubbard, however, had an almost childlike belief in doing the right thing, and having been given this unfortunate job, he was determined to see it through correctly. Owing to the closeness of his ties to NASA, he understood an aspect of the situation that others might have overlooked: despite overwhelming evidence to the contrary, many people at NASA continued stubbornly to believe that the foam strike on launch could not have caused the *Columbia*'s destruction. Hubbard argued that if NASA was to have any chance of self-reform, these people would have to be confronted with reality, not in abstraction but in the most tangible way possible. Gehman found the argument convincing, and so the foam shot proceeded.

The work was done in San Antonio, using a compressed-nitrogen gun with a thirty-five-foot barrel, normally used to fire dead chickens – real and artificial – against aircraft structures in bird-strike certification tests. NASA approached the test kicking and screaming all the way, insisting, for instance, that the shot be used primarily to validate an earlier debris-strike model (the so-called Crater model of strikes against the underside tiles) that had been used for decision-making during the flight, and was now known to be irrelevant. Indeed, it was because of NASA obstructionism – and specifically the illogical insistence by some of the NASA rocket engineers that the chunk of foam that had hit the wing was significantly smaller (and therefore lighter) than the video and film record showed it to be – that the CAIB and Scott Hubbard finally took direct control of the testing. There was in fact a series of foam shots, increasingly realistic according to the evolving analysis of the actual strike, that raised the stakes from a glancing blow against the underside tiles to steeper-angle hits directly against leading-edge panels. The second to last shot was a 22-degree hit against the bottom of panel six: it produced some cracks and other damage deemed too small to explain the shuttle's loss. Afterward there was some smugness at NASA, and even Sean O'Keefe, who again was badly advised, weighed in on the matter, belittling the damage. But the shot against panel six was not yet the real thing. That was saved for the precious panel eight, in a test that was painstakingly designed to duplicate (conservatively) the actual impact against the *Columbia*'s left wing, assuming a rotational 'clocking angle' 30 degrees off vertical for the piece of foam. Among the engineers who gathered to watch were many of those still living in denial. The gun fired, and the foam hit the panel at a 25-degree relative angle at about 500 mph. Immediately afterward an audible gasp went through the crowd. The foam had knocked a hole in the RCC large enough to allow people to put their heads through. Hubbard told me that some of the NASA people were close to tears. Gehman had stayed away in order to avoid the appearance of gloating. He could not keep the satisfaction out of his voice, however, when later he said to me, 'Their whole house of cards came falling down.'

NASA's house was by then what this investigation was really all about. The CAIB discovered that on the morning of January 17, the day after the launch, the low-level engineers at the Kennedy Space Center whose job was to review the launch videos and film were immediately concerned by the size and speed of the foam that had struck the shuttle. As expected of them, they compiled the imagery and disseminated it by e-mail to various shuttle engineers and managers – most significantly those in charge of the shuttle program at the Johnson Space Center. Realizing that their blurred or otherwise inadequate pictures showed nothing of the damage that might have been inflicted, and anticipating the need for such information by others, the engineers at Kennedy then went outside normal channels and on their own initiative approached the Department of Defense with a request that secret military satellites or ground-based high-resolution cameras be used to photograph the shuttle in orbit. After a delay of several days for the back-channel request to get through, the Air Force proved glad to oblige, and made the first moves to honor the request. Such images would probably have shown a large hole in the left wing – but they were never taken.

When news of the foam strike arrived in Houston, it did not seem to be crucially important. Though foam was not supposed to shed from the external tank, and the shuttle was not designed to withstand its impacts, falling foam had plagued the shuttle from the start, and indeed had caused damage on most missions. The falling foam was usually popcorn sized, too small to cause more than superficial dents in the thermal protection tiles. The CAIB, however discovered a history of more serious cases. For example, in 1988 the shuttle *Atlantis* took a heavy hit, seen by the launch cameras eighty-five seconds into the climb, nearly the same point at which the *Columbia* strike occurred. On the second day of the *Atlantis* flight Houston asked the crew to inspect the vehicle's underside with a video camera on a robotic arm (which the *Columbia* did not have). The commander, Robert 'Hoot' Gibson, told the CAIB that the belly looked as if it had been blasted with shotgun fire. The *Atlantis* returned safely anyway, but afterward was found to have lost an entire tile, exposing its bare metal belly to the re-entry heat. It was lucky that the damage had happened in a place where a heavy aluminum plate covered the skin, Gibson said, because otherwise the belly might have been burned through.

Nonetheless, over the years foam strikes had come to be seen within NASA as an 'in-family' problem, so familiar that even the most serious episodes seemed unthreatening and mundane. Douglas Osheroff, a normally good-humored Stanford physicist and Nobel laureate who joined the CAIB late, went around for months in a state of incredulity and dismay at what he was learning about NASA's operational logic. He told me that the shuttle managers acted as if they thought the frequency of the foam strikes had somehow reduced the danger that the impacts posed. His point was not that the managers really believed this but that after more than a hundred successful flights they had come blithely to accept the risk. He said, 'The excitement that only exists when there is danger was kind of gone – even though the danger was not gone.' And frankly, organizational and bureaucratic concerns weighed more heavily on the managers' minds. The most pressing of those concerns were the new performance goals imposed by Sean O'Keefe, and a tight sequence of flights leading up to a drop-dead date of February 19, 2004, for the completion of the International Space Station's 'core.' O'Keefe had made it clear that meeting this deadline was a test, and that the very future of NASA's human space-flight program was on the line.

From Osheroff's scientific perspective, deadlines based on completion of the International Space Station were inherently absurd. To me he said, 'And what would the next goal be after that? Maybe we should bring our pets up there! "I wonder how a Saint Bernard urinates in zero gravity!" NASA sold the International Space Station to Congress as a great science center – but most scientists just don't agree with that. We're thirty years from being able to go to Mars. Meanwhile, the only reason to have man in space is to study man in space. You can do that stuff – okay – and there are also some biology experiments that are kind of fun. I think we are learning things. But I would question any statement that you can come up with better drugs in orbit than you can on the ground, or that sort of thing. The truth is, the International Space Station has become a huge liability for NASA – expensive to build, expensive to fly, expensive to resupply. 'Now members of Congress are talking about letting its orbit decay – just letting it fall into the ocean. And it does turn out that orbital decay is a very good thing, because it means that near space is a self-cleaning place. I mean, garbage does not stay up there forever.'

In other words, completion of the Space Station could provide a measure of NASA's performance only in the most immediate and superficial manner, and it was therefore an inherently poor reason for shuttle managers to be ignoring the foam strikes and proceeding at full speed. It was here that you could see the limitations of leadership without vision, and the consequences of putting an executive like O'Keefe in charge of an organization that needed more than mere discipline. This, however, was hardly an argument that the managers could use, or even in private allow themselves to articulate. If the Space Station was unimportant – and perhaps even a mistake – then one had to question the reason for the shuttle's existence in the first place. Like O'Keefe and the astronauts and NASA itself, the managers were trapped by a circular space policy thirty years in the making, and they had no choice but to strive to meet the timelines directly ahead. As a result, after the most recent *Atlantis* launch, in October of 2002, during which a chunk of foam from a particularly troublesome part of the external tank, known as the 'bipod ramp,' had dented one of the solid rocket boosters, shuttle managers formally decided during the post-flight review not to classify the incident as an 'in-flight anomaly.' This was the first time that a serious bipod-ramp incident had escaped such a classification. The decision allowed the following two launches to proceed on schedule. The second of those launches was the *Columbia*'s, on January 16.

The videos of the foam strike reached Houston the next day, January 17. They made it clear that again the offending material had come from the area of the bipod ramp, that this time the foam was larger than ever before, that the impact had occurred later in the climb (meaning at higher speed), and that the wing had been hit, though exactly where was not clear. The astronauts were happily in orbit now, and had apparently not felt the impact, or been able to distinguish it from the heavy vibrations of the solid rocket boosters. In other words, they were unaware of any trouble. Responsibility for disposing of the incident lay with engineers on the ground, and specifically with the Mission Management Team, or MMT, whose purpose was to make decisions about the problems and unscripted events that inevitably arose during any flight. The MMT was a high-level group. In the Houston hierarchy it operated above the flight controllers in the Mission Control room, and just below the shuttle program manager, Ron Dittemore. Dittemore was traveling at the time, and has since retired. The MMT meetings were chaired by his protégé, the once rising Linda Ham, who has come to embody NASA's arrogance and insularity in many observers' minds. Ham is the same hard-charging manager who, with a colleague, later had to be forcefully separated from the CAIB's investigation. Within the strangely neutered engineering world of the Johnson Space Center, she was an intimidating figure, a youngish, attractive woman given to wearing revealing clothes, yet also known for a tough and domineering management style. Among the lower ranks she had a reputation for brooking no nonsense and being a little hard to talk to. She was not smooth. She was a woman struggling upward in a man's world. She was said to have a difficult personality.

As the head of the MMT, Ham responded to news of the foam strike as if it were just another item to be efficiently handled and then checked off the list: a water leak in the science lab, a radio communication failure, a foam strike on the left wing, okay, no safety-of-flight issues here – right? What's next? There was a trace of vanity in the way she ran her shows. She seemed to revel in her own briskness, in her knowledge of the shuttle systems, in her use of acronyms and the strange, stilted syntax of aerospace engineers. She was decisive, and very sure of her sense for what was important and what was not. Her style got the best of her on day six of the mission, January 21, when at a recorded MMT meeting she spoke just a few words too many, much to her later regret.

It was at the end of a report given by a mid-ranking engineer named Don McCormack, who summarized the progress of an ad hoc engineering group, called the Debris Assessment Team, that had been formed at a still lower level to analyze the foam strike. The analysis was being done primarily by Boeing engineers, who had dusted off the soon to be notorious Crater model, primarily to predict damage to the underwing tile. McCormack reported that little was yet resolved, that the quality of the Crater as a predictor was being judged against the known damage on earlier flights, and that some work was being done to explore the options should the analysis conclude that the *Columbia* had been badly wounded. After a brief exchange Ham cut him short, saying, 'And I'm really . . . I don't think there is much we can do, so it's not really a factor during the flight, since there is not much we can do about it.' She was making assumptions, of course, and they were later proved to be completely wrong, but primarily she was just being efficient, and moving the meeting along. After the accident, when the transcript and audiotapes emerged, those words were taken out of context, and used to portray Ham as a villainous and almost inhumanly callous person, which she certainly was not. In fact, she was married to an astronaut, and was as concerned as anyone about the safety of the shuttle crews. This was a dangerous business, and she knew it all too well. But like her boss, Ron Dittemore, with whom she discussed the *Columbia* foam strike several times, she was so immersed in the closed world of shuttle management that she simply did not elevate the event – this 'in-family' thing – to the level of concerns requiring action. She was intellectually arrogant, perhaps, and as a manager she failed abysmally. But neither she nor the others of her rank had the slightest suspicion that the *Columbia* might actually go down.

The frustration is that some people on lower levels were actively worried about that possibility, and they understood clearly that not enough was known about the effects of the foam strike on the wing, but they expressed their concerns mostly to one another, and for good reason, because on the few occasions when they tried to alert the decision-makers, NASA's management system overwhelmed them and allowed none of them to be heard. The question now, of course, is why.

The CAIB's search for answers began long before the technical details were resolved, and it ultimately involved hundreds of interviews and 50,000 pages of transcripts. The manner in which those interviews were conducted became a contentious issue, and it was arguably Gehman's biggest mistake. As a military man, advised by military men on the board, he decided to conduct the interviews according to a military model of safety probes, in which individual fault is not formally assigned, and the interviews themselves are 'privileged,' meaning forever sealed off from public view. It was understood that identities and deeds would not be protected from view, only individual testimonies to the CAIB, but serious critics cried foul nonetheless, and pointed out correctly that Gehman was using loopholes to escape sunshine laws that otherwise would have applied. Gehman believed that treating the testimony as privileged was necessary to encourage witnesses to talk, and to get to the bottom of the story, but the long-term effect of the investigation will be diminished as a result (for instance, by lack of access to the raw material by outside analysts), and there was widespread consensus among the experienced (largely civilian) investigators actually conducting the interviews that the promise of privacy was having little effect on what people were willing to say. These were not criminals they were talking to, or careful lawyers. For the most part they were sincere engineering types who were concerned about what had gone wrong, and would have been willing even without privacy to speak their minds. The truth, in other words, would have come out even in the brightest of sunshine.

The story that emerged was a sad and unnecessary one, involving arrogance, insularity, and bad luck allowed to run unchecked. On the seventh day of the flight, January 22, just as the Air Force began to move on the Kennedy engineers' back-channel request for photographs, Linda Ham heard to her surprise that this approach (which according to front-channel procedures would have required her approval) had been made. She immediately telephoned other high-level managers in Houston to see if any of them wanted to issue a formal 'requirement' for imagery, and when they informed her that they did not, rather than exploring the question with the Kennedy engineers she simply terminated their request with the Department of Defense. This appears to have been a purely bureaucratic reaction. A NASA liaison officer then e-mailed an apology to Air Force personnel, assuring them that the shuttle was in 'excellent shape,' and explaining that a foam strike was 'something that has happened before and is not considered to be a major problem.' The officer continued, 'The one problem that this has identified is the need for some additional coordination within NASA to assure that when a request is made it is done through the official channels.' Months later one of the CAIB investigators who had followed this trail was still seething with anger at what had occurred. He said, 'Because the problem was not identified in the traditional way – "Houston, we have a problem!" – well, then, "Houston, we don't have a problem!" Because Houston didn't identify the problem.'

But another part of Houston was doing just that. Unbeknownst to Ham and the shuttle management, the low-level engineers of the Debris Assessment Team had concluded that the launch films were not clear enough to indicate where the foam had hit, and particularly whether it had hit the underside tile or a leading-edge RCC panel. Rather than trying to run their calculations in the blind, they had decided that they should do the simple thing and have someone take a look for damage. They had already e-mailed one query to the engineering department, about the possibility of getting the astronauts themselves to take a short spacewalk and inspect the wing. It later turned out that this would have been safe and easy to do. That e-mail, however, was never answered. This time the Debris Assessment engineers decided on a still simpler solution – to ask the Department of Defense to take some high-resolution pictures. Ignorant of the fact that the Kennedy group had already made such a request, and that it had just been peevishly canceled, they sent out two requests of their own, directed, appropriately, to Ron Dittemore and Linda Ham, but through channels that were a little off-center, and happened to fail. Those channels were ones they had used in their regular work as engineers, outside the formal shuttle-management structure. By unfortunate circumstance, the request that came closest to getting through was intercepted by a mid-level employee (the assistant to an intended recipient, who was on vacation), who responded by informing the Debris Assessment engineers, more or less correctly, that Linda Ham had decided against Air Force imagery.

The confusion was now total, yet also nearly invisible – and within the suppressive culture of the human space-flight program, it had very little chance of making itself known. At the top of the tangle, neither Ron Dittemore nor Linda Ham ever learned that the Debris Assessment Team wanted pictures; at the bottom, the Debris Assessment engineers heard the 'no' without suspecting that it was not an answer to their request. They were told to go back to the Crater model and numerical analysis, and as earnest, hardworking engineers (hardly rebels, these), they dutifully complied, all the while regretting the blind assumptions that they would have to make. Given the obvious potential for a catastrophe, one might expect that they would have gone directly to Linda Ham, on foot if necessary, to make the argument in person for a spacewalk or high-resolution photos. However, such were the constraints within the Johnson Space Center that they never dared. They later said that had they made a fuss about the shuttle, they might have been singled out for ridicule. They feared for their standing, and their careers.

The CAIB investigator who asked the engineers what conclusion they had drawn at the time from management's refusal later said to me, 'They all thought, "Well, none of us have a security clearance high enough to view any of this imagery." They talked about this openly among themselves, and they figured one of three things:

'"One: The 'no' means that management's already got photos, and the damage isn't too bad. They can't show us the photos, because we don't have the security clearance, and they can't tell us they have the photos, or tell us the damage isn't bad, because that tells us how accurate the photos are – and we don't have the security clearance. But wait a minute, if that's the case, then what're we doing here? Why are we doing the analysis? So no, that can't be right.

'"Okay, then, two: They already took the photos, and the damage is so severe that there's no hope for recovery. Well . . . that can't be right either, because in that case, why are we doing the analysis?

'"Okay, then, three: They took the photos. They can't tell us they took the photos, and the photos don't give us clear definition. So we need to do the analysis. That's gotta be it!"'

What the Debris Assessment engineers could not imagine is that no photos had been taken, or ever would be – and essentially for lack of curiosity by NASA's imperious, self-convinced managers. What those managers in turn could not imagine was that people in their own house might really be concerned. The communication gap had nothing to do with security clearances, and it was complete.

Gehman explained the underlying realities to me. He said, 'They claim that the culture in Houston is a "badgeless society," meaning it doesn't matter what you have on your badge – you're concerned about shuttle safety together. Well, that's all nice, but the truth is that it does matter what badge you're wearing. Look, if you really do have an organization that has free communication and open doors and all that kind of stuff, it takes a special kind of management to make it work. And we just don't see that management here. Oh, they say all the right things. "We have open doors and e-mails, and anybody who sees a problem can raise his hand, blow a whistle, and stop the whole process." But then when you look at how it really works, it's an incestuous, hierarchical system, with invisible rankings and a very strict informal chain of command. They all know that. So even though they've got all the trappings of communication, you don't actually find communication. It's very complex. But if a person brings an issue up, what caste he's in makes all the difference. Now, again, NASA will deny this, but if you talk to people, if you really listen to people, all the time you hear "Well, I was afraid to speak up." Boy, it comes across loud and clear. You listen to the meetings: "Anybody got anything to say?" There are thirty people in the room, and slam! There's nothing. We have plenty of witness statements saying, "If I had spoken up, it would have been at the cost of my job." And if you're in the engineering department, you're a nobody.'

One of the CAIB investigators told me that he asked Linda Ham, 'As a manager, how do you seek out dissenting opinions?'

According to him, she answered, 'Well, when I hear about them . . .'

He interrupted. 'Linda, by their very nature you may not hear about them.'

'Well, when somebody comes forward and tells me about them.'

'But Linda, what techniques do you use to get them?'

He told me she had no answer.

This was certainly not the sort of risk-versus-risk decision-making that Michael Bloomfield had in mind when he described the thinking behind his own shuttle flights.

At 7:00 AM on the ninth day, January 24, which was one week before the *Columbia's* scheduled re-entry, the engineers from the Debris Assessment Team formally presented the results of their numerical analysis to Linda Ham's intermediary, Don McCormack. The room was so crowded with concerned observers that some people stood in the hall, peering in. The fundamental purpose of the meeting would have been better served had the engineers been able to project a photograph of a damaged wing onto the screen, but, tragically, that was not to be. Instead they projected a typically crude PowerPoint summary, based on the results from the Crater model, with which they attempted to explain a nuanced position: first, that if the tile had been damaged, it had probably endured well enough to allow the *Columbia* to come home; and second, that for lack of information they had needed to make assumptions to reach that conclusion, and that troubling unknowns therefore limited the meaning of the results. The latter message seems to have been lost. Indeed, this particular Power-Point presentation became a case study for Edward Tufte, the brilliant communications specialist from Yale, who in a subsequent booklet, *The Cognitive Style of PowerPoint*, tore into it for its dampening effect on clear expression and thought. The CAIB later joined in, describing the widespread use of PowerPoint within NASA as one of the obstacles to internal communication, and criticizing the Debris Assessment presentation for mechanically underplaying the uncertainties that remained. Had the uncertainties been more strongly expressed as the central factor in question, the need to inspect the wing by spacewalk or photograph might have become obvious even to the shuttle managers. Still, the Mission Management Team seemed unprepared to hear nuance. Fixated on potential tile damage as the relevant question, assuming without good evidence that the RCC panels were strong enough to withstand a foam strike, subtly skewing the discussion away from catastrophic burn-through and toward the potential effects on turnaround times on the ground and how that might affect the all-important launch schedule, the shuttle managers were convinced that they had the situation as they defined it firmly under control.

At a regularly scheduled MMT meeting later that morning McCormack summarized the PowerPoint presentation for Linda Ham. He said, 'The analysis is not complete. There is one case yet that they wish to run, but kind of just jumping to the conclusion of all that, they do show that [there is], obviously, a potential for significant tile damage here, but thermal analysis does not indicate that there is potential for a burn-through. I mean, there could be localized heating damage. There is . . . obviously there is a lot of uncertainty in all this in terms of the size of the debris and where it hit and the angle of incidence.'

Ham answered, 'No burn-through means no catastrophic damage. And the localized heating damage would mean a tile replacement?'

'Right, it would mean possible impacts to turnaround repairs and that sort of thing, but we do not see any kind of safety-of-flight issue here yet in anything that we've looked at.'

This was all too accurate in itself. Ham said, 'And no safety of flight, no issue for this mission, nothing that we're going to do different. There may be a turnaround [delay].'

McCormack said, 'Right. It could potentially [have] hit the RCC . . . We don't see any issue if it hit the RCC . . .'

The discussion returned to the tiles. Ham consulted with a tile specialist named Calvin Schomburg, who for days had been energetically making a case independent of the Debris Assessment analysis that a damaged tile would endure re-entry – and thereby adding, unintentionally, to the distractions and false assumptions of the management team. After a brief exchange Ham cut off further discussion with a quick summary for some people participating in the meeting by conference call, who were having trouble hearing the speakerphone. She said, 'So, no safety-of-flight kind of issue. It's more of a turnaround issue similar to what we've had on other flights. That's it? All right, any questions on that?'

And there were not.

For reasons unexplained, when the official minutes of the meeting were written up and distributed (having been signed off on by Ham), all mention of the foam strike was omitted. This was days before the *Columbia*'s re-entry, and seems to indicate sheer lack of attention to this subject, rather than any sort of cover-up.

The truth is that Linda Ham was as much a victim of NASA as were *Columbia*'s astronauts, who were still doing their science experiments then, and free-falling in splendor around the planet. Her predicament had roots that went way back, nearly to the time of her birth, and it involved not only the culture of the human space-flight program but also the White House, Congress, and NASA leadership over the past thirty years. Gehman understood this fully, and as the investigation drew to a close, he vowed to avoid merely going after the people who had been standing close to the accident when it occurred. The person standing closest was, of course, Linda Ham, and she will bear a burden for her mismanagement. But by the time spring turned to summer, and the CAIB moved its operation from Houston to Washington, D.C., Gehman had taken to saying, 'Complex systems fail in complex ways,' and he was determined that the CAIB's report would document the full range of NASA's mistakes. It did, and in clean, frank prose, using linked sentences and no PowerPoint displays.

As the report was released, on August 26, Mars came closer to earth than it had in 60,000 years. Gehman told me that he continued to believe in the importance of America's human space-flight effort, and even of the return of the shuttle to flight – at least until a replacement with a clearer mission can be built and put into service. It was a quiet day in Washington, with Congress in recess and the President on vacation. Aides were coming from Capitol Hill to pick up several hundred copies of the report and begin planning hearings for the fall. The White House was receiving the report too, though keeping a cautious distance, as had been expected; it was said that the President might read an executive summary. Down in Houston, board members were handing copies to the astronauts, the managers, and the families of the dead.

Gehman was dressed in a suit, as he had been at the start of all this, seven months before. It was up to him now to drive over to NASA headquarters, in the southwest corner of the city, and deliver the report personally to Sean O'Keefe. I went along for the ride, as did the board member Sheila Widnall, who was there to lend Gehman some moral support. The car was driven by a Navy officer in whites. At no point since the accident had anyone at NASA stepped forward to accept personal responsibility for contributing to this accident – not Linda Ham, not Ron Dittemore, and certainly not Sean O'Keefe. However, the report in Gehman's hands (248 pages, full color, well bound) made responsibility very clear. This was not going to be a social visit. Indeed, it turned out to be extraordinarily tense. Gehman and Widnall strode up the carpeted hallways in a phalanx of anxious, dark-suited NASA staffers, who swung open the doors in advance and followed close on their heels. O'Keefe's office suite was practically imperial in its expense and splendor. High officials stood in small, nervous groups, murmuring. After a short delay O'Keefe appeared – a tall, balding, gray-haired man with stooped shoulders. He shook hands and ushered Gehman and Widnall into the privacy of his inner office. Ten minutes later they emerged. There was a short ceremony for NASA cameras, during which O'Keefe thanked Gehman for his important contribution, and then it was time to leave. As we drove away, I asked Gehman how it had been in there with O'Keefe.

He said 'Stiff. Very stiff.'

We talked about the future. The report had made a series of recommendations for getting the shuttle back into flight, and beyond that for beginning NASA's long and necessary process of reform. I knew that Gehman, along with much of the board, had volunteered to Congress to return in a year, to peer in deeply again, and to try to judge if progress had been made. I asked him how genuine he thought such progress could be, and he managed somehow to express hope, though skeptically.

By January 23, the *Columbia's* eighth day in orbit, the crew had solved a couple of minor system problems, and after a half day off, during which no doubt some of the astronauts took the opportunity for some global sightseeing, they were proceeding on schedule with their laboratory duties, and were in good spirits and health. They had been told nothing of the foam strike. Down in Houston, the flight controllers at Mission Control were aware of it, and they knew that the previous day Linda Ham had canceled the request for Air Force photographs. Confident that the issue would be satisfactorily resolved by the shuttle managers, they decided nonetheless to inform the flight crew by e-mail – if only because certain reporters at the Florida launch site had heard of it, and might ask questions at an upcoming press conference, a Public Affairs Office, or PAO, event. The e-mail was written by one of the lead flight controllers, in the standard, overly upbeat style. It was addressed to the pilots, Rick Husband and William McCool. Under the subject line 'info: Possible PAO Event Question,' it read:

Rick and Willie,

You guys are doing a fantastic job staying on the timeline and accomplishing great science. Keep up the good work and let us know if there is anything that we can do better from an MCC/POCC standpoint.

There is one item that I would like to make you aware of for the upcoming PAO event . . . This item is not even worth mentioning other than wanting to make sure that you are not surprised by it in a question from a reporter.

The e-mail then briefly explained what the launch pictures had shown – a hit from the bipod-ramp foam. A video clip was attached. The e-mail concluded,

Experts have reviewed the high speed photography and there is no concern for RCC or tile damage. We have seen this same phenomenon on several other flights and there is absolutely no concern for entry. That is all for now. It's a pleasure working with you every day.

The e-mail's content honestly reflected what was believed on the ground, though in a repackaged and highly simplified form. There was no mention of the inadequate quality of the pictures, of the large size of the foam, of the ongoing analysis, or of Linda Ham's decision against Air Force imagery. This was typical for Mission Control communications, a small example of a long-standing pattern of something like information-hoarding that was instinctive and a matter as much of style as of intent: the astronauts had been told of the strike, but almost as if they were children who didn't need to be involved in the grown-up conversation. Two days later, when Rick Husband answered the e-mail, he wrote, 'Thanks a million!' and 'Thanks for the great work!' and after making a little joke, that 'Main Wing' could sound like a Chinese name, he signed off with an e-mail smile—:). He made no mention of the foam strike at all. And with that, as we now know, the crew's last chance for survival faded away.

Linda Ham was wrong. Had the hole in the leading edge been seen, actions could have been taken to try to save the astronauts' lives. The first would have been simply to buy some time. Assuming a starting point on the fifth day of the flight, NASA engineers subsequently calculated that by requiring the crew to rest and sleep, the mission could have been extended to a full month, to February 15. During that time the *Atlantis*, which was already being prepared for a scheduled March 1 launch, could have been processed more quickly by ground crews working around the clock, and made ready to go by February 10. If all had proceeded perfectly, there would have been a five-day window in which to blast off, join up with the *Columbia*, and transfer the stranded astronauts one by one to safety, by means of tethered spacewalks. Such a rescue would not have been easy, and it would have involved the possibility of another fatal foam strike and the loss of two shuttles instead of one; but in the risk-versus-risk world of space flight, veterans like Mike Bloomfield would immediately have volunteered, and NASA would have bet the farm.

The fallback would have been a desperate measure – a jury-rigged repair performed by the *Columbia* astronauts themselves. It would have required two spacewalkers to fill the hole with a combination of heavy tools and metal scraps scavenged from the crew compartment, and to supplement that mass with an ice bag shaped to the wing's leading edge. In theory, if much of the payload had been jettisoned, and luck was with the crew, such a repair might perhaps have endured a modified re-entry and allowed the astronauts to bail out at the standard 30,000 feet. The engineers who came up with this plan realized that in reality it would have been extremely dangerous, and might well have led to a high-speed burn-through and the loss of the crew. But anything would have been better than attempting a normal re-entry as it was actually flown.

The blessing, if one can be found, is that the astronauts remained unaware until nearly the end. A home video shot on board and found in the wreckage documented the relaxed mood in the cockpit as the shuttle descended through the entry interface at 400,000 feet, at 7:44:09 Houston time, northwest of Hawaii. The astronauts were drinking water in anticipation of gravity's redistributive effect on their bodies. The *Columbia* was flying at the standard 40-degree nose-up angle, with its wings level, and still doing nearly 17,000 mph; outside, though the air was ultra-thin and dynamic pressures were very low, the aerodynamic surfaces were beginning to move in conjunction with the array of control jets, which were doing the main work of maintaining the shuttle's attitude, and would throughout the re-entry. The astronauts commented like sightseers as sheets of fiery plasma began to pass by the windows.

The pilot, McCool, said, 'Do you see it over my shoulder now, Laurel?'

Sitting behind him, the mission specialist Laurel Clark said, 'I was filming. It doesn't show up nearly as much at the back.'

McCool said to the Israeli payload specialist, Ilan Ramon, 'It's going pretty good now. Ilan, it's really neat – it's a bright orange-yellow out over the nose, all around the nose.'

The commander, Husband, said, 'Wait until you start seeing the swirl patterns out your left or right windows.'

McCool said, 'Wow.'

Husband said, 'Looks like a blast furnace.'

A few seconds later they began to feel gravity. Husband said, 'Let's see here . . . look at that.'

McCool answered, 'Yup, we're getting some Gs.' As if it were unusual, he said, 'I let go of the card, and it falls.' Their instruments showed that they were experiencing one hundredth of a G. McCool looked out the window again. He said, 'This is amazing. It's really getting, uh, fairly bright out there.'

Husband said, 'Yup. Yeah, you definitely don't want to be outside now.'

The flight engineer, Kalpana Chawla, answered sardonically, 'What – like we did before?' The crew laughed.

Outside, the situation was worse than they imagined. Normally, as a shuttle streaks through the upper atmosphere it heats the air immediately around it to temperatures as high as 10,000°, but largely because of the boundary layer – a sort of air cushion created by the leading edges – the actual surface temperatures are significantly lower, generally around 3,000°, which the vehicle is designed to withstand, if barely. The hole in the *Columbia*'s leading edge, however, had locally undermined the boundary layer, and was now letting in a plume of superheated air that was cutting through insulation and working its way toward the inner recesses of the left wing. It is estimated that the plume may have been as hot as 8,000° near the RCC breach. The aluminum support structures inside the wing had a melting point of 1,200°, and they began to burn and give way.

The details of the left wing's failure are complex and technical, but the essentials are not difficult to understand. The wing was attacked by a snaking plume of hot gas, and eaten up from the inside. The consumption began when the shuttle was over the Pacific, and it grew worse over the United States. It included wire bundles leading from the sensors, which caused the data going into the MADS recorder and the telemetry going to Houston to fail in ways that only later made sense. At some point the plume blew right through the top of the left wing, and began to throw molten metal from the insides all over the aft rocket pods. At some point it burned its way into the left main gear well, but it did not explode the tires.

As drag increased on the left wing, the autopilot and combined flight-control systems at first easily compensated for the resulting tendency to roll and yaw to the left. By external appearance, therefore, the shuttle was doing its normal thing, banking first to the right and then to the left for the scheduled energy-management turns, and tracking perfectly down the descent profile for Florida. The speeds were good, the altitudes were good, and all systems were functioning correctly. From within the cockpit the ride appeared to be right.

By the time it got to Texas the *Columbia* had already proved itself a heroic flying machine, having endured for so long at hypersonic speeds with little left of the midsection inside its left wing, and the plume of hot gas still in there, alive, and eating it away. By now, however, the flight-control systems were nearing their limits. The breakup was associated with that. At 7:59:15 Mission Control noticed the sudden loss of tire pressure on the left gear as the damage rapidly progressed. This was followed by Houston's call 'And *Columbia*, Houston, we see your tire-pressure messages, and we did not copy your last call,' and at 7:59:32 by *Columbia*'s final transmission, 'Roger, ah, buh . . .'

The *Columbia* was traveling at 12,738 mph, at 200,000 feet, and the dynamic pressures were building, with the wings 'feeling' the air at about 170 mph. Now, suddenly, the bottom surface of the left wing began to cave upward into the interior void of melted and burned-through bracing and structure. As the curvature of the wing changed, the lift increased, causing the *Columbia* to want to roll violently to the right; at the same time, because of an increase in asymmetrical drag, it yawed violently to the left. The control systems went to their limits to maintain order, and all four right yaw jets on the tail fired simultaneously, but to no avail. At 8:00:19 the Columbia rolled over the top and went out of control.

The gyrations it followed were complex combinations of roll, yaw, and pitch, and looked something like an oscillating flat spin. They seem to have resulted in the vehicle's flying backwards. At one point the autopilot appears to have been switched off and then switched on again, as if Husband, an experienced test pilot, was trying to sort things out. The breakup lasted more than a minute. Not surprisingly, the left wing separated first. Afterward the tail, the right wing, and the main body came apart in what investigators later called a controlled sequence 'right down the track.' As had happened with the *Challenger* in 1986, the crew cabin broke off intact. It assumed a stable flying position, apparently nose high, and later disintegrated like a falling star across the East Texas sky.

# 9

## *The Devil at 37,000 Feet*

What were the odds? There were so many chances for the accident not to occur – so many ways to break the chain that led to it – that a crash investigator later told me it seemed the Devil himself was at play. The men responsible were American pilots and Brazilian air-traffic controllers working the high-altitude jet routes above the Amazon basin in central Brazil. If these were not the sharpest guys around, they were ordinary for the type, until then functional enough, and not so stupid that stupidity alone can explain the disaster that they brought about. It was Friday, September 29, 2006, toward the end of the dry season in northern Mato Grosso State, where the Amazon jungle reaches south along the broad, brown Xingu River. The sky that afternoon was pale and hot. Dolphins swam in the river, as they always have. Turtles lazed on the banks. On the rough dirt road that cuts for hundreds of miles through the forests and clearings, a few vehicles crept along as usual, boiling the dust in second gear and drifting clouds of it across the occasional settlements. The road has a federal designation, BR-80, but it is less a road than a track. It leads from nowhere to the same. During the rainy season it becomes nearly impassable. The settlers who followed it into the jungle call themselves the Forgotten Ones. Those who feel superior to the Indians nearby seem nonetheless resigned to low ambitions in life. When strangers drive by, the settlers pause to watch. This and television pass for entertainment. Otherwise most days go by like all the others. September 29 was a day like those, too. There were no strangers on the ground that I know of. If there was any sense of urgency, it was in the late afternoon, when the few drivers within range of the Xingu River crossing began pushing to make the final ferry, at sundown.

The crossing is in the heart of Caiapó Indian territory, a large and densely forested reserve. The ferry is a barge side-tied to a small tugboat piloted by taciturn Indians. The ferry operation is their only source of income beyond government handouts. The main village is nearby. About 300 Caiapós live there in airy thatch-roofed huts that are tidier than the squalid shacks of the Forgotten Ones. They paint their bodies with geometric designs, but wear Western clothes on top. Some have a penchant for camouflage shirts. Some stretch their lower lips around lip plates. It is an impractical fashion, which makes spitting hard. The men call themselves 'warriors,' which must do something for their pride. They are hunters and fishermen who go disappearing into the jungle for days at a time. The women stay home, where they tend to the children and village chores. The village is noisy because of all the comings and goings, the babies who cry, and the constant din of chickens. But on the afternoon of September 29, about a minute before 5 PM, two women who had gone into the silence by a stream to wash heard a single roll of heavy thunder. The thunder was strange because the sky was clear. The women returned to the village and reported what they had heard.

In the aftermath the press made much of this Caiapó group, describing them as people close to nature and therefore pure, and with experience so limited to their traditional ways that they understand airplanes as distant iron birds. The reality is more complex. I counted five satellite television dishes in the village, and, out beyond an imposing schoolhouse, found a groomed dirt runway long enough to accommodate high-performance turboprops. The Caiapós certainly know what airplanes are. In fact their leader, a heavyset man named Megaron, sometimes gets around on government-paid chartered ones, and several years ago was flown to New York by the musician Sting to join a campaign for the preservation of Indian lands. Sitting in a council space in the shade of trees, Megaron described his arrival in New York to me – looking out his window and seeing other airplanes in flight, and then watching them land, one after the other, just minutes apart. He had been impressed by the performance of New York air traffic control. So much for the 'iron bird' part of the story. Nonetheless, it is true that the Caiapós are not sold on modernity as it is typically defined. They have not, for instance, been Christianized or persuaded to abandon their traditional beliefs, which include the proximity of a parallel world 'on the other side,' roamed by the souls of the sudden-dead, with whom only a shaman can talk. Was it possible that the thunder had escaped from there? In some sense it had. But to ride in airplanes is not to have them foremost in mind. No one among the Caiapós imagined that the thunder was the sound of a Boeing 737 hitting the ground. The same bewilderment afflicted others within earshot of the impact. To the west of Caiapó territory, at the headquarters of a 21,000-head cattle ranch called Fazenda Jarinã, many of the employees heard the thunder and could make nothing of it. The manager of Fazenda Jarinã is a small, lonely man named Ademir Riebero, who told me he knew that the north–south traffic between Manaus and Brasília passes high overhead, and that at night you can hear the airplanes and see their lights. On the evening of September 29, however, when he heard talk of the unexplained thunder, he did not wonder if one had crashed. To me he said, 'We just couldn't imagine it could happen here. Only in São Paulo or places like that.' Indeed, the airplanes that passed overhead were in the least critical phase of flight, cruising high and straight through the cold clean sky, unstressed, and organically resistant to almost any error their crews might make. But then Riebero received a radiophone call from an official he knew, who said, 'Ademir, there is a Gol airplane that has disappeared, and it seems to have gone down near you.' Gol is a discount airline named after the drawn-out victory cry in soccer – G-O-O-O-O-L!!!

Riebero switched on the television news and saw a map labeled Jarinã on the screen. It was odd how this authenticated the situation in his mind. From the lack of reports from the outstations, he surmised that the airplane had not crashed on the ranch's holdings. But given the size and density of the bordering jungle, it was not surprising that an entire Boeing could have disappeared.

Later that night, with more radiophone calls coming in, Riebero heard that workers at the neighboring farm had seen an airplane fall. These are the only known eyewitnesses to the accident. The farm where they live and work is small compared with Fazenda Jarinã, but large nonetheless. As something of a plaything it is luxurious and extremely well kept. It belongs to a twenty-four-year-old man in São Paulo, to whom it was gifted by his grandfather. Being rich can be especially pleasant in Brazil – and the Amazon, let's face it, looks better after it is cut down. The workers were laying a new brick wall when they heard a roar and spotted the Boeing perhaps a dozen miles to the east. It was pointed straight down and seemed to be wobbling and trailing a cloud. At that distance the airplane looked just a few inches long. It disappeared over a tree line and into the forests beyond. No dust or smoke rose into the sky. Some seconds later came the thunder. The workers ran to find their boss, who hurried to a radio and made the first call. That night people at the farm had a hard time sleeping.

Riebero had a long night as well. The Brazilian Air Force called asking to use Fazenda Jariná for rescue and recovery operations once the airplane was found. Riebero acquiesced because the ranch had the facilities to handle a crowd. God willing, the crowd would include survivors. At 11 PM a four-engine Hercules lumbered overhead and began searching through the darkness to the east, ultimately without success: the Boeing's emergency locator transmitter had apparently failed, because no homing signal was received. The Air Force kept calling Riebero to keep him abreast. Riebero finally switched off the radiophone to catch some rest. He got up at dawn. For a while the morning was calm, but at 8:30 another Hercules flew low overhead, equipped with a magnetometer of use in detecting metal masses. At 9 AM, Riebero heard that the wreckage had been found. It lay in heavy forest on Caiapó territory, and was almost impossible to see from above. Air Force helicopters began to settle onto the ranch's soccer field. A rescue team went out, rappelled down to the crash site, and came back with the news that there would be no survivors. The scene was grim. One hundred and fifty-four people had died. They were innocent men, women, and children. People are insignificant blips on the scale of history, but these had not died peacefully, as one might wish. They had endured a period of absolute terror, and had been torn apart by the force of the impact. It was the worst accident in Brazil's long aviation history.

*

The recovery operation began with the clearing of a helipad in the forest. When word came to the Caiapós that the Boeing lay on their land, Megaron mobilized twenty-two men – warriors all – and drove to Fazenda Jarinã, where they launched two aluminum boats into the Jarinã River and set off downstream, a full day's travel to the site. The Caiapós wanted to help. Their shaman was with them. The heavens had rained ruin into their trees. They did not believe that people are insignificant blips in history. They believed that in a parallel world in the forest 154 tortured souls were crying out for tending.

A thousand miles to the south on the afternoon of September 29, a few hours before the Boeing's impact, two American pilots were preparing to fly home in a brand-new business jet made by the Brazilian manufacturer Embraer. The airplane stood gleaming in the sunshine at the Embraer plant in São José dos Campos, near São Paulo. It was a Legacy 600, an imposing $25 million beauty capable of accommodating thirteen passengers in luxury at 41,000 feet, at more than 500 miles an hour, and, with a reduced passenger load, of flying 3,700 miles between stops. The Legacy occupies a position toward the high end of private jets – among airplanes like Gulfstreams, Challengers, and Falcons – which by political, ethical, and environmental measures are abhorrent creations, but which nonetheless are masterworks of personal transportation. The Legacy weighs 50,000 pounds fully loaded, and is powered by twin Rolls-Royce turbofan engines mounted aft against the fuselage, delivering a total of 16,000 pounds of thrust at a price to the atmosphere and global oil reserves of about 300 gallons an hour. It has a high T-tail and thin swept-back wings which span 69 feet and turn upward at the tips into graceful winglets – six-foot vertical extensions meant to tame the airflow and improve efficiency (entirely in relative terms). It has a cockpit with the latest in electronics and instrumentation, including a Flight Management System computer, ultra-accurate GPS receivers, strong radios, a superb autopilot, and the ultimate in onboard collision-avoidance devices. It has a cabin equipped with a full galley (personal flight attendant suggested), an entertainment system, a satellite phone, a large lavatory, and three distinct seating areas, including one in the back that can be converted into a private bedroom. If you insist on treating yourself really well, and at considerable cost, flying in a Legacy comes highly recommended.

This one had been bought by a Long Island-based aircraft-management company called ExcelAire, which planned to charter it out as a global air taxi. It had been given an American registration, N600XL, which in radio phonetics would become November Six Hundred X-ray Lima. The 'XL' referred to ExcelAire. Over the days preceding the homeward flight, four company employees had inspected the airplane before consummating the purchase. The employees included two ExcelAire vice presidents and the flight crew – the captain, Joseph Lepore, aged forty-two, and his copilot, Jan Paul Paladino, age thirty-four. Lepore had a reputation for being a pleasant man who had always wanted only to fly; Paladino was said to be more articulate and perhaps to have a quicker mind. Neither pilot spoke Portuguese or demonstrated much enthusiasm for Brazil beyond the standard stuff about Rio de Janeiro. Judging from the cockpit voice recordings captured by the Legacy's black box and later recovered by investigators, their English was New York-accented – and no less so when they enunciated for the locals. In the recordings, they didn't enunciate often. But so what – English is aviation's lingua franca, controllers everywhere are required to speak it to non-native pilots, air-traffic procedures are much the same globally, and Lepore and Paladino had signed on to fly airplanes, not wander around contemplating cultural nuances.

These were the same pilots later pilloried in the press for having dropped off the radar to stunt-fly over the Amazon – an accusation that was ridiculous from the start and was soon disproved by the records of their flight. Lepore and Paladino were not the joyriding type. In fact, quite the opposite. Beneath their cockpit banter, they come across in the voice recordings as almost childishly dutiful toward their superiors and their job. In that sense they represented the industry ideal. They were also experienced pilots and officially qualified to handle an airplane of this kind. In the United States they had recently completed Legacy training at FlightSafety International, the world's best-known private-jet flight school, where they had demonstrated proficiency in the various check-box categories. FlightSafety training is classroom and simulator-based. It is also stilted and formalistic – designed to impress bureaucracies as much as to impart knowledge to pilots – and is therefore less useful than it pretends to be. It is not, however, without value, and ExcelAire had gone still further, arranging for both men to fly a Legacy twice before sending them off to Brazil for the purchase. Additionally, during the inspection-and-acceptance process in São José dos Campos, they had test-flown the new airplane under the guidance of Embraer factory pilots and engineers, who had briefed them on the cockpit systems and provided practical tips. Furthermore, the copilot, Paladino, had previously flown a similar Embraer regional jet during a stint at American Airlines. And these jets are easy to fly. There was no reason to doubt that Lepore and Paladino would bring N600XL safely home.

It was not a fun stay in Brazil. São José dos Campos is a dull town, and there were repeated delays as the ExcelAire team found small problems with the airplane, and Embraer technicians struggled to resolve them. Particularly difficult was a problem with flickering L.E.D. cabin lights, which nearly caused the purchase to fall through. Embraer treated the Americans well, and insisted on sending a staffer along for the first leg of the homeward flight, apparently to ease their exit from the country. Things didn't work out that way, but the plan was to fly 1,725 miles north to Manaus, where they would spend the night in a good hotel and take a boat ride on the Amazon, before heading to the United States later in the day. Also along for the flight was Embraer's North American sales representative Henry Yandle and a *New York Times* contributor named Joe Sharkey, who writes a business-travel column for the newspaper and was doing a story on another Embraer model for a U.S. magazine called *Business Jet Traveler*. Sharkey was the outsider among them, and potentially an influential one. It was unusual to have invited him on a maiden voyage with a freshly trained crew. But this was to be a rare run without a client aboard, or the shyness that typically accompanies the use of such airplanes.

Embraer and ExcelAire welcomed the publicity. Sharkey was not there to write about the Legacy now. But he was well positioned to write about it in the future – perhaps. A description of the Legacy in *Business Jet Traveler* might help persuade someone to buy or charter one. It was hard to know what Sharkey could write of genuine content – that riding in a Legacy is comfortable? That the cabin offers legroom, desk space, and a walk-in luggage compartment? That the cabin lighting does not flicker? At $25 million it had better not. Anyway, Sharkey seemed a decent sort, and unlikely to delve into the airplane's dark side – the fuel burn per passenger-mile, the expense to company shareholders, the disproportionate use of public resources like air traffic control and landing slots. No, it was a safe bet that *Business Jet Traveler* would not be publishing that. Nonetheless, Sharkey's presence placed additional pressure on the pilots as they taxied the unfamiliar airplane toward the runway.

It was just before 3 PM on Friday, September 29. Embraer had submitted a computer-generated flight plan to air traffic control for the run north to Manaus. Flight plans are trip requests, or advance notices of an imminent flight. This one was for a routing that would take N600XL over Brasília, where, after a slight left turn, an airway would lead the airplane 1,200 miles to Manaus. That airway is called UZ6. It passes over Caiapó Indian territory and Fazenda Jarinã, but of course the flight-planning computer did not know this, or even of the Amazon's existence. On the basis of forecasted winds and the Legacy's performance, it requested a climb to 37,000 feet, or Flight Level 370, an altitude appropriate for the initial direction of flight. Until Brasília, that direction was slightly to the east side of magnetic north. Airplanes cruising on such easterly headings are usually assigned 'odd' altitudes (35,000, 37,000, 39,000), while airplanes cruising on westerly headings are given 'even' altitudes (36,000, 38,000, 40,000). This is basic stuff, the vertical equivalent of drive-on-the-right highway rules. Virtuoso air traffic controllers sometimes allow exceptions to be made when traffic is light (and exceptions are systemic along certain one-way routes), but generally these cruising rules dictate the altitudes at which airplanes fly worldwide. The flight-planning computer knew it, and since the airway to Manaus required a westerly turn over Brasília, it proposed a descent to 36,000 feet at that point.

Lepore and Paladino had a printout of the flight plan in the cockpit, with the route highlighted in yellow, and the altitudes shown. But a flight plan is merely a proposal, and it becomes something of an artifact after air traffic control mulls it over and issues a formal clearance into controlled airspace, assigning a route and altitude according to its own needs. Afterward the original flight plan becomes operational only in narrow circumstances related to communications failure. Lepore and Paladino received their clearance by radio from the control tower at São José dos Campos prior to taxiing. The local controller spoke the bare minimum of English. Lepore and Paladino eventually gleaned the essential: they were cleared to Manaus via a standard departure procedure and then the flight-plan route, at an initial cruising altitude of 37,000 feet. They were assigned a unique transponder code, which they set. The transponder is a radio beacon which responds to air traffic control radar, enhancing the display on the controllers' screens and automatically transmitting the aircraft's altitude in flight. Like most of the Legacy's electronics, this one was made by the American company Honeywell. At 2:51 PM, with Lepore in the left seat and at the controls, N600XL accelerated smoothly down the runway and lifted off. I presume that Sharkey was pleased. He was embarking on a trip in the style of a latter-day pasha. Neither he nor the pilots could have known that at the same time, in the humble world 1,725 miles to the north, the ordinary passengers of Gol Flight 1907 were crowded around the gate at the airline terminal in Manaus, preparing to board a Boeing 737 for their flight south.

The Legacy's cockpit voice recordings are closed loops two hours long. The one recovered from N600XL opens forty-two minutes into the flight like a curtain rising on a scene of normalcy, but with the Devil lurking just out of sight. It was 3:33 in the afternoon. The airplane was cruising on autopilot, about 150 miles south of Brasília, at the assigned altitude of 37,000 feet. Paladino, as copilot, was working the radio, checking into a new air traffic control sector. The sector was a subdivision within Brasília Center's airspace. Brasília Center is a radar facility that controls traffic across a huge expanse of central

Brazil, approximately to the northern boundary of Mato Grosso State. Paladino keyed a transmitter and said, 'N600XL level, Flight Level 370.' The controller's response was garbled and incomprehensible. Paladino tried again, and this time the controller's transmission was only slightly more clear. Lepore said, 'I think he just said "radar contact."' Paladino took the captain on faith and radioed, 'Roger, radar contact.' To Lepore he added, 'I have no idea what the hell he said.' Lepore made no comment. Radio communications in cruise are largely routine, the necessary exchange had occurred, and pilots don't tend to get excited. Back home in the United States they might have pushed the issue, alerted the controller to the poor quality of his transmissions, and tried to get him to switch to a better frequency or a closer antenna. They did none of that here. Was it cultural arrogance? Probably not. Was it linguistic timidity? Possibly, and perhaps compounded by the mental inertia that can lull pilots in flight. All was well for now, but in retrospect the crew's lack of follow-up was not a good sign.

To pass the time, they explored the airplane's Flight Management System and the related flat-panel displays, as well as a stand-alone laptop computer loaded with Legacy flight-planning software provided by the Embraer factory. Paladino had the laptop. A passenger came forward. It may have been Sharkey, because he asked about the altitude as if he couldn't simply read the instrument panel, as one would expect the others to have done. Whoever it was, Paladino greeted him with an overbright tone. 'Hello! How ya doin'?'

'Good. You?'

'Very good. We're just, ah, playin'. Trying to get used to the airplane.'

'She's flying nice, no?'

The use of the feminine was awkward, but Paladino went along. 'Yeah! She's flying real nice!'

They spoke about the weather, which for the moment was nice, too. The passenger left. Paladino got back to poking at the laptop. Speaking of the screen, he said, 'Aw shit, I lost it . . .'

Lepore said, 'What's the matter?'

Paladino said, 'I lost a page. Where'd it go? I musta hit something.'
Lepore said, 'Aw, it's all right.'

With nothing better to do, Lepore and Paladino kept fiddling
with the computer. There was little reason to look outside. The
earth lay far below as an irrelevant concern, and the surrounding
sky was huge. Traffic at those altitudes was under radar control, and
though other airplanes could be heard on the radio, the Legacy's
collision-avoidance system would warn of any that might stray near
should the controllers make a mistake. That was the nature of the
flight then under way. The cockpit was a cocoon. Lepore and
Paladino were operating an inherently simple jet that had been
stuffed with electronic capabilities – most of them nested, and therefore hidden from immediate view. The nesting of flight information,
much of it non-essential, is a development now several decades old
and somewhat out of control. It is driven on the one hand by market
pressures to create clean cockpit displays, and on the other hand by
the technical possibilities offered to overly enthusiastic designers
and engineers. The problem for pilots is the idiosyncratic architecture of the systems that are created, the need to fathom the logic
that has been applied, and the reliance on manuals laced with
invented terminology to which practitioners are expected to submit
their minds. In principle a pilot with sufficient time and patience
can figure it all out in advance, but such pilots are rare, and Lepore
and Paladino were not among them. They were stick-and-rudder
men, confident in their control of the jet itself and comfortable with
the first rule of aerial navigation, which is to point the airplane in
the right direction and let it fly. In the Legacy, with its refined autopilot and its navigational systems, they had no problem doing that.
The record shows that they remained at exactly 37,000 feet along
the perfect centerline of the route they had been assigned. Meanwhile, they set about learning the airplane, as pilots must, through
trial and error and practical use.

The North American sales rep, Henry Yandle, came forward to
visit. He had a hail-fellow manner that some passengers adopt in the
company of pilots. Radio transmissions can be heard in the background, most in Portuguese, some from other airplanes, some from

air traffic control. Yandle emphasized the need to give Sharkey a good flight. Eventually he said, 'All right. How much longer, guys?'

Lepore said, 'Aw shit, good question,' and laughed.

Paladino said, 'It's fair enough.'

Yandle said, 'We were wondering because . . .'

Lepore apologized. 'We didn't have it loaded up till after we got up here.'

Paladino may have tried to pull up a clock. Speaking of the flight-planned duration, he said, 'It's three hours and twenty-three minutes from takeoff, so it's gonna be, uh . . .'

Lepore said, 'Hour and . . .' He began to finger his keypad, hoping to extract the answer from the Flight Management System. He said, 'Still working out the kinks on how to work this stuff. This FMS.' It now seems sad and even tragic, the reach for automation by these working pilots, their button-pushing response. They must have known at what time they had taken off. They had been in the air for forty-five minutes, give or take. The winds were not significant. With an additional ten minutes tacked on for arrival turns, this meant they probably had about two hours and forty-five minutes to go. It was the simplest sort of mental calculation and would have been accurate enough.

Yandle tried to let it slide. He said, 'Not a problem.' But the question had been raised. Duty Time, Block Time, Local Time, Push Time, Release Time, Time Off, Time en Route, Time of Arrival, Fuel-Remaining Time, Void Time, Expect-This-or-That Time. There is also Coordinated Universal Time, called Zulu Time, which rolls nicely off the tongue.

Lepore said, 'Where's the one that gives us Total Time?'

Paladino said, 'The Current, right?'

'Current' is the one you get from an ordinary watch. Lepore said, 'Landing – that ain't it.' He kept fingering the keypad. 'The arrival, the arrival, the arrival.' He wasn't giving up on the quest.

But it was Paladino who had success. He said, 'Here we go! Two hours and forty-seven minutes.' He had unearthed Time Remaining.

Yandle said, 'Two forty-seven.' The electronics had made it official. And so it went. This was an interval which might have been better spent in quiet concentration on the flight, but in private jets you don't shut the door on the passengers. Yandle was a colleague, and Sharkey was important. The conversation continued as Lepore and Paladino tried to pull up weather information on the Flight Management System. They had a hard time finding it. They had similar trouble with the laptop. Their uncertainties were not to their discredit, and did not mean that they were reckless even to be flying that airplane, as has since been claimed. In retrospect they were perhaps too active in the cockpit. However, in this they were not alone. The best pilots are masters of minimalism who rely less on the equipment and more on their brains, but such pilots are rare.

Airplane salesmen are different, because they profit from the add-ons. Yandle returned to the cabin and his guest. Alone in the cockpit, Lepore and Paladino kept fussing with the buttons as they approached the turn point over Brasília. The controller gave them a frequency change as they entered a new Brasília Center sector. That sector is large, stretching nearly 500 miles north to the edge of Brasília's airspace, just beyond the Caiapós' skies, where Manaus assumes control. In the new sector the first frequency was 125.05 megahertz, which normally would be functional for about the next 250 miles. Paladino acknowledged the handoff, set the new frequency, and checked in with a standard call. 'Brasília, N600XL, level, Flight Level 370. Good afternoon.' The controller's response was fast and strong. He said, 'N600XL, squawk ident. Radar surveillance.' Paladino answered, 'Roger.' Though the airplane had the entire large sector still to traverse, and all the radios were fine, this was the crew's last full exchange with Brasília Center.

Air traffic control in Brazil is a military function for historical reasons, none of them good. In the new sector, the controller on duty was an Air Force sergeant, aged thirty-eight, named Jomarcelo Fernandes dos Santos. His instruction to the Legacy to 'squawk ident' was a request for the crew to push a button associated with the transponder, which would highlight the airplane's electronic symbol on the control-room console, making it easier for dos Santos to distinguish N600XL from other targets in flight. Why dos Santos felt the need is not clear, since the sector was particularly quiet at the time. In any event, high above Brasília, Paladino briefly neglected to comply. When he caught his error, he said, 'Oh fuck, I forgot to do that.' The ident button was on the Radio Management Unit, a control screen for the radios and transponder. Paladino pushed it. Belatedly, Lepore said, 'ID's right there.' Paladino said, 'I think I did it, yeah.' Then he said, 'I think you see that . . .' He didn't finish the thought. He said, 'Oh shit!' On the same device, the communications frequency had suddenly disappeared. But Paladino knew the number. He said, 'Twenty-five-oh-five. That's why I write it down.' It was a good practice. Despite what engineers may think, there is no cockpit tool as solid as a pen. Paladino reset the frequency. Lepore said, 'Yeah.' Between the two men a subtle change was under way, and Paladino was ascending.

Together they got back to the electronic maze, trying to calculate landing distance at Manaus, and takeoff performance for the following day. In the midst of this, the Legacy arrived over Brasília and was turned by the autopilot to track the airway, UZ6, on a course 24 degrees to the west of north. The Current Time was 3:55 PM.

The pilots made no mention of the turn that the airplane had just made. That in itself is not surprising. But the Legacy was now cruising at 37,000 feet, in contradiction to the convention that would have shifted it to an 'even' flight level in the new direction. This was not illegal – and operationally it did not matter that the original flight plan had proposed a descent here to 36,000 feet. Indeed, the rules are very clear. Lepore and Paladino had been assigned 37,000 feet, and barring an emergency they were obligated to remain there until air traffic control approved a change. There had been no such instruction. They may have assumed that with so little traffic in the air the controller was doing them a favor and allowing an exception, as sometimes occurs in the United States. They certainly knew that they were in radio and radar contact with Brasília Center, and that their transponder was transmitting their altitude and showing it accurately on the radar screens. Nonetheless, 1,200 miles of airway now lay straight ahead – a long stretch to fly against convention – and it is odd that they did not comment on the unusual flight level or bother to verify it with the controller, all the more so in a Latin

American system that felt loose to them and that they had reason to distrust. Their failure to speak up may never be fully explained. But it seems to have been a human thing, a slap-your-head lapse of the sort that invites the familiar question 'How could I have been so dumb?'

Explanations are harder for the performance of Sergeant dos Santos. His tasks as a high-altitude controller were similar to those faced by Internet gamers, but significantly slower and less complex, and although the consequences of his errors were potentially grave, the dimensions of the airspace overhead provided him with large margins for safety, even discounting cockpit-based collision-avoidance systems and the fact that some pilots do still look outside. In the United States a controller doing simulation research once mentioned to me the difficulty of directing two airplanes into each other even if you try. I answered that I was not surprised. Even the largest airplanes are small, and the starting point of collision avoidance has traditionally been a reality known as the theory of 'the big sky.' Dos Santos may not have thought about it as such, but his actions indicate a faith that airplanes left alone just naturally don't collide.

He sat at an electronic display that was as crisp and capable as any in the world. When the Legacy first checked in, just south of Brasília, it appeared on the screen as an encircled cross indicating an enhanced transponder return, with a vector line showing its direction of flight and a data block displaying its call sign and two altitudes. The first altitude was the transponder's report of the Legacy's current altitude, 37,000 feet, which Paladino had just confirmed by radio. It was followed by an equal sign (=) indicating a functioning transponder in level flight. This in turn was followed by the second displayed altitude, whose function is unique to the Brazilian system and operationally awkward. Elsewhere in the world that second altitude is the flight level to which an airplane has been cleared, a number entered manually by controllers when they call for a descent or climb. In Brazil it may be the same, but if no manual entry has been performed, automation takes over and the second altitude displayed becomes the one proposed by the original (archival) flight plan for the segment of the route. Does Santos must have known of the distinction. He was a working controller, and the nature of the second altitude is not difficult to understand. Nonetheless, on this particular day he seems to have become confused. When N600XL first entered his sector, just south of Brasília, the two altitudes were the same, both showing 37,000 feet with the equal sign between them, and the nature of the second altitude did not matter. But five minutes later, when the Legacy crossed overhead Brasília and turned left to track the airway, the second altitude display automatically switched to 36,000 feet, the original flight plan's proposal, and a conventional level for the new direction of flight. Apparently dos Santos took this to mean that the Legacy had been instructed to descend, though he was the controller in charge and had made no such request. Mysteriously, he then ignored the indicator of the Legacy's actual altitude – the transponder return, which showed the airplane still level at 37,000 feet. Against solid indications to the contrary, he believed that the Legacy had descended to 36,000 feet.

I have tried to understand why. It may be that dos Santos would have so expected the Legacy pilots to speak up about flying at a non-standard altitude that their radio silence got him to believe they were doing the conventional thing. But as errors go, this one was more than a head slapper. Furthermore, it was sustained, and it turned out to be contagious.

For 50 miles beyond Brasília, the symbol for the Legacy showed a clear transponder return at 37,000 feet, and dos Santos did nothing about it. Then the Devil stepped onto the stage. It happened at 4:02 PM, when the Legacy's transponder stopped transmitting. The loss was apparent in two ways on dos Santos's screen: the circle surrounding the cross that marked the airplane's position disappeared, and the sign between the two displayed flight levels (FL370 and FL360) changed from an equal sign to a 'Z.' The Legacy now existed as an unenhanced 'primary' target, a raw metal mass reflecting radar beams, with no altitude-reporting capacity. In the militarized environment of Brasília Center, however, an Air Force radar kicked in with a crude height-finding function intended to help fighter jets intercept hostile intruders who would naturally try to penetrate Mother Brazil with their transponders turned off. Because the Legacy was still close to the radar dish on the ground, the height finder was able to calculate the altitude correctly, and briefly showed it on the screen as 37,000 feet. Be that as it may, the loss of the transponder should have been no big deal. Indeed, transponder failures are fairly routine, and because they normally elicit a reaction from controllers (generally a request to the pilots to reboot the unit), this one might have gotten the two sides at least to talk. The transponder problem would have been sorted out, and with it the question of altitude. Dos Santos, however, did not bother to call. It is as if he never noticed that the transponder had quit.

Fifteen minutes later dos Santos went off duty. His replacement was another sergeant, age twenty-seven, named Lucivando Tibúrcio de Alencar. Dos Santos briefed him on the sector's traffic, including a Legacy headed for Manaus – at Flight Level 360, he said. By then the Legacy was about 150 miles past Brasília, still within effective communication distance on the frequency assigned, but moving beyond the accuracy range of the military height-finding radar, which began to show the airplane's altitude erroneously – coincidentally first at 36,000 feet, and then at variations so large that the Legacy would have had to zoom wildly to achieve them. This explains the later reports that the pilots had been stunting. Belatedly, de Alencar realized that the Legacy showed as a 'primary' target only, unenhanced by transponder and altitude reporting – but at soonest this appears to have been a full ten minutes after he came on duty, when he bothered for the first time to make a call. It was 4:27 PM, about a half-hour shy of Caiapó territory. The Legacy by then had flown for thirty-six minutes since the last communication with air traffic control, and for fully twenty-five minutes since the transponder had failed. It was roughly 250 miles north of Brasília; and already beyond the range of reliable two-way communication on the assigned frequency. When de Alencar called, the Legacy did not answer, because the transmission was not heard in the cockpit. De Alencar called again, to the same effect.

One might expect that de Alencar would have risen to the occasion.

He now knew that he had a jet without a transponder, unresponsive to the radio, that was flying fast toward the boundary of his electronic vision and moving against possible opposing traffic as yet unseen. Closing speeds between jets in cruise may exceed 1,000 miles an hour, which can make a speck glimpsed in the distance very quickly fill the windshield. Admittedly, de Alencar believed that N600XL was at 36,000 feet, and that any opposing traffic would be 1,000 feet higher or lower – but even if correct, these were self-evidently unverified assumptions. Furthermore, until recent years a 2,000-foot vertical separation was the minimum considered safe between airplanes at those altitudes, and though a 1,000-foot separation is now the norm, it is based on the mandatory use of a new generation of precision equipment, including advanced autopilots and altimeters, and closely calibrated transponders. Until communications with the Legacy could be re-established, and the transponder problem resolved, N600XL for all its expense and elaboration was a rogue airplane, precisely flown but inadequately equipped for the tight tolerances of the airspace. There was no reason for panic, but by procedure and common sense de Alencar should have consulted with the Manaus sector, which adjoined his airspace ahead, and made a special effort to keep any traffic there far away. Instead, over the next twenty-six minutes he did little but call five times to the Legacy, in the unhurried hope that the crew might hear him and answer. All but the last call were on the same line-of-sight frequency that had already proved unavailing. De Alencar could have tried to relay a message through other airplanes in flight – this would have been normal – but perhaps because of the language barrier he did not. Through much of that time he had another controller by his side to assist him. Toward the end, as the Legacy approached the limits of Brasília's airspace, the assistant called Manaus and advised a controller there that the airplane was coming at him at 36,000 feet. He neglected to mention that there had been no communications for 500 miles, and that by the way the Legacy's transponder had failed. It was nearly 5 PM. Gol Flight 1907 was speeding steadily south. Unseen in the jungle below, two Caiapó women had gone down to a stream to wash.

\*

Back to 50 miles north of Brasília – and back nearly an hour in time, to the moment of the Legacy's transponder failure. At that time, the transponder did not power off but switched from 'Altitude' to 'Standby.' It did this either by itself or because one of the pilots unknowingly pushed a button. Though both are possible, and the latter seems likely, the distinction does not really matter. Pilots, no less than controllers, are expected to notice such events. Far to the north and near Manaus, the southbound Boeing had just leveled at 37,000 feet. In the northbound Legacy at the very same altitude, and on the very same flight path, Lepore and Paladino were alone in the cockpit, continuing to plan the next day's trip, and relying on electronic elaborations for help.

Copilot Paladino said, 'Naw, we can do 48, eight eight four.'

Captain Lepore said, 'If we do, uh . . . A.T.O.? That's basically, uh, full fuel, isn't it?'

At that moment, 4:02 PM, the transponder quit. No chime sounded in the cockpit. Instead, a small warning silently appeared on each of the two Radio Management Units, showing an abbreviation for 'Standby.' The understated warnings must have made good sense to Honeywell's engineers, who inhabit offices in Arizona, but they were not helpful to the pilots far away in flight, who were drowning in their products. For the next 500 miles the 'Standby' warnings remained in view but unseen. The pilots were occupied with other things: their automated flight-performance calculations, fraternal visits from the passengers in the cabin, offers of water and soft drinks. The runway at Manaus was a particular concern – it had been shortened because of construction. At one point Lepore said, 'We can do the landing, all right. Just have to get on it.' He was not acutely worried. He laughed wryly. 'Nothin' like banging the first flight of the friggin' airplane.'

Bang it, prang it, really fuck it up. But first you have to screw the pooch in your mind. Paladino matched Lepore's tone. He said, 'We couldn't get a nice long runway, you know? You get stuck in a fucking place in the middle of the Amazon Unknown.' He glanced out at the brown-green expanses below. He said, 'Aw, beautiful. But it don't look so Amazonish.'

Lepore said, 'Nah, it doesn't either.'

It didn't because it wasn't yet. Later, for a while, it still wouldn't, because that part of the forest has been cut down. Aw, beautiful. A few clouds floated ahead. Paladino considered a turn to smooth the ride. He said, 'I guess we'll have to deviate.' It was a proposition. He thought again. He said, 'Aw, maybe we'll be all right.' They were doing 500 miles an hour. It seemed slow because the clouds were large, and they could see them far ahead. Lepore said, 'Aw, probably will.' He dropped something on the cockpit floor. 'Aw, goddamn it.'

Navigational precision poses dangers not immediately apparent. In the Legacy, it was based on three systems. The first was an ultra-accurate altimeter, capable of measuring the atmosphere with such finesse that at Flight Level 370 it could distinguish the Legacy's altitude within perhaps five feet. The second was almost as accurate. It was the airplane's satellite-based GPS receiver, a positioning system that kept track of the airplane's geographic location within a distance of half of its wingspan, and that, linked to a navigational database, defined the assigned airway with equal precision. The third was an autopilot that flew better than its human masters, and, however mindlessly, worked with the altimeter and GPS to keep the airplane spot-on. Such capability is relatively new. Until recently, head-on airplanes mistakenly assigned the same altitude and route by air traffic control would almost certainly have passed some distance apart, due to the navigation slop inherent in their systems. But this is no longer true. The problem for the Legacy was that the Boeing coming at them on the same assigned flight path had equipment that was every bit as precise.

Paladino referred to a high-altitude navigational chart. It was made of paper as strong as money. He said, 'In case we lose radios, we have a bunch of frequencies we can use.' The radios occasionally sounded with exchanges between the controllers and other airplanes. Slowly, however, a change occurred. As the Legacy sailed beyond the range of the antenna on the ground, eventually the controller's side of the transmissions could no longer be heard. Lepore and Paladino did not wake up to this as they might have in the United

States, perhaps because they discounted Portuguese and did not realize that the transmissions they continued to hear were one-sided affairs, exclusively from other pilots in flight. At the start of this unknown condition of communications loss – about when de Alencar made his unsuccessful first call – Paladino pulled out a new digital camera and started to play with it. He said, 'I don't know how to get video on this thing.' It was as if the Legacy's system had not been confusing enough.

Lepore said, 'Press the video button. No, I don't know.'

'Where would that be?'

'I don't know. Hold on.' Lepore took the camera. A minute of silence went by, broken by an aircraft transmission in Portuguese. Lepore said, 'It's probably one of these, on the rotators.'

'Yeah. You'd think. Right?'

Lepore said, 'I'm not sure. I don't . . . don't know if you can with this camera. I mean, gotta be something with setting up here . . .'

'Yeah.'

'But I don't know which one. You'd have to probably read the manual, see which setting it would be.'

Paladino had the camera again. He said, 'I'm afraid to read anything else right now.'

'Yeah, well that's fine. Don't do. Yeah, just shut it off.'

It was good advice. But with their attention again focused on the cockpit, the pilots still did not notice that the transponder was on standby. Another warning they missed was a small sign saying TCAS OFF, shown at the bottom of each pilot's Primary Flight Display, the screens they would have referenced for basic flight control had the autopilot not by law been handling that chore. TCAS stands for Traffic Collision Avoidance System. It is a nested safety device independent of air traffic control that converses electronically with other airplanes in flight, and in the case of imminent collision alerts the pilots of both airplanes and negotiates a solution – typically instructing one crew to descend and the other to climb. It is required equipment in almost all airliners and jets, and is considered to be so reliable that its instructions supersede those of air traffic controllers. It works, however, only between airplanes with active transponders.

In the Legacy cockpit, therefore, the TCAS necessarily dropped out when the transponder switched to standby. Again, there were no warning chimes. But as a consequence the Legacy was now flying blind to the presence of other airplanes, and was itself invisible to their otherwise functional TCAS displays.

Lepore said he needed to use the toilet. He twisted out of his seat, saying, 'How the fuck do I get back?' and left the cockpit. He must have been waylaid by the passengers, because he was gone for almost seventeen minutes. During that time Paladino had some peace. The jet was fast approaching the limits of Brasília's airspace. Two transmissions came over the radio, both from distant airplanes in Portuguese. Paladino spoke once to himself. He said, 'Fuck did I put my glasses?' For long minutes afterward the radio was silent. Paladino must finally have wondered why, because at last he attempted to raise air traffic control. On the frequency 125.05 he radioed twice, 'Brasília, N600XL.' When he got no reply, he began to 'shop' the other frequencies listed on the navigation chart, systematically giving each frequency two tries, for a total of twelve calls over a period of five minutes. It is now known that none of the calls got through to de Alencar, and for a variety of reasons, including that some receivers were simply switched off at Brasília Center, and that by a vicious fluke at least two of Paladino's calls were blocked by other airplanes transmitting at the same time.

By chance, Paladino's attempts to raise air traffic control left the Legacy's radio on a frequency which de Alencar then used for his final attempt to get through. As a result, de Alencar's voice suddenly came across the Legacy's radio, instructing the flight to check in with Amazonia Center, the facility at Manaus. De Alencar radioed, 'N600XL, Brasília blind. Contact Amazonia Center, 123.32. If unable, ah, 126.45. N600XL.' His English was accented but clear enough – or almost. The record shows that three minutes remained. If Paladino had fully understood the call, he would have switched to Manaus's frequency and checked in with a routine report of the Legacy's altitude. It is possible that the Manaus controller, who had been working the Gol flight at 37,000 feet and had just handed it off to Brasília, would have had the reflexes and skills to turn the Legacy, or get it immediately to descend or climb. But Paladino did not wholly hear the new frequency. He responded to de Alencar, 'No, just trying to reach you. I'm sorry, what was the first frequency for N600XL? 1-2-3 . . . I didn't get the last two . . .' There was no answer. Paladino tried several more times, but without success. Lepore returned to the cockpit and strapped himself in. He said 'Sorry,' about his absence. Paladino explained the trouble they seemed to be having with radio communications. They began experimenting with frequencies, expecting eventually to raise Manaus.

Maybe a minute remained. The Boeing was approaching fast from about thirty miles away. As a narrow head-on silhouette it would have been hard to spot had the Legacy pilots been looking outside. Furthermore, because of illusions associated with the curvature of the earth, the oncoming airplane would have appeared to be significantly higher until the last few seconds before impact. For the Boeing pilots, spotting the Legacy would have been harder still. The captain was one of Gol's most seasoned men, a line instructor named Decio Chaves Jr, who at age forty-four had logged 14,900 hours in flight, nearly a third of them in the latest 737s. His copilot was Thiago Jordao Cruso, aged twenty-nine, an advanced apprentice with 3,850 hours. The 737 they were flying was fresh from Boeing's production line and had been in service with Gol for merely two weeks. The flight south so far had been routine, with the airplane cruising on autopilot, at all times exactly where it was supposed to be. The pilots spent much of the flight looking through photographs of their colleagues and friends. About ten minutes before the end, a flight attendant entered the cockpit for a flirtatious chat. She asked them if they had seen a video of Brazilian model Daniela Cicarelli having sex on a beach. One of the pilots said, 'Love, come here. Can you bring something like that for us?' They laughed. As she was leaving, the pilot called out, 'Come back, my love!' Soon afterward the controller in Manaus gave them a frequency change to Brasília Center and instructed them to delay checking in until they got to a certain waypoint a few minutes ahead. The pilots switched to the new frequency and, in an odd twist to the story, heard de Alencar's last broadcast to the Legacy – clearly audible on the Boeing's cockpit voice recording – because the controller had shotgunned it across multiple frequencies simultaneously. The Boeing's pilots did not, however, hear the Legacy's requests for clarification, which Paladino made across a frequency that they were not on. It would not have mattered anyway. The Boeing's TCAS was clear. The pilots had no reason to suspect that the Legacy was near. They continued to look at pictures. There was one of a pilot named Bruno, of a marathon, of a waterfall, and of a *quati* – a funny four-legged creature that had torn into some bags.

The Legacy came streaking at the Boeing about 30 feet to the left of the fuselage and 2 feet lower. The displacement was infinitesimal on the scale of the sky, and a measure of impressive navigational precision. The Legacy's winglet acted like a vertically held knife, slicing through the Boeing's left wing about halfway out and severing the wing's internal spar. The outboard section of the wing whipped upward, stripping skin as it went, then separated entirely, spiraling over the fuselage and demolishing much of the Boeing's tail. In the Boeing's cockpit the sequence sounded like a car crash. Instantly the Boeing twisted out of control, corkscrewing violently to the left and pitching straight down into a rotating vertical dive. The cockpit filled with alarms – an urgent klaxon and a robotic voice insistently warning, *Bank angle! Bank angle! Bank angle!*, as if the crew might need the advice. Back in the cabin the passengers screamed and shouted. The pilots reacted as one might expect, fighting desperately to regain control. They probably did not know what had gone wrong. They certainly never mentioned it. What is unusual is that they also did not swear. Ten seconds into the dive, one of them did cry '*Aye!*,' but the other urged him to stay calm. '*Calma!*' he said, and seconds later he said it again. If pilots must die in an airplane, all would choose to finish so well. Of course these two knew they were gone, but they did what they could, even extending the landing gear to slow the dive. The gesture was hopeless. Twenty-two seconds into the plunge the airplane's over-speed warning came on with a rattle that continued to the end. Forces inside the airplane rapidly grew until, thirty seconds into the dive, they exceeded four Gs – the gravity-load threshold beyond which some passengers must have begun to black out as the forces drained blood from their minds. Maybe they were the lucky ones or maybe it didn't matter. In the cockpit the pilots kept trying to fly, struggling with the controls and exchanging a few words which are impossible to discern over the bedlam of alarms. Forty-five seconds into the dive came another '*Aye!*' Seven seconds later, at 7,000 feet, the Boeing broke into three parts, which plummeted in formation into the forest below.

In the Legacy the collision sounded like a snap. Lepore grunted as if he had been punched in the gut. The airplane rolled left, and the autopilot disengaged with a robotic warning and three chimes. Lepore grabbed the controls. He said, 'What the HELL was that?' He sounded swamped in adrenaline. Paladino for his part sounded pumped up for the game. He said, 'All right, just fly the airplane, dude! Just fly the airplane!' He checked the cabin pressurization. He said, 'It's not . . . We don't have explosive decompression.' He may have thought that Lepore was shaky, or that on the basis of his own greater experience with that category of jet he perhaps should take over. He said, 'You want me to fly it, dude? You want me to fly it?' Lepore did not hear the question, or he chose not to answer. The Legacy was badly out of whack, insisting on rolling to the left, and requiring Lepore to hold the controls a half-throw to the right just to maintain wings-level flight. He was handling the airplane well enough. But he was extremely anxious. He said, 'What – we got fucking HIT?'

Paladino said, 'I dunno, dude. Lemme fly it.'

Lepore acquiesced. Paladino then not only took the controls but assumed command. This passed unsaid between the two men. Paladino was decisive. Lepore had not completely folded, but under the stress his mental processes had slowed. Paladino said, 'All right, declare an emergency,' and Lepore hesitated over the most basic frequency known. He asked, 'What is it, twenty-one five?' Paladino said, 'Yeah, twenty-one five.' That exchange placed Paladino firmly in charge. He said, 'Whatever the fuck that was . . . we have to get down.'

Lepore said, 'Go!' A passenger came to the cockpit and said, 'You know we lost a winglet?' Lepore said, 'Did we? Where the fuck did he come from?' To the passengers back in the cabin Paladino said, 'All right, we're going down! We're declaring an emergency! Sit down!' Breathing heavily into his microphone, Lepore made the first emergency call to air traffic control. There was no response. Paladino pulled the throttles back and pushed the airplane into a descent. The left winglet had torn away, leaving a jagged stump, the left wing had bent upward, and along its upper surface some of the skin was separating from the internal structure. The passengers could see the heavily deflected aileron necessary to maintain control. What they could not see was that the Legacy's tail had been hit as well.

From the cockpit none of this damage was in view, but the pilots knew that the airplane was badly wounded and might at any moment die. They needed to land as soon as possible, but to do that they had to descend to low altitudes, where if they were not careful with airspeeds the thicker air might tear the plane apart. Paladino said, 'Want to keep the speeds low.' But he also knew that if he got too slow he might lose the ability to control the roll. Someone whispered 'Fuck it!' into a microphone. At that very moment the Boeing hit the ground unseen somewhere behind and below. Paladino pushed a button on the Flight Management System and found that the nearest airport lay one hundred miles ahead. The airport was identified by its four-letter code, SBCC, whatever that meant. For all they knew it was a jungle strip of the sort that missionaries use, and completely inadequate for a Legacy. They needed more information, like field elevation and runway length. Paladino said, 'I got the nearest airport right there. Look that up if you want.' Looking it up might have been possible electronically, but they did not know how. Somewhere they had paper charts that might contain the information. Breathing hard, Lepore asked, 'It was books on your side?' Paladino said, 'Yeah, no, yeah, I got it.' Lepore reached again for the controls, saying, 'I got the . . .' Paladino wouldn't have it. He said, 'Let me just fly the thing, dude, 'cause I just think . . .'

Lepore said, 'Where the FUCK did he come from?'

Paladino said, 'Did we hit somebody? Did you see that? Did you see something?'

Lepore was hesitant. 'I thought I saw . . . I looked up . . .' He made another Mayday call, but remained behind the game. Struggling to look up information about the nearest airport, he said, 'What is it . . . S?'

Paladino answered, 'S-B-C-C. We'll just go direct to it.'

'I don't know if it's big enough.'

Paladino said, 'I know. We'll just fly. We'll find out. Trying to contact these fuckers. They won't answer the radio.'

Lepore said, 'S . . . B . . . C . . . C?'

Paladino said, 'Yeah.' Somebody gasped. Apparently Paladino had scanned the displays. He said, 'Dude! [Do] you have the TCAS on?'

Lepore said, 'Yes, the TCAS is off.' There are two ways to understand the reversal in his answer – either that he was fumbling his words or that right after 'Yes' he finally noticed the warnings on the cockpit displays, showing that the TCAS was off and the transponder was on standby. From his intonation on the recordings it is impossible to tell. But far away on air traffic control screens, at that moment, the airplane's transponder suddenly reappeared.

In the cockpit, the implications of an inoperative TCAS would have been obvious: the airplane would have been electronically invisible to other airplanes in flight, and would itself have been blind. For ten seconds neither pilot spoke. Then Paladino said, 'All right, just keep an eye out for traffic. I'll do that, I'll do that, I'll do that. I got that.'

The descent was a one-man show. It lasted about twenty minutes. While Paladino flew the airplane, Lepore struggled with the charts, trying to find information about the airport ahead. He never came up with much, except that SBCC is the identifying code for an airport called Cachimbo. He said, 'I wish I had a fucking thing that I knew.' He was frustrated and probably embarrassed. He had ceded a command which could not now be reclaimed. He continued to participate, but Paladino for his part kept taking over tasks that Lepore could have done. There was something overreaching about this behavior, as if Paladino had been waiting years to show his mettle, and would not now be denied. He was worried about dying – as much as anyone aboard. But he was a soldier with a battlefield promotion, and engaged in the fight of his life. On the recordings his exhilaration is clear.

A dangerous landing lay ahead. There was no telling what the extension of flaps and wheels would do. The control forces already were high, and Paladino was afraid to relieve them with trim. When he tried to slow below 230 miles an hour, he had a harder time maintaining wings-level flight, and had to accelerate again. This was bad. They descended through 10,000 feet. The salesman Henry Yandle came forward and stood by to help. At high altitude a passing Boeing 747 cargo flight had answered the Mayday call and was talking to air traffic control on the Legacy's behalf, trying to extract information about Cachimbo. Paladino felt the control forces getting heavier. He sent Yandle back to see if the wing was coming apart.

Lepore said, 'We may just need to get on the ground.' He meant, no matter what kind of runway they found, or if they found none. A forest landing would likely kill the pilots, but might allow some passengers to survive. He said, 'I hate to say this.'

Paladino answered with a clipped, soldierly 'I understand that.'

Cachimbo lay twenty-one miles ahead. Paladino had accelerated to 275 miles an hour and was trying to slow. Speed control was difficult, perhaps because of damage to the tail. The air below 10,000 was Amazonish – thick with smoke from forests being fired to clear the land. Paladino was fighting to raise the nose. 'I'm not sure if I can get this thing slow, I have to be honest with you. So I'm gonna have to come in fast.' Lepore said. 'Come in fast, and we'll just do what we can.' He seemed to be better now. Yandle returned with news that the damage did not seem to be spreading.

They spotted the airport ahead, a slash in the landscape, discernible to the practiced eye. As they approached they saw that it was a single paved runway and apparently long, oriented at a sharp angle to their direction of flight. The question of why such a runway exists in the middle of the jungle did not arise. But it is a military field, built by the Air Force for its own reasons and maintained complete with a control tower, however rarely it is used.

The stricken Legacy overflew Cachimbo high and fast just as the 747 provided it with a frequency with which to contact distant Manaus. This led Lepore into a wasteful exchange with an irrelevant controller, who at least finally provided the frequency for the

Cachimbo control tower. Sitting in his glass booth, presiding over a dormant field with no other airplanes in motion, the tower controller then occupied Lepore with his own confusions. Eventually he cleared the airplane to land, as if he had a choice in the matter. Those pilots were going to put the airplane on the ground regardless. That turned out to be quite difficult to do – a piece of flying that pushed Paladino and Lepore to their limits, and probably the Legacy as well. The problem was the damaged airplane's inability to slow and its limited ability to bank to the left, a condition compounded by poor visibility aft from the cockpit, and burdened by the controller's chatter as well as a chorus of automated alarms triggered by the airplane's necessarily unusual configuration. But Paladino flew well, and Lepore took up the slack, and in the end they landed safely at Cachimbo, doing more than 200 miles an hour over the runway threshold, touching down firmly, then braking hard to bring the airplane to a stop. In the cabin the passengers cheered and clapped.

Lepore said, 'Good job, good job, funny, good, we're good.'

Paladino said, 'Fucking we're alive!! FUCK YOU!!!' It was a victory cry, a shout of exuberance and relief. He laughed ferociously.

Lepore laughed less strongly. 'Fuck you!' he agreed. 'Good job, good job.'

The controller instructed the Legacy to taxi to the ramp for parking. Paladino gave the controls to Lepore. He said, 'I'm sorry, dude. I didn't mean to do that to you.' Briefly they talked over each other. Lepore escaped by radioing thanks to the 747. But as they slowly taxied in, Paladino got back to his apology. 'Hey, I'm really sorry.'

Lepore said, 'Nothing to be sorry about, man.'

'I didn't mean to . . .'

'Don't . . .'

'I know the speeds, I know everything about . . .'

'Don't you worry about anything. I'm not . . .'

'I just want you to understand, you're the captain.'

'I don't have . . . Don't . . . Believe me, I'm the last person you need to talk to about shit. I mean, it doesn't matter to me. It was perfectly . . .'

'I didn't mean to come across like that. I was just trying to think of what to do.'

Lepore said, 'I'm more worried about my friggin' . . .'

Paladino finished for him. '. . . life.'

It was an awkward exchange. But the greater problem, now sinking in, was the reality of a collision at 37,000 feet. Lepore especially was disturbed. He kept coming back to the consequences. When one of the ExcelAire executives, Ralph Michielli, came forward, he said, 'Fuckin' A, Ralph! What the fuck?'

Michielli said, 'What if we hit something else? I mean, we were at the proper altitude . . .'

Paladino summarized the situation just prior to the impact. He did not mention the transponder or TCAS. Accurately enough he said, 'The guys forgot about us. Previous frequency had completely forgotten about us. And I started querying them. "This is not right. I haven't talked to anybody in a long time."' He did a verbal shrug. 'We're alive.'

Lepore said, 'Yeah, but I'm worried about the other airplane. If we hit another airplane. I mean, what else could it have been?'

Paladino agreed. 'At 37,000 feet? Yeah, it was a hard hit, though, whatever it was.'

That evening at dinner on the air base they got word that a Boeing had disappeared. A search was under way. An English-speaking official from Manaus called the base for a preliminary interview with the Legacy's captain. Lepore took the call. Brazilian investigators have told me that Paladino was standing beside him as he spoke. The call was taped by the Brazilians. On the phone Lepore confirmed that the collision had occurred about one hundred miles from Cachimbo, when the airplane was level at 37,000 feet.

The official asked, 'Level at 370?'

'Level at 370.'

The official said, 'O.K.! And the TCAS system was on?'

Lepore said, 'No.'

The official said, 'What? . . . Hello?'

Lepore said, 'No, it wasn't.'

'No TCAS.'

If Paladino was there, one can only imagine his reaction. A voice can be heard insisting that the TCAS was on. Replying again to the official Lepore said, 'The TCAS was on.'

'O.K., was on? But no signal was reported.'

'No, no, we didn't get any, uh . . . any warning, no.'

With that conversation, the Brazilian government took the first step in a process of bringing criminal charges against Lepore and Paladino, essentially for reckless flying. Though safety experts deplore it, the criminalization of airplane accidents is a growing trend world-wide. It led in this case to Lepore and Paladino being detained in Brazil for two months, after which they returned to New York, where they now fight the charges from a stubborn distance, still flying for ExcelAire, but only within the United States, lest Brazil try to grab them abroad. Big law firms represent the victims, the operators, and the manufacturers in civil lawsuits, and as with every air disaster the fighting among them will go on for years.

ExcelAire and the pilots have hunkered down into a defensive position, whose general outlines can be anticipated: the pilots did nothing improper or illegal, and despite all the circumstantial evidence to the contrary, the Legacy's transponder and TCAS functioned correctly throughout the flight. According to this argument, the failures lay entirely within the Brazilian air traffic control system. Such a position would require an explanation of why the 737 did not show up on the Legacy's TCAS, and why just after the impact, when Paladino questioned Lepore about the unit, the Legacy's transponder suddenly reappeared on air traffic control screens. Competent lawyers will probably come up with reasons.

In any case, on the evening of the accident the pilots did not suspect the nightmare that lay ahead. They were relieved about their survival. Perhaps they toasted it. But they were not callous about the fate of the dead, as is claimed by some of the victims' families. They are decent guys, ordinary workaday pilots. Like the people on the ground within earshot of the impact thunder, they did not sleep easily that night.

Several days later, when Megaron and his band of Caiapó warriors launched their aluminum boats into the Jarinã River, they carried no radio, no GPS, no electronics of any kind. They had gasoline for the outboard motors, some pots and pans, and a few machetes and axes. They did not ask permission. They were not assigned a route. They chose the Jarinã River because it runs in the right direction. They were confident navigators. They understood the importance of common sense.

The river carried them eastward. Eventually it brought them to the vicinity of the crash. They realized they were near when they saw an Air Force helicopter hovering downsun ahead. They did not think that the helicopter was an iron bug. They knew that it was bringing in soldiers and carrying away the dead. There was no need to code the location or punch up displays, no need to submit their minds. They simply stayed in their boats until the river could take them no closer. There they made camp on the riverbank and spent the night. In the morning they set out to cut a trail to the crash site, a distance of about two miles. The jungle was especially dense, but with twenty-three men to swing machetes, in the afternoon they arrived. They had slopped around along the way, but in the end their accuracy was fine.

The site smelled of jet fuel, which had soaked into the soil and spilled into two small streams that flowed through the forest there. It also smelled of death, or more accurately of organic decomposition, which in the heat was well advanced. Perhaps a hundred soldiers were at work, expanding a helicopter landing zone, and collecting and bagging the victims. They had built a camp out beyond a cluster of wreckage from the Boeing's wings, where the landing gear could be seen still desperately extended. The main wreckage lay just to the north in a dispersed chaos of torn and twisted metal, shattered machinery, bent hydraulic lines, tubes, wiring harnesses, cockpit displays, cabin seats, and all the transported contents of the airplane – a sad spillage of luggage, purses, briefcases, clothes, medicines, cosmetics, photographs, trophy fish that sportfishermen had been hauling home from Manaus, and thousands of computer parts that the Boeing had been carrying in its cargo hold and that now littered the forest and slumped into a stream. The debris had dug into the earth on impact, and had drawn trees and branches into the tangle.

The condition of the dead should be left unsaid, except to note the mercilessness of the slaughter, and the fact that after Gol Flight 1907 hit the ground hardly any corpse remained intact. Carnivorous tiger-fish had braved the poisoned streams and were feeding on flesh that had fallen into the water. This is what happens when a wing is severed in flight. The Caiapós are warriors, perhaps, but they were deeply disturbed by the scene.

They did what they could, mostly by swinging axes to expand the landing zone. For the main work of collecting and tagging the human remains, they lacked the necessary skills and equipment. After a few days the Air Force asked them to leave. They understood – or later claimed to me that they had – but rather than fully comply, they withdrew to their camp by the river, where they built shelters and settled in for an indeterminate stay. As they saw it, this was their forest, and they were its guardians. Their stewardship didn't amount to much by Christian standards. The recovery effort lasted two months, while the soldiers struggled to reclaim and identify every last occupant of the Boeing, probing the ruins under difficult conditions, heavily garbed against disease and aggressive bees. During all that time the Caiapós stood by, visiting the site each day, but staying out of the way. One afternoon at the river camp three settlers appeared in a dugout canoe, drawn by the universal impulse to gawk at disaster. The Caiapós protected the site by sending them away. They did nothing about another impulse at play, which led some soldiers to pocket the watches, jewelry, and other valuables that they found. Perhaps the Caiapós didn't know, or perhaps they didn't care. Internally their agenda had more to do with souls than possessions. After the Air Force finally left, the Caiapós danced among the Boeing's remains, and with their shaman's guidance began the long, gentle process of reaching out to the dead.

When I met the men who had done this work – Megaron, the shaman, and several others – more than a year had gone by. They were angry that the Boeing still lay in their forest, and apparently would never be removed. Sitting in their council space in the shade of trees, I asked them why they cared. They said it was because of the damage being done to the environment. This was the message I was supposed to convey. I answered, however, that airplane wreckage is largely inert, and that operations to remove the Boeing would make things worse. Megaron was not convinced. He wanted a full-blown environmental-impact study performed. He and the shaman seemed to have an employment program in mind.

We spoke about the collision itself. They knew that American pilots were involved, and they assumed that I would take their side. I answered that it is pointless to use this accident for nationalisms of any kind. Certainly blame should be assigned, some to individuals directly involved, some to cultures in aviation and beyond. You can include the Brazilian generals who insist on militarizing air traffic control, and the sort of software engineers who make even digital cameras tedious to figure out. You can include the corrupted tax structures that allow airplanes as questionable as the Legacy to be built, sold, and flown. You can even include *Business Jet Traveler* for wanting to ride along. But assigning blame can only go so far. Ultimately the accident leaves you to ponder a paradox associated with progress and modern times. I asked the Caiapós to consider that in all the sky above the forest only these two airplanes had been in flight. It was as if in a space the size of the Caiapó village – no, all the way out to the road – you had shot two arrows in opposing directions, and they had collided. What were the odds? In the past it never would have happened. Even if you had assigned them identical flight paths, the arrows would have passed some distance apart because of the inherent inaccuracies of flight. But now better feathers have been invented, and have become required equipment for the high-speed designs. As a result, the new arrows are extraordinarily accurate, which allows more of them to be shot around, but with increasing reliance on tightly coupled systems of control. The sky is just as big as it ever was, but the margin for error has shrunk. And when the systems fail? That is what happened over the Caiapós' land. The paradox was precision. Mistakes were made, the Devil played, and two arrows touched nose to nose.

Printed in the United States
by Baker & Taylor Publisher Services